The Literature of Cinema

ADVISORY EDITOR: **MARTIN S. DWORKIN**
INSTITUTE OF PHILOSOPHY AND POLITICS OF EDUCATION
TEACHER'S COLLEGE, COLUMBIA UNIVERSITY

THE LITERATURE OF CINEMA presents a comprehensive selection from the multitude of writings about cinema, rediscovering materials on its origins, history, theoretical principles and techniques, aesthetics, economics, and effects on societies and individuals. Included are works of inherent, lasting merit and others of primarily historical significance. These provide essential resources for serious study and critical enjoyment of the "magic shadows" that became one of the decisive cultural forces of modern times.

BRITISH
FILM
Music

John Huntley

ARNO PRESS & THE NEW YORK TIMES

NEW YORK • 1972

Reprint Edition 1972 by Arno Press Inc.

Reprinted by permission of Peter Skelton Ltd.
LC# 72-169331
ISBN 0-405-03897-6

The Literature of Cinema - Series II
ISBN for complete set: 0-405-03887-9
See last pages of this volume for titles.

Manufactured in the United States of America

British Film Music

*Made and Printed in
Great Britain, for Skelton Robinson
22 Chancery Lane, W.C.2, by
Knapp, Drewett & Sons Ltd.,
Kingston-upon-Thames
and London*

BRITISH FILM Music

John Huntley

Foreword by

Muir Mathieson

LONDON
SKELTON ROBINSON
22, CHANCERY LANE, W.C.2

CONTENTS

Foreword

by Muir Mathieson

Film music is the youngest, and probably the most vigorous offspring of one of our oldest Arts. As such, it deserves the attention and interest it is receiving, both from the public and in this book. One point, however, I would like to make clear. Film music having availed itself of every type of music, every type from symphony to swing, must now be separated into two separate categories. Firstly, there is the standard music which is merely recorded and used *in* a film, and, secondly, there is the music specially commissioned and written *for* a film : I believe in the latter. I believe in its vast possibilities for audience and composer alike, and I believe in the importance of getting the right composer for each type of picture.

Film music was just beginning to develop at the end of the silent days : special scores were being sent round with each film instead of just relying on the ingenuity of the local cinema pianist or Musical Director, as had been the case up to that time. Then came talkies and the theme song, and with them the inglorious period of music merely used *in* films. After about five years, however, music *for* films again emerged and began to progress. With Arthur Bliss' *Things To Come*, film music established itself in its own right. Much has been done since then by producers, directors and musicians to explore the full possibilities of music in relation to the film, but even to-day we are only at the beginning. For one thing, we lack any experienced or constructive criticism in the National Newspapers. To date film music has been nobody's baby ! I imagine the difficulty is that the Film Critic is not supposed to criticize music, and equally, the Music Critic must lay off films. This seems to me to be a great pity, as so much contemporary musical thought is being expended in this direction.

The public likewise has little idea of what background music is supposed to do. Indeed, the present method of film-going does not permit it. As things are now, pictures are designed to be seen only once, and on one viewing the music cannot hope to emerge as a conscious element of the entertainment. In fact, it is not meant to, for the music should be an integral part of the construction of the picture like the direction, the decor or the dialogue. Only on closer examination do the individual factors become apparent. But John Huntley will have more to say about that. What it all comes to is that, while we have made considerable progress in this country in getting our finest contemporary composers to write music for the screen, we still find their efforts pass unnoticed, even by the music and film critics themselves. Not being a composer, I can only imagine how depressing this can be.

Of course, we are not standing still. I have conducted and presented concert performances of British film music all over the country and have met with tremendous enthusiasm. Even the critics were divided. Some said that film music should not be taken out of its context, while others said that in the concert hall it was an exciting reflection of contemporary life which should be fostered. Gramophone records of film music are beginning to appear, but in such a highly publicised art form as the cinema, music has still to receive its full due. Among recent developments have been the new series of British Film Music recordings made by the Decca Gramophone Company, the first being Arthur Bliss' music for *Men Of Two Worlds*, while Vaughan Williams has recently produced his music for *The Story Of A Flemish Farm* at the London Proms and turned his score of *The 49th Parallel* into a concert suite to join the ranks of such works as Sir Arnold Bax's *Malta G.C.*, Arthur Bliss' *Things To Come*, William Walton's *Henry V* and Constant Lambert's *Merchant Seamen*.

During the last few years I have had the fascinating job of introducing many of our leading composers to the film studio. They have not only shown an intense interest in this new medium, but an immediate grasp of its technical and dramatic demands. Thus, into British films has gone a wealth of great music, truly representative of our time in its linking of the ancient and traditional art of music-making with the modern art of the motion picture. That is the story that this book presents to you.

In every way, the film to-day is becoming more and more conscious of the importance of music. As the British film grows in importance and output, as we gradually secure better production and world-wide distribution facilities, so will our music grow, taking in all the best of this country's composers (of whom we have every reason to be proud), in order to ensure that the very finest music is available to every British picture that is recorded in the British studios now working to secure our place in the international field of motion pictures.

MUIR MATHIESON

Denham, 1947.

Introduction

This is a book about film music. Two other books have been published in this country on the subject. One was issued by Pitman in 1935 and is a translation of a Russian book by Sabaneev. It is designed mainly for the musician and music recordist, being full of practical directions on the writing and recording of film music plus a good deal of theory. It is a good book, but it is a handbook for the specialist and as such has been largely superseded by the new technical developments in sound recording, by new approaches to music composition, and by the music chapter of the book on sound recording by Ken Cameron (of Crown Film Unit), also published by Pitman. Cameron's book was written in 1946.

The second is called "Film Music," and was written in Paris by Kurt London, a pioneer of the early experiments in sound and music recording as carried out on the Continent. It was published in 1936 by Faber & Faber of London, and is an excellent survey of the silent film days and the transition from silent to sound. Beyond that, there is some reliable theory, but the advances of the last ten years find Kurt London's book now out-of-date. He finishes just at the dawn of the modern film score with fleeting references to *Things To Come* (music by Arthur Bliss) and *Escape Me Never* (music by William Walton). Apart from a brief survey of film music in the silent days and a summary of Talkies up to 1935, our story begins where Kurt London finishes.

In one respect, however, this book claims to be unique, for here we are not concerned so much with a discussion on the theory of film music as in a statement of the facts. I have tried as far as possible to avoid the technicalities of film music scoring and recording, but rather to set out the facts from which you may draw your own conclusions on the value and place of music in the British film industry. Here you will find a note of the films that have featured the music of the " Great Masters," the orchestras of the country, and the specially composed scores of Vaughan Williams and Arthur Bliss, set down just " for the record." I

9

think you will find it an impressive record. That is, if you mean " film music " in the same sense as I do.

Britain is backward in the production of musical films in the Hollywood sense. We just do not seem to understand the technique of the big, Technicolored, Betty Grable Super-Musical. Of course, in some cases we have no equipment available to tackle this type of production, but we do have the talent, the orchestras and occasionally the big sound stages necessary for this sort of picture. Many attempts have been made over here, but none have so far been up to Hollywood standards. Perhaps one day we shall do it ; perhaps it is not important whether we do it or not. It is not in this sphere of film music that our record is so impressive ; it is background and featured serious music that we have so successfully employed in British films. Especially background music.

There is still a good deal of confusion over " background music," and if it is not clear to you, you are not alone. I wanted to know who had composed the music for a certain film, so I went to Wardour Street, the London home of the British film industry. Entering one of the largest publicity offices in the street, I boldly put my question to them : " Can you tell me, please, who wrote the background music for your film . . .? " After three different people had come to know " what exactly it was I wanted," after two people had told me that there was no music in the film (it later turned out that there was 35 minutes of it), I was eventually informed that " as a matter of fact, it was a confidential matter for the film company, and such details are not usually revealed to the public." It was only after considerable discussion that I convinced them that if you were quick enough, you could write the name down from the credit titles when you saw the film in the cinema ; then they finally agreed to take the plunge and give me the information. The composer was actually very famous and the music later became extremely popular.

Despite the fact that this incident occurred some time ago, even to-day it is not easy, except by checking direct with the various composers or by carefully noting the credit titles, to obtain information about film background music. Although it is gradually coming to assume an importance of its own, in the past the film critics, trade press and the industry itself have given little thought to background music, except when a " Warsaw Concerto " or a *Henry V* brings it forcibly to their notice. The world of serious music has shown even less regard for this new outlet to the modern composer, and even to-day some composers treat their film work as " not quite the thing to do," as a commercialisation of the art of music. However, the general trend is a healthy one. Almost every modern contemporary composer has nowadays made some contribution to the film. To mention but a few, Arnold Bax, Arthur Bliss, John Ireland, William Walton and Ralph Vaughan Williams—all have composed music for the motion picture, and their work has been recorded by such orchestras as the London Symphony, the National Symphony and the London Philharmonic. A wealth of the country's musicians, the product of the Royal College of Music and the Royal Academy, devote themselves to the writing and recording of British film music. Guided by a small group of specialists, composers in ever-increasing numbers are introduced to the new medium with its promise of vast dramatic possibilities and its extensive field for musical experiment and exploration, offering to the enthusiastic writer an audience of perhaps ten million people. Here the composer comes face to face with the realism of the cinema, with the greatest form of mass entertainment the world has ever seen ; with a chance to bring music back to the mass of the people who seem at the present time to be in acute danger of losing that vital contact with the world of serious music, while simultaneously, the musician himself becomes more distant from his audience. And incidentally, film composition offers the modern composer a reasonable livelihood, perhaps the greatest contribution that the cinema has so far made to the arts.

Naturally, there are set-backs for the pioneers of to-day, and innumerable problems. The composer often feels his music is being wasted in films. Time will alter that, as we see the creation of a new public for films, a public demanding better standards of entertainment, a public that can distinguish good photography from bad, good art direction from bad, and eventually, good music from bad. Already we have film societies springing up everywhere, which examine films beyond the casual viewing of the ordinary cinemagoer, to probe the construction and artistic values of a picture. If there is good music to be had, film society audiences will discover it. And their membership increases all the time. Music and film magazines are taking an increasing interest in the subject, and in some cases we now have special reviews devoted to background and featured scores. As one writer puts it, to-day we can see the beginning of the movement of " background music

11

to the fore " as it prepares to take its place among the specialised forms of modern musical development.

This book is intended to give a background of fact to this exciting new approach in music. Here you will find a list of composers, over a hundred of them, with the films they have scored, a list of gramophone records to enable you to get more out of the music, and an account of the history of film music so that you can see just what has been done so far. Although background scoring is frankly our main interest, we have not ignored the other aspects of picture music, and you will find quite a section of our index devoted to featured music, including notes on the dance bands and the popular song writers of the British screen. First, however, we take note of a famous Brains Truster, because " it all depends on what you mean by film music." And so to the first chapter.

JOHN HUNTLEY

Kew, 1947.

ACKNOWLEDGEMENTS

"British Film Music" attempts to present the views of as many people as possible, both in and out of the industry. Therefore the author wishes to thank all the composers, directors, technicians and critics who helped by their outspoken comments to make this book an expression of, I hope, most of the approaches to film music. In addition, I have to acknowledge most gratefully the special assistance of the following magazines and books from which quotations have been made :—

The British Film Institute, for permission to quote from their publications " Sight and Sound " and the " Monthly Film Bulletin."

Kurt London, for permission to reproduce large sections of his book " Film Music " (Faber & Faber, 1936).

" Tempo," the music magazine of Messrs. Boosey and Hawkes, to whom I am indebted for numerous comments by Dr. Hubert Clifford and Ernest Irving as well as the article on Aspects of Film Music by Muir Mathieson ; in this connection, I wish to thank the editor, Edward Chapman, for his help.

" Documentary News Letter " for leave to quote from their various film reviews.

" Film Music Notes " in Hollywood and New York ; the editors, Constance Purdy, Margery Morrison and Grace Mabee.

and the following :—

(Chapter II).   Caroline Lejeune (" Modern Woman ").
H. G. Wells (Cresset Press).
" Sound Magazine " and Sam Heppner.
A. Vesselo (" Amateur Cine World ").
Marjorie Deans, Eagle Lion Distributors and Macdonald & Co. Ltd.

(Chapter III). Miss M. E. Calthrop ("The Piping Times").

(Film Music Forum). "Documentary Film" (Paul Rotha). Faber & Faber, 1936.

"Sound Magazine" and Sam Heppner for the quotations by Arthur Bliss and Sir Arnold Bax.

Rollo Myers for quotations from his book "Music in the Modern World" (Edward Arnold & Co., Ltd.).

Arthur Unwin ("Music Parade").

The article by Louis Levy is reproduced by kind permission of "Kinematograph Weekly."

The article by Ralph Vaughan Williams is reprinted from the Royal College of Music Magazine by the generous permission of the author, and by courtesy of the editor.

The articles by George Burgess and Margery Morrison were specially written for "British Film Music," and the author expresses his gratitude to them both for their collaboration.

The index section, "Film Music in Broadcasting," was made possible through the courtesy of the B.B.C.

Extracts from "The British Film Yearbook" and "Transatlantic Jazz" are by kind permission of the Publishers, British Yearbooks.

The article "A Film Music Recording Session" is reproduced by permission of "Our Time."

The author gratefully acknowledges the assistance given by Marjorie Salter, May Huntley and Philip Evans.

CHAPTER I

FILM MUSIC
Its Composers, Orchestras and Functions

───────────◆───────────

(A). FEATURED FILM MUSIC

All songs, dances, orchestral, instrumental or choral items which are specially featured in a film, and all well-known music which is used either as a background or as a specially presented part of any film, music that in any way, either because of its familiarity or on account of its method of presentation, is not an integral part of the film itself, but which emerges as a unit of its own constitutes " Featured Film Music."

About thirty-three million people a week are visiting the cinema to-day in England and they all go expecting to be entertained. Consider the problem the film producers face in setting out to please all the different tastes and fancies of such a vast audience. Yet the cinema does manage to satisfy everyone somehow, for when the magazine " Kinematograph Weekly " held an extensive investigation of a cross-section of the British public they failed to find anyone who had not at some time or another gone to the pictures. For the film student there is *Thunder Rock, Man Of Aran* and *Drifters* ; for the historian *The Young Mr. Pitt* ; for the literary man *The Stars Look Down* ; for the educationist the *Secrets Of Life* series ; for the theatre fan *They Came To A City* ; for the spectacle lover *Caesar And Cleopatra*; for the Shakespearians *Henry V* ; for the lads out for a night, a wealth of colourful musicals and comedies ; for the small country audiences there is Frank Randle and Sexton Blake ; even for those who don't go to see the film at all, the cinema designer provides a comfortable seat for dozing, or plenty of darkness in the back row for holding hands. The cinema is mass entertainment indeed.

Musically too, all tastes are catered for, so that your film-going may be enhanced by good listening as well as good looking. Perhaps you like the latest dance tunes, the big bands, the new vocalists, the recent dances. The first talkie brought you Al Jolson and *Sonny Boy* ; since then a continuous stream of musical films has flowed across from America without a break for the last twenty

years.   Although the slick modern musical is our most unsatisfactory
product at present, we have had Jessie Matthews, Henry Hall,
Ambrose, Carroll Gibbons, Geraldo, Harry Roy, Vera Lynn,
Evelyn Dall, Harry Parry and Pat Kirkwood, backed by such
composers as Noel Gay and Manning Sherwin, to maintain our
modest place in the world of the fox-trot, boogie-woogie, solid
four, torch song and crooning, in films like *He Found A Star*, *Flight
From Folly*, *Miss London Limited*, *First A Girl*, *The Lambeth Walk*
and *Lisbon Story*.

To the lover of light music, there is always a wide selection,
as people like Reginald Foort, Alfredo Campoli, Flanagan and
Allen, Vic Oliver, Rawicz and Landauer record a wealth of music
on British sound tracks to suit the people who enjoy " a good solid
tune."   Good march tunes are likewise in excellent supply (often
coming under the second film music category, " Background
Music ") with films like Desert Victory and *Nine Men*.

Maybe you are a Ballet-goer. The motion picture has catered for
you in your turn with the Ballet Russe of Monte Carlo in two
superb Technicolor short films, *The Gay Parisian* and *Spanish Fiesta*
shown extensively in this country, and although the Ballet is not
as yet suited to film form, you will find plenty of experiments on
a little close analysis of foreign films shown here, such as *Russian
Salad*, the French Ballet films, or Ballet extracts like "Swan Lake" in
various American films, and the British Ballet items in *Latin Quarter*
(British National, 1945).

The screen has periodically sought inspiration from the Opera.
On the Continent, whole Operas have been filmed experimentally
for the film student, while in more popular vein Hollywood films
provide sequences of interest·such as *San Francisco* (large pieces of
" Faust ") or *The Phantom Of The Opera*.   A visit to the Soviet
Film Season at London's Tatler Cinema may reward you with
operatic arias by Sergei Lemeshev, whose screen work includes
parts of " Eugene Onegin " (*A Musical Story*) and " Rigoletto "
(*Russian Salad*).

Lovers of the waltz will surely find satisfaction in the dynamic
beauty of the American *Great Waltz* or the British *Waltzes From
Vienna*, dealing with the life of Strauss.   In the sphere of folk music,
the Hall Johnson Choir recording Negro Spirituals in a film like
Green Pastures, or Paul Robeson's singing in *The Proud Valley* and
Sanders Of The River are notable movie contributions to music.

16

Another example in this field is the Glasgow Orpheus Choir music in Michael Powell's British films *The Edge Of The World* and *I Know Where I'm Going*.

You like to hear the world's great orchestras? Listen to the Philadelphia Symphony in *100 Men And A Girl*, the London Symphony in over a hundred British films, the London Philharmonic in *Battle For Music* and *The Great Mr. Handel*, the National Symphony Orchestra in *Love Story* and *Caesar And Cleopatra*, the Vienna Philharmonic in the Schubert film *Unfinished Symphony*, the R.A.F. Orchestra in *Coastal Command* or the Paris Conservatoire Orchestra in *Symphonie Fantastique*.

Beethoven you want? Enjoy the Pastoral Symphony recording by Leopold Stokowski and the Philadelphia Orchestra in Walt Disney's *Fantasia*, the whole extent of Ludwig's versatile imagination in the Abel Gance film *Life And Death Of Beethoven*, his Pathetique Sonata in *The Seventh Veil*, or even his piano concerto played by the London Symphony Orchestra conducted by Stanelli with solo pianoforte by Old Mother Riley! (Film—*Old Mother Riley Overseas*). You prefer Bach? See the Soviet picture *Spring Song* for Chorales, Preludes and Toccatas (as well as the music of Handel, Gluck and Kabelevsky), or *A Canterbury Tale* for the Toccata and Fugue in D, which also appears in *Fantasia*. But Tchaikowsky is your speciality? *Fantasia* again can provide the Nutcracker Suite; *Battle For Music* has some " Romeo and Juliet " extracts, while Piano Concerto No. 1 devotees have five films to choose from, e.g., *The Song Of Russia* (Albert Coates conducting), *The Common Touch* (Mark Hambourg), or *The Great Lie*. You will find Tchaikowsky extracts everywhere; do you know that phrase from the Fifth Symphony used as the signature tune of John Nesbitt's *Passing Parade* series, for example? If it is Handel you are after, there is the first production of J. Arthur Rank's new deal for British movies *The Great Mr. Handel*, starring Wilfred Lawson and Elizabeth Allan. More subtle but quite pleasing is the arrangement of the " Water Music " scored to Ealing Studio's Fleet Air Arm film, *Find, Fix And Strike*. Hear Grieg, Rachmaninoff, Chopin and Mozart in numerous films such as *The Seventh Veil*, *Escape To Happiness*, *Brief Encounter* and *A Girl In A Million*; the cinema has drawn extensively from the world's great composers.

All this is " featured film music." Sometimes it is successfully employed to the improvement of the film, and on other occasions it has been used badly as a substitute for true " background music,"

17

when it becomes a distraction from the picture itself. The musical film has many pitfalls for the unwary. How often has a picture been brought to a complete standstill by a badly interpolated song, which consists of a series of long close-ups that only serve to accent failure to keep the story on the move. *Hellzapoppin* was one of the few films in which the pace never let up for a minute, each song and dance being cinematically designed to carry forward the action of the plot. Compare a well directed musical short film by director Jean Negulesco (Warner Bros.) to a badly directed one, such as we have seen from the Universal Studios, and note how in one case the director overcomes the dragging action of a straight song or dance routine by continual interplay of camera angle and lighting key. Compare the unimaginative handling of certain orchestral sequences in a number of British films to the strong presentation of Paul Whiteman's Orchestra in the *Rhapsody In Blue* recording from the film of that name. In *The Seventh Veil*, the music was skilfully used so as to fit naturally into the plot without slowing down the action or distracting from the story, whereas in an already dull film, songs by Handel, John Gay, James Hook and Sir Henry Bishop inserted into *Pink String And Sealing Wax* further reduced a snail-like pace. The work of popularising serious music through the medium of the cinema, however, is an excellent scheme and provided that the music can occur naturally in the picture, it should be developed as a contribution from the art of cinema to the art of good music.

(B). BACKGROUND MUSIC

" We do not go to the cinema to hear music. We require it to deepen and prolong in us the screen's visual impressions."

MAURICE JAUBERT.

" Background music " suggests the silent days of a battered piano, " Hearts and Flowers," and no unemployed musicians, but it is a term not yet replaced by something more adequate. " Incidental music " suggests something spurious to the film itself, and this is just what true background music is not. " Integral music " has been suggested, but this is clumsy. So it remains " Background music," a score specially written to fit the film, an integral part of the script, a vital link in the technical assembly of a movie in which the composer takes his place alongside the film editor, the cameraman and the sound recorder as a member of a film producing team. It calls for a composer who has a keen interest in films, a strong sense of the dramatic in music, and the ability to write music spontaneously and to the strict discipline of a stop-watch. He must be prepared to give and take with the other technical departments of film making ; to their require-ments the music must be orchestrated, balanced and re-recorded to fit the scenarist's dialogue, the quality of the actor's voice or the use of natural sound, while elsewhere it must dominate the screen. " Here is a bowler hat in close-up ; the whole story hinges on this hat. Write music to convey the implications of the bowler hat on the plot ; the shot lasts fifteen seconds." And the composer must attempt to convey the sense of sinister horror, of unseen terror, of fateful events foreshadowed, in those brief seconds of screen time.

Who are these composers of British films ? Almost every contemporary writer of music in the country, and no list could do full justice to the number of men engaged in this type of work. To instance a few, we include men like William Alwyn, Richard Addinsell, Arthur Bliss, Lennox Berkeley, Arnold Bax, Hubert Clifford, Gordon Jacob, Constant Lambert, Leighton Lucas, Alan Rawsthorne, R. Vaughan Williams and William Walton. Their work is unified and recorded by a handful of musical directors, led by the outstanding figure of the British film music world, Muir Mathieson ; others in this specialised job of Musician-Composer-Conductor-Sound Expert are Louis Levy, Ernest Irving and Charles Williams. The orchestras who record the music in-clude the London Symphony, the London Philharmonic and the National Symphony Orchestra.

Some composers go into films for the money, some for the experience, some for the rigid discipline of film scoring, some because they have a leaning towards the dramatic and find it a substitute for the almost dead art of Opera. If it is for money, well, a composer must live. He can spend two months in the year writing film music which he despises, but which earns him enough to spend the rest of the year writing chamber music which he loves, but which never earns him a penny. If he is a good composer and enters into the spirit of the thing, he may make money and preserve his artistic integrity as well. Bach earned his living from the Church, Mozart from the Court of Princes, Rossini from the Theatre ; to-day the film industry provides a living for many contemporary composers of serious music. From the film studios we may look for music representative of our time as we might once have looked at the chorales and preludes of a German organist to discover Bach, the Court Music files of German principalities to discover Mozart, the Opera House of Naples to discover Rossini. To-day we may look for strips of celluloid, 35 mm. wide, in large flat round tins. Film music takes second place to the story, the cast, the visuals of the medium, but that need not bother us. Bach's music was secondary to the celebration of the Holy Mass, Mozart's to the Court social functions and Rossini's to the splendour of the stage and the singing. Great music can still emerge in competition with other forms of artistic expression ; film music can do just this. It simply makes the search a little keener.

If a composer enters the film studio for the experience, he must have some interest in films for their own sake. He must believe in films. The man who never goes to the cinema and who arrives to score a film because he thinks it will be a nice rest after his latest Symphony is doomed to disappointment. To write good film music, you must like good films. If he comes for the discipline of film scoring, he may find the teamwork beyond him. Some composers are born individualists, and when it comes to sharing the honours and trials of producing a film, they fail. Without the team spirit, back to chamber music is the only solution. If he comes to the film as a substitute for Opera, the composer may find exactly what he has been looking for. Vaughan Williams has said that " the film contains potentialities for the combination of all the arts such as Wagner never dreamt of," and judging by the number of eminent men who now claim a strong liking for film scoring, this may be very true.

From the listener's point of view, background film music offers some problems. " We do not go to the cinema to hear music. We require it to deepen and prolong in us the screen's visual impressions." When you see a film you should not be conscious of the music as a separate entity, but if it is a good score, your enjoyment of the film will be greatly increased. It is the old question of teamwork. If the photography is good, the sound recording is good, the film editing is good, you will not be aware of any these items as separate parts, but you will come away saying that it was a thundering good film. The same applies to the music. How, then, to get to know something about film music ?

When you buy a new symphony on gramophone records, do

you play the records once and then throw them away? You listen once, twice, three times to get the overall effect of what the composer is getting at. Then you listen again to see how he works out his themes, you listen again to see how he uses his strings, again for the woodwinds, then there is that little passage on the French horn that you missed before, again and you note the piquancy added by the triangle in the third movement, and so on. You don't read a really good book and forget it; you read it perhaps ten times. You don't glance at a great painting as you would a comic strip in the "Daily Mirror." You examine the painting in detail, at a distance, expanding your appreciation by a knowledge of the artist and his work. Nor then will you appreciate a film score at one screening. You will be too interested in the story and if it is a good score you will not hear it consciously. But your enjoyment of the picture as such will be greatly increased. Pick your films carefully, reject the vast array of mediocre productions, and concentrate on the good stuff. See the really top-notch films more than once; study the credit titles, that boring list of names at the beginning of a film which is usually ignored, and you will soon get to know those names as well as the stars. They are far more reliable for gauging the quality of a film than the list of stars. You have not seen a good film until you have seen it three times; once as a film, once for direction, story, dialogue, and once for photography, sound, art direction, and music. You cannot judge a symphony, a good book, a great painting at one go; how much less then a vastly complex piece of art like a film. Get to know your movies, check on the composer, then go and see the film—really see it! If the task seems big, remember that there are only about twenty really good films produced in a year, plus a few documentaries and foreign pictures.

The best way by far to study film music is at the cinema. The music was designed that way, its whole existence is bound up with the visual impressions, it is as much a part of the film as the sound, the photography, and the acting. Movie music must be judged first and foremost in its correct context, judged by its suitability to the visuals to which it is related. However, there are three supplementary ways of studying it out of context; the printed score, the concert hall, the gramophone. The first method does not offer much scope. Of course we have a full piano transcription for Richard Addinsell's "Warsaw Concerto" and some "Tea Time Music" that he wrote for the film *A Day Will Dawn*,

Hubert Bath's "Cornish Rhapsody" from the Gainsborough picture *Love Story*, likewise orchestral scores of *Things to Come* and *Men of Two Worlds*, but there it ends. An American magazine "Film Music Notes" publishes a typical page of an American movie writer's scoring each month which is very useful, but on the whole there is little available in this direction.

Some composers have made orchestral suites from their film scores, which have received concert hall airings. William Walton's music "Spitfire Prelude and Fugue," Arthur Bliss' music from *Things To Come* and *Conquest Of The Air*, the Arnold Bax score *Malta G.C.*, Constant Lambert's *Merchant Seamen*, the R. Vaughan Williams' scores *49th Parallel* and *The Flemish Farm*, William Walton's *Henry V* music and Lennox Berkeley's "On The Beach" scene from *Hotel Reserve* have all received broadcast and concert hall performances. By carefully scanning Symphony Concert programmes it is possible to hear film music in this exciting way.

But by far the most convenient of the three methods is with a gramophone and you will find on page 239 a list of recommended records for both "Featured" and "Background" British film music. The best scheme is to see the film first and then go through the record, finishing up with a further viewing of the film to observe how the music checks both out of, and especially in, its correct context.

CHAPTER II

THE STORY OF BRITISH FILM MUSIC

" There is one department in which English studios can be fairly claimed to excel Hollywood—that of musical direction."

1. THE SILENT FILM

Film music began in Britain, as it did all over the world, in the dingy fairground sideshows, the music-halls and the little shop-front cinemas of the early 1900's. Music and films have been inseparable right from the start. First, it was simply a matter of drowning the noise from the projector which was set up often in the middle of the audience, its primitive mechanism creating quite a clatter, cranked at a terrific speed by hand from an operator who was solely concerned with screening his film as quickly as possible. Perhaps the greatest authority on silent film music is Kurt London and it is to his book that we are indebted for many fascinating descriptions of those early days of picture music. The old showman's technique of narration was still employed, in the best tradition of the fairground side-show. " Let us try to picture to ourselves the cinema of those days," says Kurt London. " Some out-of-the-way hall, probably rectangular in shape, with a screen in front, the projector at the back, and chairs in the intermediate space. The projector made a terrible noise ; the commentator had to have good lungs to make his discourse audible. And, between them, we can imagine the young couples rejoicing in the darkness of the place—the biggest attraction of the cinema in those days ! In places such as this film music was born.

" It began, not as a result of any artistic urge, but from the dire need of something which would drown the noise made by the projector. For in those times there were as yet no sound-absorbent walls between the projection machine and the auditorium. This painful noise disturbed visual enjoyment to no small extent. Instinctively cinema proprietors had recourse to music, and it was the right way, using an agreeable sound to neutralise one less agreeable. The first instruments to be used for the purpose were mechanical : barrel-organ, musical box, orchestrion and—phonograph."

23

After a few years, the projector was finally settled in a sound-proof box and its chatter was heard no more, so that now the audience sat in complete silence. But just as music had instinctively been used to neutralise the noise, so it was found necessary in order to neutralise the silence. Although we talk about the " silent cinema," in practice a real " silent " show is almost intolerable. Perhaps you can recall parts of a film show which were run in silence ; how odd they seemed. Even to-day, in a talkie programme, it sometimes occurs that part of the film is shown in silence ; the effect can be startling if used ingeniously, because we are now so accustomed to hearing as well as seeing. In fact, we have reached the stage where even a silent " cinema " with no film on the screen seems odd. In London on a Sunday the cinemas open their doors at 4 p.m., but the Sunday Cinema Opening clauses in the L.C.C. licences forbid the showing of films or a performance of any kind in a cinema before 4.30 p.m., so that we sit in the hall for half-an-hour without even the " non-sync " going (that is, without gramophone records being played—a bit of projection room parlance). How queer it sometimes feels. People tend to talk in a hushed manner and an air of impatience is felt ; whereas with music playing, all seems normal. One hardly listens to the music, but it is there and we associate music so strongly with the cinema that its absence makes us feel " all wrong."

So first and foremost the silent cinema needed music in order to give it an existence at all, as a vital factor in its make-up, to give the film depth and a reality which its lack of voice demanded. More than that, " the reason which is aesthetically and psychologically most essential to explain the need of music as an accompaniment of the silent film, is without doubt the *rhythm of the film as an art of movement*. We are not accustomed to apprehend movement as an artistic form without accompanying sounds, or at least audible rhythms. Every film that deserves the name must possess its individual rhythm which determines its form. (Form is here taken in the widest sense as a ruling concept). It was the task of the musical accompaniment to give it auditory accentuation and profundity." (Kurt London).

After a brief beginning with mechanical music we come to that great institution, the cinema pianist. " Don't shoot the pianist, he's doing his best," they used to say. It was, of course, no easy job to play a piano for six or eight hours a day, straining the neck to see what was on the screen, improvising with all the latest tunes in an attempt to keep up with the moods of the picture. In some cases the pianist even played a harmonium with one hand and the piano with the other, and " his right hand knew not what his left hand did." For many years the cinema pianist stayed on in the small country halls, but as the film progressed as a medium of popular entertainment so the cinemas themselves improved, and orchestras began to replace the extemporising pianist. What were these orchestras like? Once again Kurt London can give a full answer. "The composition of the silent-film orchestra was subject in general to the same rules and conditions in every case, if we take as our example the larger picture-theatres, in which alone a kind of musical culture could flourish at all. These used flutes, clarinets, trumpets, trombones, percussion and pianoforte. Usually there was an organ (built in to the big houses) or harmonium to compensate for the missing wind-instruments and to give greater effect to dynamic variations. Only in rare cases were horns employed. Of course, the strings in the shape of a few violins, violoncello and a double-bass, were not dispensed with ; but only quite a few cinema orchestras could afford the luxury of viola parts. The advantage of an orchestra so composed, capable of having its numbers strengthened, in the strings especially, lay not alone in the saving in individual players, but also in the fact that it had at its disposal a huge literature without extra arrangement of the parts ; for either it could easily be adapted, or it was available in the parts that made up the so-called chamber orchestra. This literature included the whole of light music and also, in arranged form, portions of favourite works by famous masters, the use of which became more and more frequent. For the needs of film music, this form of orchestra was fully adequate. The peculiar qualities of film music in those early days already permitted a much slighter orchestral scheme, and could dispense with a huge symphonic body of players who might possibly kill the picture with their mass of sound, because the spectator's attention would be distracted from the screen."

We have looked at the reason for having music, and at the method of presenting it ; now to have a look at the music itself and the men who were involved in its composition and performance. Two types of music were used for silent pictures. First there were original compositions and occasionally complete scores. These were few and far between, for the technical difficulties were tremendous, and there were hardly any cases of special scores for British films. Elsewhere, however, the tradition of original com-

25

position for motion pictures does show a slow and modest development dating back as far as 1908 when Saint-Saens wrote music for an old French film. In London, for example, we heard original music by Edmund Meisel to a number of the Russian silent classics like *Potemkin* and *October*, and the music written for *The Four Horsemen Of The Apocalypse*, or some of the Charles Chaplin films, but original music for silent films never became more than an additional publicity boost to the general run of commercial pictures.

Far more intrinsic to the silent days was the use of already existing music strung together in musical " hot-pots " and known as " compilations " or film music " illustrations." Every conceivable type of music was called into service to provide material for the film orchestras—opera, the classics, light music, symphonies, musical comedy, jazz, everything—all arranged and orchestrated, published and labelled so that it could be ordered from a catalogue depending on what type of effect was required :—

" TENSION—Agitato.
- (*a*) Pursuit, flight, hurry.
- (*b*) Fight.
- (*c*) Heroic combat.
- (*d*) Battle.
- (*e*) Disturbance, unrest, terror ;
- (*f*) Disturbed masses : tumult ;
- (*g*) Disturbed nature : storm, fire."

In addition, there was a vast collection of " hurry " music, invaluable for the inevitable " chase " sequence which still finds a modern counterpart in cowboy and comedy films. Naturally, there was a full range of Indian, Chinese and other Eastern music listed, while for the " blighted love " scenes there was no better tearjerker than " Hearts and Flowers " which you can hear to-day on a gramophone record (for example, Columbia DB690). This moving piece by Jessel became so overworked in the early days that in the end it brought a laugh each time it was played under a scene of pathos, as its intent had become altogether too obvious. So it was that for over twenty years the public heard music on a scale rarely equalled before or since. A boom hit the music industry and the hundreds of cinema orchestras and pianists put the musicians of the country on a new level—financially, if not æsthetically. The public heard a lot of semi-classical music, many of them for the first time, but they heard it unconsciously. It may be argued that music heard unconsciously may have a

26

stronger long-term effect on a person's musical outlook than that which is listened to in cold analysis, and in fact it is often claimed that the present trend towards greater interest in modern and classical music is due partly to a predetermined receptivity, founded on unconscious reactions to the inculcation of musical forms and patterns which accompany to-day's films. That is difficult to prove satisfactorily, but examples even from the silent days show that the Tchaikowsky Piano Concerto No. 1 was not the first piece of serious music to owe its popularity to films. Part of the score sent out with the silent classic *The Ten Commandments* used Dvorak's New World Symphony to set the emotional tempo for the scene in which Moses leads 2,500 Israelites in flight from Egypt, with the result that the Dvorak Symphony became a more popular " request " item.

Quite a number of you will recall the great days of the silent cinema. So also do many of the older generation of our present-day music composers and directors. Percival Mackey, born in 1894, began his film music career at the age of 14, touring as a pianist with a one-man show which included a ventriloquist, conjuring and comedy act—and the showing of a film. The projector was set up in the middle of the audience with two large gas cylinders stuck behind to provide the incandescent projection illumination. The machine itself was fixed up on a pile of old boxes, and as the showman-operator turned the handle, young Percival provided the improvised piano accompaniment. During this tour of the Midlands and Southern England he received 2/6 a week and his keep. Afterwards he went to Ireland to join the " Royal Irish Animated Picture Company " in Tipperary, run by that old pioneer, Arthur Jameson, who began exhibiting in 1898. Mackey had a rough crossing but eventually arrived in Tipperary and contacted the travelling film show where he became a member of the " Royal Irish Animated Picture Company Grand Orchestra." This consisted of a trumpeter from a circus, aged 72, a drunken fiddler of 45, and young Mackey, aged 18, on the piano, occasionally augmented for special overtures and intermissions by a harmonium with six notes missing. He recalls the one-night stands, the continual improvisation of the rough-and-ready scores (especially when the fiddler was too drunk to play), and the time when they stood aside during the visit of a special touring symphony orchestra who brought their own score, complete with trumpet calls played with echo effect in the rear of the hall and machines for producing

" horse's hooves " noises. This was for the premiere performance of *The Four Horsemen Of The Apocalypse* in Belfast, after Mackey had been in Ireland for a number of years. Back in England during the middle 20's, he got a job one day as relief pianist at a cinema in Harrow Road, but after playing non-stop from 2 till 5, and having developed a bad neck-ache, he packed up and left at 5.15 when the regular man failed to arrive, leaving the picture to continue in silence. Another " short-term engagement " he recalls with gusto was at a little " flea-pit " in Brick Lane, Aldgate. Passing down a series of dirty, dark streets, populated by tough East-enders, he arrived to find a collection of six burly individuals gathered in the orchestra pit. After getting under way, Mackey happened to slip up on a note, whereupon the conductor swore savagely at him. This was enough for the pianist ; putting on his coat he left there and then while the orchestra and the picture rattled on to the accompaniment of curses and mutterings from the swarthy M.D.

Other music directors who had experience of the silent days include Louis Levy, Charles Williams and composer Hans May. Levy began work on film music well over 35 years ago, and by 1916 was conductor at the New Gallery in London, while in 1921 he went to the Shepherd's Bush Pavilion prior to joining Gaumont-British in Lime Grove when talkies first began. Charles Williams likewise had considerable experience both as a conductor and an orchestral player for " the silents." To-day he is still conducting for films like *The Way To The Stars*, *Colonel Blimp* and *Carnival*. Hans May, composer for such films as *The Wicked Lady*, *Waltz Time*, *Madonna Of The Seven Moons* and *The Stars Look Down*, was a pioneer of the old days, arranging music for about one thousand films and composing hundreds of special pieces for " Kinothek," the original cinema music library set up in Berlin in 1919 by an Italian called Guiseppe Becce. He wrote original scores for the Russian film *Potemkin* (in addition to Meisel's music) and also to the silent version of *A Midsummer Night's Dream*, made by UFA. Kurt London likewise was associated with silent film music in Germany and in France.

Just at the end of the silent era, we began to see signs of a gradual approach to a more serious outlook on film music, as evidenced by some of the original scores written at that time. And then suddenly Al Jolson—1928—*The Singing Fool* ; and overnight the art of the silent cinema disappeared for ever.

2. THE SOUND FILM

The violence with which talking pictures arrived in a big way with the last desperate gamble of the financially embarrassed Warner Brothers in 1927 is apt to give the impression that a synchronised sound film was something absolutely new. Actually it was simply a matter of developing previous knowledge and experiment into a technically and economically solid proposition which could establish itself with the majority of the film-going public. In the same way as it took thirty years to bring sound to vision in the cinema, so it took thirty years to bring vision to sound in radio (since the first time in about 1910 when the first practical cathode-ray tubes were being worked out). The fact is that talking pictures had been the goal from the very beginning when the staff of the Edison company greeted their leader on his return from the Chicago Exhibition with a short length of film which screened the firm's chief technician, synchronised to a gramophone record of his voice, saying " Good morning, Mr. Edison. I hope you are satisfied with the Kinetophonograph." In 1903 we find a British company, Walturdaw Pictures, issuing a large series of musical short films (for example, extracts from "The Mikado" and "Yeomen Of The Guard"), which used a method of linking sound and film basically the same as one of our modern " post-sync " systems found in most studios to-day. A gramophone record is made and played back to the artist in the studio, who then carries out the appropriate action before the camera. Nowadays that is only a prelude to a long series of dubbing and re-recording processes, but in 1903 the films were screened in the cinema accompanied by the gramophone record in approximate unison. In 1908, Cecil Hepworth, one of the pioneers of the British silent film, developed a Vivaphone, a talking picture method which, unfortunately, failed to find commercial backing in this country and was eventually sold to America.

The basic principle of photographing sound on a strip of film was known even before 1900, but it was not until 1911 that it was actually achieved by M. Lauste ; no headway, however, could be made until 1920 when Theodore Case patented the photo-electric cell. Simultaneously as the Western Electric Company of America were perfecting their Vitaphone system of sound-on-disc, which they eventually sold to Warner Brothers, a number of sound-on-film talkies were being produced in England. It is ironic that the first talking picture system to sweep through the world should be a throwback to the old Edison days of gramophone records in synchronisation with the film, whereas in 1925, an American inventor, Lee De Forest, was producing sound-on-film talkies, in which a photographic record of the actor's voice is recorded along the edge of the celluloid strip of film—the system which has been universally employed for the last fifteen years. Not far from Clapham Junction is a social club and billiard room, slightly blitzed but still functioning. Few of the club members know that once the hall was the home of the Lee De Forest Phono-films and that in 1925, they too cursed the roar of steam and electric trains that thundered over the nearby railway bridge every few minutes. Miles Mander directed these early sound-on-film pictures with people like Lilian Hall Davies, Owen Nares, Dorothy Boyd, Malcolm Keen and Mary Clare appearing in them. Two of the early pictures, *As We Lie* and *The Sentence Of Death*, contained sound, dialogue and " compilation " musical scores which were simply a recorded version of the normal silent-cinema orchestral background. The films were initially exhibited (as were the first silent movies) as items in music-hall programmes, and in England the very first picture theatre built and equipped specially for the showing of talkies was at the Wembley Empire Exhibition in 1925. Admission was 6d. In September 1926, the De Forest sound films were successfully shown at the old Capitol Cinema in Haymarket. At the original Lime Grove Studios in Shepherd's Bush, the first British acoustic sound film was made by erecting a bell tent in the ordinary studio for sound-proofing, and banging two saucepan lids as " clappers " ; later this unit filmed the Changing of the Guard at Buckingham Palace, complete with natural sound. Although this was all a full year before *The Singing Fool* was shown in London, the Americans went ahead and we languished behind, with the result that when *The Jazz Singer* was shown at the Piccadilly Theatre at the end of 1928, we were caught on the hop.

What happened to film music for the next few years of the mighty American theme song " all talking, all singing, all dancing " period is best described by listening to the gramophone record of Al Jolson singing " Sonny Boy " from the film *The Singing Fool* (Brunswick 3879), and by reading the comments of an eminent film musician of the day, Kurt London :—

" When the great frenzy consequent on the sound-film invasion broke out in full force, and the technical factories were in vain trying to cope with all the demands made by studio and theatre for new apparatus, they lost their heads. A huge number of silent films lay there finished, others were just in the middle of production, hundreds of them still had to be paid for ; were these to show a dead loss, like all the printed music in the stocks of the unfortunate publishers of film compilations ? That would have spelt ruin for the whole European film industry. No effort was to be spared at least to postpone the coming of that 'evil,' the sound film ; for, in the first place, the funds were not there for the reorganisation that was necessary, and, in the second place, the technicians had not had time to adapt themselves to the needs of the new sound-industry. They had gained much electro-acoustical experience in their work on wireless and gramophone recording, but the sound-film confronted them with problems that were much more complex and varied.

" In the sphere of film music, the state of affairs was even more catastrophic. Thousands of orchestral musicians were in the greatest danger of losing their livelihood. Inevitably the great demand for musicians in the heyday of the silent film had brought in its train a kind of boom in musicians. Amateurism flourished. Among the many thousands of ensemble players, only a small fraction could be called first-rate artists— a fact which did very much harm to the bona fide professionals.

" And now the sound-film had arrived, the music became mechanised, and at once almost all film musicians were out of a job. Their associations lodged despairing protests with the public and the authorities concerned, but, of course, could do nothing at all to stem the tide of events. In every cinema the orchestra was the first item to be abolished, in favour of music produced electro-mechanically.

"For without any delay, the public, crazy as it was over the sound-film, was offered something which pretended to be a ' sound-film,' but in fact was nothing else than a silent film with mechanised music. The film forthwith hovered between silence and sound, and the artistic bastardy made the cinema loathsome even to the most patient of audiences. It is impossible to describe the lack of taste which was displayed in that period of about one or two years."

In the case of Great Britain, the situation regarding musicians applied to us as much as to any other part of the world ; only the first-rate artist had a chance for anything else, and the disaster became all the more tragic with the approach of a far more widespread period of unemployment and distress, affecting every trade and industry in the country. As regards the panic caused by the sudden arrival of the talkies from the States, a good example is the case of the film *Kitty*. This was half completed at Elstree when British producers finally took the plunge to go over to sound, and so the whole film, cast and all, was shipped to Hollywood for conversion to a talking picture. The scheme was quite crazy, but it was financially successful now that it could be issued as a British " all-talking " picture, despite the fact that some scenes started off silent and began talking in the middle. And the pioneer British sound film music composer for this production was Hubert Bath, who not only scored *Kitty* (part sound) but also the first genuine " all-talking " British film *Blackmail*, made in 1929, in which director Alfred Hitchcock showed a brilliant and speedy grasp of the potentialities of the new medium. Both these pictures were made by British International in 1929 and were closely followed by Gaumont's *High Treason* (music direction by Louis Levy). Indeed, for the first few years of sound, the film industry in this country remained remarkably stable, turning out a series of good pictures of excellent taste. This contrasts strongly with the " theme song " craze of those early days, claimed to have originated from an idea developed by Louis Levy when musically directing silent films, and later adopted so overwhelmingly by America. Kurt London describes this phase in detail :—

" The first period of the purely noise films was followed by undiluted dialogue films and sound-film operettas. The dialogue film, first created by Hollywood, soon came to an end for the time being : the language difficulty precluded export, and post-synchronisation in the present sense of the term was not yet known. As a result, a return was made to music, but admittedly only in a very negative way. The dullest and most stale devices of operetta were transplanted into the cinema, and the plague of the ' song hit ' infected the world's industries.

" In the last year of silent films, such theme-songs had already begun to be tacked on to a few individual films, to gain increased propaganda for them by means of records and other methods of publicity. This germ of the theme-song spread with terrible rapidity, became an epidemic, and systematically disintegrated the sound-film. For its style has been totally destroyed by this craze, always excepting genuine musical comedies that have been filmed. Thus serious plays became operettas and drama changed into farce. The dramatic texture was torn out of even the neatest manuscript, and still is sometimes, though nowadays far more care is taken to motivate these songs properly.

" The theme-song broke the tension at the most important points in the film, because it held up the action. And a film must never linger without reason : requiring, by its very nature, incessant motion. The song hit with its usually stupid and insipid text, lowered the general level of the early sound-films even below that in the period of mechanical interludes. In consequence of the inevitable mass production of songs, a veritable ' song-hit boom ' occurred, until it was barely possible to distinguish between one number and the next."

And to think that it all started over here !

The first five years of British film music was naturally a period of experiment, as it was with the whole process of movie making, but the position of our films was firmly established, and many exhibitors were voluntarily showing as much as 50 per cent. of the home product in their cinemas, making the then recently introduced Quota Act quite superfluous. These films included Anthony Asquith's *Tell England* (1930), *Under The Greenwood Tree* (music by Hubert Bath), *Baroud, Ball At The Savoy* and *Wife Of General Ling* (music by Jack Beaver), *Flame Of Love* (music by Hans May), *Autumn Crocus, Water Gypsies* and *Java Head* (music by Ernest Irving) ; also a very excellent set of pictures made by the Gaumont-British company, in which resident music director Louis Levy introduced a whole series of composers who were later to become a strong nucleus of the lighter type of British film musicians. Such pictures include *The Man Who Knew Too Much* (music by Arthur Benjamin), *The Lucky Number* (music by Mischa Spoliansky), *The Constant Nymph* (music by Eugene Goossens, John Greenwood), *Chu Chin Chow* and *Waltzes From Vienna* (music by Hubert Bath), *Channel Crossing* (music by Jack Beaver), *Dr. Syn* and *The Thirty-Nine Steps* (music by Jack Beaver, Hubert Bath) and *Britannia Of Billingsgate* for which five composers collaborated : Jack Beaver, Bretton Byrd, Walter Collins, Noel Gay and Leighton Lucas. Then there was the series of Jack Hulbert and Jessie Matthews pictures, with song hits and scoring by Bretton Byrd and Leighton Lucas. We recall such titles as *Jack's The Boy, Gangway, Head Over Heels, The Good Companions, Evergreen* and *First A Girl.* The solid work of Hubert Bath during this 1930-35 period did much to lay a firm foundation for future development, though even to-day he has received little public recognition for his musical integrity and masterful handling of some of the early scores.

In 1931, Alexander Korda, under the auspices of Paramount Pictures, directed the Leslie Howard film *Service For Ladies* ; the music score was by Percival Mackey. This was followed by the formation of Korda's own company, London Films, and their first production appeared in 1932. Entitled *Wedding Rehearsal*, it was musically directed by Philip Braham. In the following year, Korda made the photoplay that put him in the front rank of British film makers, where he stayed to become the outstanding producer of the next five-year period (1935-40). It was called *The Private Life Of Henry VIII*, featured Charles Laughton, and was musically directed by Kurt Schroeder, a German opera conductor who took over the music department for Korda at that time. Having had the satisfaction of working on one of the classics of the early English sound era, Schroeder retired from Korda's unit. He was succeeded by the man who was destined to become the most important single figure in the history of British film music.

3. MUIR MATHIESON

" *There is one name that appears very frequently in British screen credits—the name of Muir Mathieson, the musical director. Note that name, please. Remember it. Honour it. Of all the people who have served the British cinema brilliantly in wartime, I should put this young, ardent little Scotsman very near the top of the list. Muir Mathieson is not only a solid conductor and a scholarly musician in his own right ; not only has he arranged countless scores for films and conducted film orchestras, large and small ; but his enthusiasm and engaging personality have cajoled one after another of the great composers into writing original music for the cinema. Vaughan Williams, Arthur Bliss, William Walton, William Alwyn, Richard Addinsell, and the Master of the King's Music, Sir Arnold Bax ; these people trust Muir Mathieson. He has musical integrity. He is one of their own kind. The film people trust him, too. He is a swift and practical worker. He knows the screen. To him, the alliance of image and sound is something of a burning mission. He is an idealist— with all the solid caution of a Scot.*"

C. A. LEJEUNE, *November*, 1944.

James Muir Mathieson was born at Stirling, Scotland, in 1911, the son of Mr. John G. Mathieson (the well-known painter and etcher) and Mrs. Mathieson (a fine violinist). Two other film personalities who were born in the same area are Norman M'Laren and John Grierson.

Muir Mathieson commenced piano studies in Glasgow with Philip Halstead, and by the age of 13 his musical knowledge had developed so rapidly that he was able to found the Stirling Boys' Orchestra, and their youthful leader made his debut as conductor and pianist on the platform of the Albert Hall in Stirling. This led to the orchestra being taken up by the newly-formed Scottish branch of the old British Broadcasting Company resulting in a number of broadcasts being presented by Muir Mathieson and his juvenile group of musicians from " 5 S C," the original Glasgow station of the B.B.C.

Soon Muir was on his way to London, having won a scholarship to the Royal College of Music in conducting. The Katherine Boult and Leverhulme Scholarships soon followed. At the Royal College, he studied piano and composition under Arthur Benjamin and conducting under Dr. Malcolm Sargent, both of whom have since had considerable associations with the cinema.

Immediately he left the R.C.M., Mathieson began in films as assistant musical director for Alexander Korda, but before assuming full responsibilities, he quite rightly spent a year or two conducting music of all types. Thus we find him in Toronto and Montreal, conducting ballet at the age of twenty.

In 1932 he appeared at the R.C.M. College Concerts, conducting single movements from symphonies or one act of an opera as is the custom at the College. In 1933 he was music director to performances of Gilbert and Sullivan's "Pirates of Penzance" with the Winchester Operatic Society, while a year later he conducted the orchestra for an open-air performance of "A Midsummer Night's Dream" at Ovington Park, Hampshire.

1935, however, is, perhaps, the most significant year of his early career. First there was Kurt Weill's operetta " My Kingdom For a Cow" staged at the Savoy Theatre in London with Mathieson as musical director. All the time since leaving the College he had been building up his film music experience, starting as an assistant music director at the age of twenty, and eventually he succeeded Kurt Schroeder as full-time musical director to Korda's London Films Company. His first film score was for *The Private*

Life Of Don Juan (1934) and his first composer was the Russian-born Mischa Spoliansky, one of a group of experienced theatrical and film music men who had scored for Max Reinhardt on the Continent and had come to London in 1933 to do such early pictures as *Lucky Number* (Gaumont, 1933) and *Tell Me To-night* (Jan Kiepura, Edmund Gwenn and Sonnie Hale, also 1933). The result was a good score for *Don Juan*, and the song " Senorita " was recorded by H.M.V. following the release of the film. Next year again produced a successful combination between Spoliansky and Mathieson in *Sanders Of The River*, with more H.M.V. records for which the orchestral accompaniment was conducted by Muir Mathieson. Also, in 1935, came one of his teachers from the R.C.M., Arthur Benjamin, to join him for music to *The Scarlet Pimpernel* and *Wharves And Strays*, both excellent scores. The year culminated, however (from a film music viewpoint) with Mathieson's first major cinematic triumph—the Arthur Bliss score for the H. G. Wells' film *Things To Come*. It was also in 1935 that he first deputised for Dr. Malcolm Sargent by conducting performances of " Hiawatha " at the Royal Albert Hall, and amongst the great cast of 1,000 performers, he first met his future wife, the ballerina Hermione Darnborough, cousin of the Duke of Portland and the Duke of Argyll. They were married at Brompton Oratory in January, 1936, and their first child was born the following year. They now have three lovely children ; composer William Alwyn dedicted his " Suite of Scottish Dances " recently to the arrival of a Mathieson son and heir. With his first big film music success, the conducting of "Hiawatha" at the Albert Hall, and getting engaged as well, 1935 was, indeed, a notable year in Muir's active life.

For the next four years he settled down to direct the music for a steady stream of top-flight films ; these include *The Ghost Goes West, Fire Over England, Vessel of Wrath, St. Martin's Lane, Sixty Glorious Years, South Riding*, and many other notable pictures. A full list of Muir Mathieson's films appear in the Biographical Index to this book. During this time, it was a case of hard, solid film work, made especially interesting by such films as *Wings Of The Morning* (1937), Britain's first full-length feature film in Technicolor, with music by Arthur Benjamin and a fine gypsy dance sequence with Hermione Darnborough, solo dancer of the Sadler's Wells Ballet, and now Mrs. Mathieson.

In 1938 he presented a highly successful series of six film music concerts for the B.B.C. with the London Film Symphony Orchestra (the unit he had formed at the studios for film work), made up chiefly of members of the London Symphony Orchestra. During March, 1939, Queen Mary came to Denham Studios in a tour which included a visit to the music recording stage where Her Majesty saw Mathieson recording part of the Miklos Rozsa score for *The Four Feathers*. She watched him conducting three choirs accompanied by a tom-tom, while scenes from the film were flashed on to the screen.

During this period Mathieson put British movie music on the map. In five years he built up a tradition of quality on the sound-track by using only the best available composers for his pictures, establishing a perfect film orchestra and working in close collaboration with the recordists. Through a highly erratic period of " quota quickies " and second-rate musicals, he blazed a trail of distinction for British film music so that even the American film critics wrote " Hollywood has nothing like this." When Alexander Korda had said that British films should have the best stars, the best directors, the best technicians, Mathieson had quietly added " and the best composers and musicians." He succeeded admirably in ensuring that those fine films which kept the standard of our cinema from going under completely in the days of the great film slump of 1935 to 1939 were all sent out with music that was technically and artistically equal to anything in the world.

During the course of the war, Mathieson became busier than ever before. First he worked as a producer of documentary and propaganda films at the Film Centre. Throughout the war he was musical director to the Crown Film Unit, the Army, Navy and R.A.F. Film Production Units and to many of the small groups engaged in instructional and training films. Elsewhere in this book is a list of these pictures, often with scores by famous contemporary writers ; in nearly all cases Mathieson directed the music and frequently the composers were introduced to films by Muir himself, as in the cases of Ralph Vaughan Williams and Sir Arnold Bax. Then there was still the work of recording feature scores at Denham, where he continued as music director to a number of Arthur Rank companies after the break-up of the old Alexander Korda group. For long periods he worked at the B.B.C. on various Overseas Broadcasts, such as the famous " Britain to America " series. He has directed the music for that traditional feature of the B.B.C., the " Christmas Round the World " programme. In October, 1942, Muir Mathieson made his first appearance as a " straight " orchestral conductor for a public concert, conducting the London Symphony Orchestra at the Cambridge Theatre, London. The programme included Beethoven's Fourth Symphony, the Mozart B Flat Piano Concerto and (the only concession to films) a performance of the " Warsaw Concerto," with Eileen Joyce at the piano.

This began his career as a concert hall conductor (distinct from a B.B.C. and film studio specialist) and since then he has conducted in all parts of the country and with almost every British orchestra. Most of his programmes have been on conventional lines, but occasionally he includes suites from films. In March, 1943, for example, he presented one of the earliest public film music recitals at the Stoll Theatre, playing music from five pictures. In 1944 he conducted a season for the Sadler's Wells Opera, while in 1945, he organised and conducted a notable series of concerts in Edinburgh, travelling to Scotland every week-end after a busy week recording for Denham and Pinewood. He did numerous concerts for E.N.S.A. all round the country during the war.

To-day he continues his work as the most progressive single element in British film music. During 1946 he directed his first picture, *Instruments of the Orchestra*, while in the same year he initiated a series of gramophone records of film composers, starting with a fine recording of music by Arthur Bliss for *Men Of Two Worlds*. Still in his thirties, Mathieson can already look back on a full and fruitful career. He lives in a beautiful old farmhouse only a short way from Denham Studios, with his wife and fine children. For recreation he enjoys riding, and keeping his car in order, but he is always willing to " talk films " at all times of the day so great is his enthusiasm for his job. Oddly enough he and his wife very rarely go to the cinema ; says Muir, " my interest lies in the picture that is in the process of having music fitted to it and as it is in practically finished form at that stage I see most of the new films ten or twenty times anyway." An energetic and enthusiastic worker, Mathieson is completely devoid of the theatrical airs and graces so often beloved by some of our leading musical personalities ; rather does he possess that down-to-earth, forthright sincerity and frankness that is the mark of true genius and ability in a man who knows his job and gets on with it.

4. " THINGS TO COME "

Appropriately enough, it was Muir Mathieson himself who initiated the great film music event in 1935 which brought the first five years of film music development in Great Britain to a climax and had a widespread effect on all subsequent progress, the event that first brought film music to the attention of the serious music lovers of this and other countries, the score that even to-day holds a unique position in any history of film music—*Things To Come*. This picture was one of the most ambitious projects ever attempted by British film units and remains to-day as one of the major achievements of Alexander Korda's London Films company. The story was based on the H. G. Wells book " The Shape of Things to Come," and Wells himself closely collaborated on every stage of production with the director and special effects expert, William Cameron Menzies (now in Holly-wood). Muir Mathieson put his theories into practice on a big scale by obtaining Arthur Bliss, prominent British contemporary composer, to write the music. Although he had no experience whatsoever of film work, Bliss belonged to the generation of symphonic composers after Elgar, who had remained amazingly young and up-to-date. " The music is a part of the constructive scheme of the film," writes H. G. Wells, " and the composer, Mr. Arthur Bliss, was practically a collaborator in its production. In this as in many other respects, this film, so far as its intention goes, it boldly experimental. Sound sequences and picture sequences were closely interwoven. This Bliss music is not intended to be tacked on ; it is a part of the design. The spirit of the opening is busy and fretful and into it creeps a deepening menace. Then comes the crashes and confusions of modern war. The second part is the distressful melody and grim silences of the pestilence period. In the third, military music and patriotic tunes are invaded by the throbbing return of the air men. This throbbing passes into the mechanical crescendo of the period of reconstruction. This becomes more swiftly harmonious and softer and softer as greater efficiency abolishes that clatter of strenuous imperfection which was so distinctive of the earlier mechanical civilisation of the nineteenth century. The music of the new world is gay and spacious. Against this plays the motif of the reactionary revolt, ending in the stormy victory of the new ideas as the Space Gun fires and the moon cylinder starts on its momentous journey. The music ends with anticipations of a human triumph in the heroic finale amidst the stars."

The result was something revolutionary in film music, but as with all experiments, it is open to criticism. Even H. G. Wells himself admits : " It cannot be pretended that in actual production it was possible to blend the picture and music so closely as Bliss and I had hoped at the beginning. The incorporation of original music in film production is still in many respects an unsolved problem." To this Arthur Bliss replies : " My argument is that in the last resort film music should be judged solely as music— that is to say, by the ear alone, and the question of its value depends on whether it can stand up to this test." In support of the idea of a completely filmic score, however, Bliss admits that " while I was writing my *Things To Come* music, I felt that I was to some extent surrendering my musical individuality to the needs of the film itself ; so, as a kind of mental purgative, I wrote my ' Music for Strings,' which, of course, is absolute music." The score for the H. G. Wells film certainly satisfied the critics from the point of view of pure music ; as a concert hall suite, *Things To Come* was an outstanding success when it was performed at the Queen's Hall Promenade Concert series in 1935, winning many new friends for film music and resulting in a set of three gramophone records being issued by Decca, recorded by the London Symphony Orchestra conducted by Arthur Bliss himself. The recording for the film sound track involved fourteen full orchestral sessions at a London theatre. In addition to a full symphony orchestra, an extra percussion orchestra, including several experimental instruments and a large choir were used in the original sound track. The sale of the gramophone records has remained consistently good right up to this day, and all film music enthusiasts should have them. There is no doubt that, although Bliss' film scores are few and far between, the quality is always first-class, all his works being later arranged as concert suites and publicly performed. First came the *Things To Come* music, then another London Films production, *Conquest Of The Air* (performed as a suite at the " Proms " in 1938), and most recently, the music to *Men Of Two Worlds*.

5. THE YEARS 1936-1939

The period from 1936 to 1939 was an erratic one for British films. In the field of background music, Muir Mathieson continued to make progress at Denham. He introduced the Hungarian, Miklos Rozsa, in 1936, with

CAESAR AND CLEOPATRA. The Music Room scene, showing the young British star Jean Simmons. The score was by Georges Auric.

Knight Without Armour, followed by *The Squeaker*, *Divorce Of Lady X*, *Four Feathers*, *South Riding* and *The Thief Of Baghdad*. All showed excellent musical quality. *Divorce Of Lady X* for example, was a light, witty and humorous score, delightfully off-setting the slick comedy of the long, opening, bedroom sequence with wailing brass, grunting bassoons and trilling flutes in the Walt Disney style. *The Thief Of Baghdad* was full of attractive themes with some ingenious orchestration, notably in the temple sequence. After completing this film, Rozsa went to America with Alexander Korda and has since been very successful in writing for Hollywood films, including the Korda pictures *Jungle Book* and *Lady Hamilton*, both made in the States. Another fruitful associate with Muir Mathieson was the film music specialist Richard Addinsell; during this period he entered films with *The Amateur Gentleman* followed by *Farewell Again*, *Fire Over England* and *Vessel Of Wrath* (all London Film productions). It was on such films as these that Addinsell built up his experience which eventually led to the " Warsaw Concerto."

In 1937, Benjamin Britten (of " Peter Grimes " fame) produced his only feature film score, *Love From A Stranger*, a remarkable piece of cinema directed by Rowland V. Lee. William Walton followed his *Escape Me Never* success with music for *As You Like It*, produced in 1936. The London Philharmonic Orchestra recorded the score in which the strings were prominently used in the excellent Oratorio Finale (based on Elizabethan songs), in the heraldic grand Introduction and, indeed, throughout a restrained musical background. In 1939 he scored the Elizabeth Bergner film *Stolen Life*.

A member of the French group "Les Six" visited us in 1938 with music for the first G. B. Shaw film, *Pygmalion*, produced by Gabriel Pascal; it was Arthur Honegger, well-known as a film composer for Continental motion pictures including *Mayerling* (Danielle Darrieux, Charles Boyer), *Crime et Chatiment* and *Les Miserables*.

Spoliansky, already mentioned in connection with *Sanders Of The River*, did the songs and background music for another Robeson film *King Solomon's Mines*, produced in 1936, based on a story by Rider Haggard. Paul Robeson went on to make *Jericho* (with musical numbers by the song-hit writers Michael Carr and Jimmy Kennedy), *The Song Of Freedom* (in which Robeson played opposite Elizabeth Welch in a sincere story of a London Negro dockhand in search of his true home), and in 1939 *The Proud Valley*, a tale of the Welsh

MUIR MATHIESON conducting a film recording.

41   B*

coalfields, Eisteddfods and a pit disaster, musically directed by Ernest Irving and featuring Mendelssohn's "Elijah" as well as the glorious music of the Welsh choirs. Although they were often marred by production faults, the Paul Robeson films of this period were considerably above the standard of the "big band" musicals of their day, and a film like *King Solomon's Mines* still makes good entertainment.

Featured music included a screen presentation of Mozart's life with the composer's songs and parts of "Figaro" and "The Magic Flute" played by the London Philharmonic Orchestra conducted by Sir Thomas Beecham. The picture was called *Whom The Gods Love*, being made at Ealing Studios in 1936; it was a weak story and the chief interest lay in the music of Mozart which was smoothly recorded. For the Elizabeth Bergner film *Dreaming Lips*, a reconstruction of the Queen's Hall was built in the studios, and the Boyd Neel Orchestra accompanied Raymond Massey in his part as a world-famous violinist. John Greenwood wrote the background score for the first British Technicolor feature film *Wings Of The Morning* in which John McCormack sings three songs. In 1937, director Michael Powell recorded the Glasgow Orpheus Choir for his picture *The Edge Of The World*; eight years later Powell again used the same choir in that delightful story of the Scottish Isles *I Know Where I'm Going*.

At this time the team of musicians under Louis Levy at Shepherd's Bush included Hubert Bath, who scored a hit in *Rhodes Of Africa*, from which came the stirring March "Empire Builders." He was responsible for *Tudor Rose* and *A Yank At Oxford* as well as a number of Alfred Hitchcock pictures. Also with Gaumont at the time were Leighton Lucas and Bretton Byrd doing scores for the Jessie Matthews, Jack Hulbert and Will Hay films.

Anthony Collins, who has spent much time in Hollywood on American films, scored *Sixty Glorious Years* and *Nurse Edith Cavell* for Herbert Wilcox in 1938 and 1939. For his earlier picture *Victoria The Great* (1937), Anthony Collins dealt with the largest job of its kind that had at that time been attempted. Conceived on a big scale, the score was recorded by the finest instrumentalists available, with members of the London Symphony Orchestra, singers from the London College for Choristers and the Life Guards Band. The actual music used at the Coronation of Queen Victoria in 1838 was incorporated into the score, with the "Gloria" by Handel, "The Queen Shall Rejoice" and "I Was Glad" by

Attwood, all being used as in the original Coronation service. The final sound track was such that the film critic of the " New York Herald Tribune " devoted two columns to the music of *Victoria The Great* saying that " the British take their film music seriously and despite the fact that American screen music has been improving at a rapid pace, no permanent symphonic ensemble in the United States has yet the record in the screen world that the English group has." This was in reference to the London Symphony Orchestra, recording under the direction of Muir Mathieson.

In 1937, we had *Rembrandt* with Charles Laughton in the title role, and a score by Geoffrey Toye, full of true Dutch colour in songs like " The Naughty Girls of Kieldrecht " or the impressive singing by the huge crowd gathered at the Town Gates awaiting the Prince of Orange. In a tavern at Leyden, the home of Rembrandt's father, singing and dancing is shown to a setting of old seventeenth century folk songs, accompanied by genuine instruments of the period such as the rommel-pot, serpent, bagpipes and clarinet.

John Greenwood was active during this period on a number of important pictures including *The Drum, Elephant Boy, A Tale Of Two Cities* and *East Meets West.* At Ealing Studios, Ernest Irving worked on all the George Formby and Gracie Fields pictures and was Music Director to Associated Talking Pictures from 1933 onwards.

The Muir Mathieson series of British Film Music broadcasts during 1938 were a landmark in the gradual recognition by musicians and public alike of the possibilities of background music, though at this time Mathieson was only in the " pioneering stage " and much was still to be done. Alexander Korda and Denham dominated the scene from 1936 to 1939 especially as regards music, for this was the day of the " quota quickie " and although there are many other films that could be quoted here to make a comprehensive list, I have followed the advice of one composer (who, incidentally, has since done some excellent scores) when he says, in submitting his list of pictures—" 1936 to 1939. Several films which I would prefer to forget."

However, very firm foundations were being laid and great individual achievements were obtained by the work of the central core of film music specialists of this period who continually strove to raise the standard of their music during an erratic four years. It was during the war years that the real value of the spade work made itself felt.

6. SCREEN OPERA

Most film-producing countries have attempted to film operas at one time or another. America has often incorporated operatic sequences into her pictures, as for example the large extract from " Faust " in the M.G.M. production *San Francisco*, or the Susanna Foster film *Phantom Of The Opera*. The Soviet Union have made a top-flight film star out of operatic tenor Sergei Lemeshev, singing parts of Tchaikowsky's " Eugene Onegin " in the picture *A Musical Story*, or performing " Rigoletto " and " Martha " in a Moscow movie, which was known over here as *Russian Salad*. In 1933 we saw the production of *Tell Me To-night* with Sonnie Hale, Edmund Gwenn, Athene Seyler and the European tenor, Jan Kiepura, directed by Anatole Litvak, and featuring music by Mischa Spoliansky, plus arias from " La Boheme," " Rigoletto," " Traviata " and " Martha," a film which survived to receive a re-issue by Ealing Distribution during the war. The period from 1936 to 1938, however, is the most active for screen opera experiments, some of which succeeded, while others were a decided flop.

First there was *The Robber Symphony*, claimed at the time as the first specially composed screen opera, written, scored and conducted by Friedrich Feher, featuring Hans Feher, Magda Sonja, Webster Booth and George Graves and recorded by the London Symphony Orchestra at Ealing. A film critic and musicologist wrote :—

" In order to assess this film properly, it is necessary first of all to forget the word ' symphony ' in the title, with its uneasy suggestion of recondite but muddled analogies between films and music, and to ignore altogether the affectation of the hoarding announcement, displayed for all to see but few to comprehend, asserting that this is the first ' composed ' film. Such pretentious generalizations serve only to obscure the ultimate issue : to the viewer all that matters is whether the thing itself is effective, and any innovations of approach or technique, supposing they exist, must be allowed to speak with their own voices. Theory—to be supported only by the most thorough and explicit analysis—comes afterwards.

" What the film does show is a sound appreciation of the screen-value of fantasy, made strong and assisted towards atmospheric unity by an exhilarating lightness of touch, by the pervading presence of a series of attractive musical motifs, and by a tempo as revealing as it is deliberate. The fairy-tale plot, which concerns itself with the pursuit through Alpine country of a small boy belonging to a band of street-performers, by a company of robbers who have hidden a stocking full of gold coins inside his piano-organ, is rightly simple in idea, and allows full scope for ingenious development. The importance of the music is unmistakably stressed in the opening, where an overture is played through at length by a complete orchestra, a brief shot of which appears once more at the close. Dialogue is not absent, but has been reduced roughly to a minimum ; it is interesting to observe that after the long musical beginning the entry of the human voice is actually a trifle disturbing.

" Technically, the production is in many ways excellent. There is little indication of any confused striving after effects— the directness of the dream-passage, linked transparently to reality by the barking of the dog, is a case in point—and the photography is good, the camera-positions expressive, and the cutting neat and accurate. The acting is as finished and professional as most of the other elements. The first part of the film is thus largely successful, but the second half is less assured. This is due not to length as such, nor to any disabilities inherent in the method, but to a common difficulty of construction—the working-out of the theme to a smooth and still convincing conclusion.

" The intimate alliance of music and fantasy is in principle wholly commendable. But, whatever the form of the music in itself, the combination is not symphonic, but, rather, operatic. Here, perhaps, may even be opera's legitimate successor—the transmutation of that hitherto over-synthetic medium into something more complete and closely-knit."

The Robber Symphony, with the singing of Webster Booth and George Graves and the music of the London Symphony was not a box-office success and has long since disappeared from the screen.

Also in 1936, the world-famous Italian singer Beniamino Gigli spent a week or two in Worton Hall Studios, where he recorded " O Sole Mio " and extracts from " Pagliacci " for a London film production directed by Zoltan Korda. *Forget Me Not*, as it was called, proved to be a moderately successful picture, but it was below the general high standard of the Korda works and it too has not been seen for many years. Attempting to find copies of this immortal voice as it was recorded in 1936, I failed to discover any trace of the film in Wardour Street to-day.

In 1937, another opera experiment was made, this time a complete screen interpretation of Leoncavallo's famous *Pagliacci*, produced by Trafalgar Films. This tale of the tragic clown, who ends by killing his faithless wife and her soldier-lover on the stage during a performance of a play, is peculiarly fitted to screen adaptation, since the stage-setting is an actual element in the plot and can, therefore, be reproduced on the screen more or less straightforwardly. With Richard Tauber and Steffi Duna, a reasonable presentation of the opera was achieved, in which the Prologue and the moving Epilogue (both sung in their entirety in the film) were shot in a British colour system that never got very far, Chemicolour. This very unnatural two-colour process, which divides the scene into bluish-green and yellowish-brown tints, was only acceptable because it did not clash with the formal conventions of opera itself. There were long periods of dialogue during the main part of the action which began to drag in the middle, while the sound recording was poor—a fatal fault in this style of picture. The strings of the orchestra were rough, while the deep full tones of the voices were over-modulated, ending in distortion. The result of using operatic technique at the beginning and end only produced an uneven effect. However, the production and photography were good while Tauber's singing, the main item of the film, did not disappoint his admirers. The cast were efficient, with Jerry Verno doing wonders in the part of Beppo and Esmond Knight appearing in an effective study of Silvio, the lover. Although an enterprising experiment in its day, *Pagliacci* again has not stood the test of time, and an afternoon trying to locate the present whereabouts of the picture ended up in a little second-floor film distributor's office where I was told that it had now been withdrawn and destroyed.

Finally, comes a note about one of the most ambitious efforts of all. A special company was formed (with considerable financial backing), Gilbert and Sullivan Films, to bring the famous comic operas of that world-famous team to the cinema. The producer of the first picture was Geoffrey Toye, with Victor Schertzinger directing at Pinewood Studios. The stars included Kenny Baker, an American singer who came over especially to make this film ; Jean Colin, Martyn Green, Sydney Granville and other members of the Gilbert and Sullivan stage team all appeared in the picture. The opera chosen first on the production schedule was *The Mikado*, photographed in Technicolor, and recorded by the London

Symphony Orchestra and the chorus of the D'Oyly Carte Company. Before the film went into production, Geoffrey Toye made an intensive study of the latest methods of sound recording and went to the United States where he contacted Leopold Stokowski and other Hollywood sound experts in order to ensure that *The Mikado* should have a perfect sound track. Returning to Pinewood, special new equipment was installed and used for the first time on the Gilbert and Sullivan picture. The technical qualities were made as near perfect as possible, with exquisite settings by Vertes, 750 specially designed costumes, and the use of delicate pastel shades of Technicolor producing a delightful effect. The music was brilliantly recorded on Western Electric ; indeed, Sullivan has never been better sung, every word of song and dialogue being perfectly clear and audible from a thoroughly competent cast. As far as possible, they kept to the original. Six numbers were omitted, also some dialogue, but nearly all the traditional stage " business " was retained, to which was added a new mimed prologue.

The picture came before the public early in 1939, being in production throughout 1938, and received a good press. Reg. Whitley said " a feast for eye and ear. Up to the highest standard of Hollywood screencraft—I have never seen more beautiful colour photography or heard the famous Sullivan melodies more effectively played—there can be nothing but praise for the magnificent singing and acting of the cast." He was supported by most of the popular critics ; Jympson Harman agreed that *The Mikado* was a winner. " The first sensation on seeing it is one of rapture. The most notable thing contributed to film entertainment in years." But the British Film Institute were more cautious. " The filming of a Gilbert and Sullivan operetta is obviously a dangerous experiment, bristling with difficulties. Countless fans on the one hand know every line of dialogue and every note of music, and cannot bear any to be omitted or altered ; a potentially vast cinema audience is possibly ignorant of both. Can the Gilbertian humour be reproduced in another medium ? Will a generation brought up on superficial verbal wisecracks appreciate the subtle and penetrating barbs of satire ? " Generally speaking, I regret to say, they did not, and *The Mikado* was only a very moderate success compared to the amount of money and work that went into it. Director Victor Schertzinger, with 100 feature films to his credit (nearly all in Hollywood) and including musical classics like *The Love Parade* (Jeanette MacDonald and Maurice Chevalier),

One Night Of Love and *Wings Of Song*, did everything possible to give *The Mikado* an up-to-date cinematic punch, but the result was only a fine technical job and an absolutely flat picture. Film critic A. Vesselo had the last word in a review written in October, 1939, on the general release of this movie. " As a film," he said, " it does not exist. The very beginning comes as a shock, for not only has it been felt necessary to insert an explanatory prologue, but this prologue is introduced by one of those old-fashioned anticipatory captions which tell you everything before it happens. Before long it grows obvious that to attempt a straightforward transference of a work like 'The Mikado' to the screen is to attempt the impossible. Look at the way in which the continuity of events is broken up and made static by the many song-passages. There is, of course, nothing wrong with them on the stage ; they are part of the technique, which is intentionally (and effectively) artificial ; and similarly the division into separate acts and scenes is a definite stage-device. But conventions of this kind have no place in films, and one is forever having forced on one's notice odd items of stage-machinery which on the screen have lost all meaning.

" Perhaps the most revealing point is the extraordinary flatness of all the well-known D'Oyly Carte stage-' business.' A single example : during one of his songs or speeches Pooh-Bah wiggles his big toe at the audience, and in the theatre the unexpectedness of this has an irresistibly comic effect. That is due in the first place to its apparent spontaneity ; in the second place, to the fact that the audience do not all notice it at once, but the word seems to creep round the house, each man eagerly nudging his neighbour ; and, in general, to the fact that it establishes a direct inter-action between the audience and the performer.

" None of this applies to the screen. The mechanical nature of the screen-photograph (added to its self-complete realism in its own sphere) precludes any direct inter-action between audience and performers ; there is no gradualness in the audience's perception, for a big toe wiggling on the screen at close quarters is big enough for everybody to see at once, so that all the subtlety is lost ; and, in the circumstances, the apparent spontaneity quite disappears."

No further attempts were made to pursue the original plans of the company for a complete series of these operas. Then came September 3rd, 1939, and further experiments in British screen opera came to an end.

It now seems reasonably safe to say that there is no future in it. Apart from the inclusion of operatic sequences (as in *San Francisco*) there is no scope for full scale adaptations from the opera house to the film studio. Even the comparatively realistic medium of the modern stage play requires drastic alteration to give scope for a good film, because of the static convention of the stage set-up. How much greater then are the problems in dealing with the far more stylised convention of the opera. In examining these expensive British experiments, one may wonder if the producers of the films read the warning that Kurt London gave in 1935 before any of the pictures had gone on the floor, for, said he, " the film version of an opera performance is impossible and intolerable. Those elements for which on the operatic stage even to-day allowance is made, under the influence of the personalities of live artists, must on the screen have an insipid, ridiculous, and anachronistic effect. The camera brings the singer's pathos much too close to the spectator ; a close-up of a photographed high C, on which the distorted face of the tenor, with wide-open mouth, is to be seen, at once destroys the effect of even the most beautiful melody and resolves it into laughter or even disgust. (Mr. London obviously hadn't seen Frankie Sinatra ! —J.H.) The unreal world of opera and the naturalistic film have nothing whatever in common.

" Even more than in the living theatre the lack of constant action would disturb the effect : opera is static, film dynamic. An alteration between detailed close-ups and panoramic effects would only be possible to a limited extent, perhaps only in panto-mimic situations with considerable dramatic action. The length-dimension of an opera could only with difficulty be made to coincide with those of a film ; abbreviated arrangements for film purposes would with most works inevitably destroy the line of the original score.

" The operatic stage keeps its spell only when it is symbolically removed from the audience by the orchestra pit : thus it retains the air of ' once upon a time,' the element of the extraordinary. Opera walks on buskins, the film on ordinary low heels. The dramatic direction of opera differs from that of the film so funda-mentally that an adoption of opera by the film can only take the form of an allusive narration."

And, indeed, there are no signs at the moment of re-attempting screen opera in this country. Before World War II, we were still groping in the dark, trying to find our best medium for a national film industry. We tried the big-scale musical and failed, we tried musical comedy and we tried opera without success. Our drama and comedy only came a poor second to the Hollywood counterparts at the box office. The war gave us the answer in the fictional-documentary film, in the period novelettes of Gainsborough Studios, in the domestic English comedy of Noel Coward, and in the realism of *The Captive Heart, 49th Parallel* and *The Way To The Stars.* I think it will be a long time before British films will want to try screen opera again.

7. " MOONLIGHT SONATA "

Ignace Jan Paderewski died in 1941 in New York at the age of eighty after a stormy life as a concert pianist (his first appearance in London was a failure, but Bernard Shaw, then a critic on a London newspaper, hailed him as a great genius) ; as a world traveller ; as a politician and one-time Foreign Secretary and Premier of Poland ; as representative of Poland at the League of Nations, and as a brilliant composer of piano music. It was while Paderewski was living in retirement at his lovely villa at Morges, near Lausanne, that film director and producer Lothar Mendes conceived the idea of introducing famous personalities to the screen in fictional stories, and in the realm of music his choice was Paderewski. Having completed *The Man Who Could Work Miracles*, a London Films production based on the story by H. G. Wells, Lothar Mendes went to Paris where he contacted Paderewski, and displayed remarkable tenacity by inducing this grand old man of 75 to emerge temporarily from retirement and make his first appearance on the studio floor. Gathering together the American actor Charles Farrell. with 72 year-old stage star Marie Tempest, and a newcomer to the screen Eric Portman, Mendes took the floor at Denham at the end of 1936 with his impressive cast, plus a weak story which simply served as a romantic background to Paderewski and his piano. The location of the plot is Sweden (actually shot at Cragside, Northumbria, on the forested estate of Lord Armstrong) where owing to an airplane mishap, three gentlemen—Paderewski, his manager, and a Chilian cook—seek refuge at the house of a Baroness, who lives with her charming stay-at-home daughter. and an American estate agent. The story works out a triangular situation, complete with kisses on the terrace after dinner and a thunderstorm at the right moment, all of which is very dull and best forgotten. The film's outstanding merit is the privilege which it presents of watching and hearing a great genius who is no longer with us.

Visitors were not allowed on the set during the time Paderewski was playing. Only the artists or technicians saw him at work, and the few weeks he spent at Denham are still remembered by the old hands from the studios. No film star ever caused such interest. The soul of courtesy, he would solemnly raise his hat to electricians and carpenters on the floor when he arrived and departed. He never started work until three o'clock in the afternoon, but came to the studios by 2.15 to see the previous day's "rushes." During the shooting of a big concert hall sequence, a crowd of 400 extras were paid a guinea a day to sit and hear Paderewski play, a privilege for which thousands would have paid five, ten and fifteen guineas themselves just to hear his performance. Needless to say, a seventy-five year-old master musician was pretty fussy about the recording of his music. Eighteen pianos were tried out before he was satisfied. When it was discovered that the wooden floor gave too much resonance, boards were torn up and a concrete floor substituted. Paderewski had a permanent " bodyguard " who followed him everywhere—his secretary, M. Strakacz, Dr. Masson, a burly Swiss doctor who was always in attendance in the last few years of his life, and Fritz Hohenstein, piano tuner to Paderewski for fifteen years, whose duty it was to tune the two pianos always kept on the set during the film. The piano you see in the film, by the way, is a Steinway.

And then there was the piano stool. Paderewski was accompanied on all his tours by his own piano stool which stood on the platform of every concert hall in the world at one time or another ; he played in practically every leading city in Europe, North and South America, Australia, New Zealand and South Africa during his life, making about twenty complete tours of the United States alone. The case in which the piano stool travelled was encrusted with over a thousand labels. The stool—which was actually a chair—was leather-seated, with a long fringe, and was adjustable. It was a very heavy affair, but without it Paderewski refused to play, so it spent a number of weeks in the studios while the film was being shot. For the first twenty minutes of the picture he plays Brahms, later his famous Minuet, and finally the whole of the first movement of the Beethoven Moonlight Sonata. He appears totally unconscious of acting a part, and except for being obviously bothered by the studio lights, he is delightfully natural,

51

like a polished and somewhat eccentric gentleman from a Russian story. Both the photography of Jan Stallich and the sound recording by C. K. Medlen are good by 1936 standards, and the film is a remarkable record of one of the world's most famous pianists. The music recording was supervised by A. W. Watkins.

In 1943, the Wardour Street racketeers got to work. *Moonlight Sonata* was re-issued as *The Charmer* and bally-hooed as an Eric Portman picture to cash in on the current popularity of the said Mr. Portman. This in itself was pretty cheap, for Portman had only a small part in the film, being practically unknown at the time. The crowning achievement, however, was that they carefully went through the picture and cut out every bit of Paderewski's playing, leaving just the exceedingly tiresome story. So, for three years, *Moonlight Sonata* became a tedious second-feature hash job for Sunday bookings. It was eventually rescued by a more public-spirited distributor, who happily re-issued it in 1946, this time in its original version.

8. THE YEARS 1939-1941

September 3rd, 1939. The cinemas all closed, a siren within an hour of declaration of war and every studio in the country closed. But not for long. In World War I, the British film industry nearly became extinct ; the mistake was not to be repeated in World War II, for Denham opened up again, and made a full length film in twelve days. It was called *The Lion Has Wings* and Richard Addinsell composed the score between his wartime duties with the Thames Patrol during the early days of September and October, 1939. It was a good score with a stirring March theme and an impressive climax. Addinsell continued his work with the film *Contraband* and outstanding music for *Gaslight* and *Love On The Dole*. Hans May, with about sixty films in France and Germany to his credit, came to the fore in 1940 with his score to *The Stars Look Down*. Walter Goehr, who also composes and conducts his own group (under the name of George Walter), has had many years experience of films, coming to England from Austria in 1933. His first wartime scores included the story of the Battle of the River Plate, made by Gainsborough under the title *Far Freedom*, and that unusual film about spiritualism, *Spellbound*. William Walton scored *Major Barbara* in 1941 with great success, while Spoliansky did one film *Jeannie* and John Greenwood scored *Pimpernel Smith*. Composer, conductor, arranger and music director Charles Williams, a veteran film music expert, scored *Kipps* for Gaumont and wrote a hit theme for *The Night Has Eyes* (James Mason, Joyce Howard) which enjoyed a number of radio broadcasts.

9. " DANGEROUS MOONLIGHT "

Like other film music composers, Richard Addinsell had met with the same experiences that confront most screen background music men. There is the interest of writing music to a moving image, the various problems which arise in working out the score, the pleasure of hearing your own music performed at the recording session, and perhaps later on when you go to the cinema. And like many other composers, Addinsell's work passed without much attention from the public. Suddenly came *Dangerous Moonlight* in 1941. And *Dangerous Moonlight* meant only one thing—" The Warsaw Concerto." Terence Young, a film script writer, was on duty one night at his army camp and was listening to a concert on the short wave from America. During the performance of a piano concerto he sketched out the idea of a Polish concert pianist who fights with the Polish Air Force until the collapse of that country, when he escapes to England and joins the R.A.F. From this outline, Young worked out the story of *Dangerous Moonlight*. It called for a short descriptive work for piano and orchestra that would give the impression of a concert pianist playing a piano concerto in the recognizable style of a romantic composer of serious music. It would have been possible to use a well-known work, as they used the Tchaikowsky Piano Concerto No. 1 in the film with Bette Davis *The Great Lie*, or in *Escape To Happiness* (Leslie Howard) which featured Grieg's Piano Concerto, played by Ingrid Bergman in the film story. The trouble with this is that people already have predetermined associations and reminiscences which they recall when they hear such music. Instead of thinking about Poland and Warsaw when the music was played, they would remember their own special reactions when they first heard the work in question ; perhaps they would recall the people who came to the concert with them, or the refreshment room at the Albert Hall when a friend said rather loudly and much to their embarrassment that " he thought it stank." In other words, the associations which individual members of the audience may have in relation to a certain piece of well-known music are quite beyond the control of the director of a film in which it is used ; indeed, it may produce an effect on the individual entirely different to

53

the one he wants, or it will almost certainly produce a distraction (which may occur at a vital moment in the plot and spoil the whole effect of the film), because of these private reminiscences which are evoked by the music. It is for this reason, of course, that it is considered vital to have specially composed background music in nearly all films as distinct from the compilations of popular semi-classical items that went to provide the musical background for silent films.

And so with *Dangerous Moonlight* it was rightly decided to have a piece of music specially written, that could be used to become associated in the mind of the audience with Poland, air raids in Warsaw, and whatever the director wanted to suggest. Richard Addinsell was given the job of producing this music, and over a period of six months he worked out a " pastiche," lasting nine minutes, giving the effect of a concert pianist playing a concerto in the romantic style (the composer most strongly suggested being Rachmaninoff). The result was an excellent piece of context film music which was duly recorded and edited into the finished film ; the Americans call them " Tabloid Concertos." The film was eventually shown at the Regal Cinema, Marble Arch, and scores of people rang up every day to ask for the title of the work and its composer ; it became known as " The Warsaw Concerto." No one had foreseen the amazing popularity that the " Warsaw Concerto " would enjoy. Thus when the film first appeared, the gramophone record had not been issued nor had the sheet music, but on discovering what a hit this elusive, haunting melody had become, the error was quickly rectified, the gramophone record being specially taken from a sound track made during the production of the film, though not as it was actually heard in the picture with dialogue and sound effects added. The music is played by the London Symphony Orchestra, conducted by Muir Mathieson. Although he was never officially credited either in the film or on the record, everyone seems to know now that it was not played by Anton Walbrook but by Louis Kentner. Even to-day it sometimes occurs that the producers prefer a veil of secrecy to be cast over the identity of instrumentalists doubling for actors on the sound track—witness the case of Jose Iturbi's piano recordings of the Chopin music in *Song To Remember*—but in the case of *The Seventh Veil* and *Love Story* it was stated in the credit titles that the music on the piano was being played by a concert pianist, without any loss of effect in the film I imagine. Concealing the identity of such people—the film stars of the sound track—recalls the old days when not even the names of the actors in a picture were quoted in the titling for fear of shattering the illusion ; besides when such things are not stated, it makes a lot of work for people like me in ferreting round the studios in order to unearth the " gen " !

The " Warsaw Concerto " naturally came in for some criticism at first from serious music fans who had never heard anything like this given the name of such a specialised musical form as the " concerto," implying to-day an elaborate work for orchestra and solo instrument with a playing time of, perhaps, thirty or forty minutes and consisting of a series of well-defined movements. The mere act of combining a piano with an orchestra does not make a concerto, and Richard Addinsell is the first to admit that " Warsaw " is not meant to be a " concerto " in the strict classical sense. However, this did not prevent it sweeping the country from end to end as a musical craze rarely equalled ; the sheet music sold in thousands of copies, it was heard almost daily on the radio, it made a tremendous hit in the United States, and during the war years wherever a pianist sat down in a N.A.A.F.I. bar, in a pub, or in the quiet of the family circle, there would come before long the request for the " Warsaw Concerto."

But to get back to the purpose for which it was written, it only remains to say that the " Warsaw Concerto " is one of the finest examples of a film music tabloid concerto, expertly written and cleverly handled to the considerable dramatic advancement of the picture, which at the same time became the first piece of film background music to attract the attention of a very large and enthusiastic audience.

10. " 49TH PARALLEL "

49th Parallel (or *The Invaders* as it was called in America) was one of the first films to found what later became a notable category in the success story of wartime motion pictures in this country, the fictional-documentary. The action of *49th Parallel* is built round the wrecking of a U-boat by Canadian bombers while a party of six Nazis have gone ashore to rifle the local trading station. Stranded, the Germans attempt to escape across Canada into the United States. Deftly woven into the framework of the plot are dramatic conflicts between the Nazis and various types of Canadians, thus giving us a picture of modern Canada set against a fictional plot, so combining the documentary approach to that of story-telling. Michael Powell, director of the film, took a unit, fully equipped, 20,000 miles across Canada in order to get authentic location sequences, going as far north as the 63rd Parallel for certain sequences—the farthest latitude at which a normal production unit has ever operated. On the trip it was necessary to take twenty-five technicians and actors, together with a seaplane that came to pieces for stowage in a ship's hold. Food, rifles, cameras and negative stock were among the other necessities, the last named requiring careful handling to prevent the celluloid from becoming brittle. At times, exposed and unexposed negative were stored in Eskimo tents, warmed by blubber oil stoves—and not one foot of film was lost owing to the weather conditions. In the Hudson Straits the unit built a complete replica of a German U-boat and arranged for it to be bombed by the Royal Canadian Air Force. Throughout the whole tour, embracing Newfoundland, Hudson Bay, Hudson Straits, Niagara Falls, Toronto, Montreal and other points east, in every case the leading local amateur dramatic societies were called upon to provide small-part players, while numerous Eskimos were also used. The stars of the picture include Leslie Howard, Laurence Olivier, Anton Walbrook, Raymond Massey, Eric Portman and Glynis Johns.

Back from the Associated Sound Studios in Montreal came the unit in order to complete their film at D. & P. Studios, Denham, England. Among the final processes to unify the job was the scoring, and it fell to Muir Mathieson to select a composer for this story set in a location where " across the great North American Continent there runs a line drawn not by bloodshed and strife, but by the common consent of the free peoples of two great countries. It is not a barrier—it is a meeting place. It is the ' 49th Parallel '— the longest undefended frontier in the world." Foremost advocate of the highest musical standards in pictures and the man responsible for greatly enhancing the reputation and prestige of the music of the cinema, Mathieson introduced yet another great name in British contemporary music to the film studio—Ralph Vaughan Williams. " When I went to see Vaughan Williams at his country home in the spring of 1940," says Muir, " I found him strangely depressed at his inability to play a fuller part in the war. He felt that the musician had done

ANN TODD as Francesca Cunningham, a concert pianist. Eileen Joyce takes the sound track ' part,' doubling for the piano playing. From *The Seventh Veil*.

little to express the spirit and resolve of the British people. At that time he was 'doing his bit' by driving a cart round the village and countryside, collecting scrap metal and salvage. (Vaughan Williams was then over 70 years of age). I told him the story of *49th Parallel* and tried to show how the cinema could help to achieve those very objects for which he was striving. His enthusiasm was wonderful. He set to work right away—and remember this was the first time he had ever consented to write for the screen."

The result was a grand score and Vaughan Williams has since done a number of other film works including *Coastal Command*, *The Flemish Farm*, *Stricken Peninsula* and *The People's Land*. The *49th Parallel* music was recorded by the Denham sound supervisor A. W. Watkins with the London Symphony Orchestra conducted by Muir Mathieson. This music was immediately taken up and often performed in the concert hall ; in 1943 the B.B.C. made a special recording of the " Prelude " (with the B.B.C. Northern Orchestra). In the meantime, Vaughan Williams arranged a " 49th Parallel " suite which received its first performance in May, 1946, and it is hoped that there will soon be a gramophone record issued of this music.

Introducing Vaughan Williams to the cinema undoubtedly ranks as one of Muir Mathieson's major achievements as the musical casting director of Denham Studios. After five years of struggle to improve the standard of movie music, it was a great day when he assembled his recording session for the performance of the first film score by one of the liveliest and most versatile of living musicians, the " Grand Old Man of English Music," composer of the "London Symphony," "Serenade to Music," operas, songs and even musical comedy, who, when over 70 years of age, was still young enough in mind to tackle an entirely new medium of composition.

11. " THE COMMON TOUCH "

The Piano Concerto No. 1 by Tchaikowsky has had a colourful career. Written in 1874, it was disappointing at first because Rubenstein, for whom it was composed, did not like it at all. However, it was revised in 1889 and rapidly became a popular item of the concert hall repertoire. It made its first screen hit in 1941 for the film *The Great Lie*, in which Mary Astor played the

THE SEVENTH VEIL. The London Symphony Orchestra accompanies Ann Todd in one of the concert hall scenes from the film.

57

part of a famous pianist in a love contest with Bette Davis. Within a couple of months we had the first movement of the Concerto again in a British production *The Common Touch*. In 1942 it featured in the last sequence of the English documentary, *C.E.M.A.*, while in 1944 the American *Song Of Russia* gave us extracts from the other movements of the Concerto instead of just the first as had so far been the case. *The Great Lie* used the music as a background and as a link in the story, whereas in *C.E.M.A.* it is partly featured as an item in a mid-day concert at a war factory canteen and partly used as a background to scenes of armament production. In *Song Of Russia* the music serves as a vehicle for Robert Taylor in his part as an American Symphony Orchestra conductor on tour in Russia, and for Susan Peters, his pianist wife. It was also played in *Anchors Aweigh* by Jose Iturbi.

The Common Touch features Mark Hambourg and the London Symphony orchestra in an impressive Tchaikowsky piano concerto sequence, but it was in a way a mistake to cast Mark Hambourg into the part of a down-and-out musician (affectionately known in the district as " Chopin," pronounced phonetically). He is so very well-known that the illusion is lost. For this picture is based on the lines of Rudyard Kipling :—

" If you can talk with crowds and keep your virtue,
    Can walk with Kings—nor lose the common touch.
If neither foe nor loving friends can hurt you,
If all men count with you, but none too much.
If you can fill the unforgiving minute
With sixty seconds worth of distance run,
Yours is the earth and everything that's in it,
And—which is more—you'll be a man, my son."

From this theme is developed a fanciful story of social drama, of two young wealthy men in search of truth among the down-and-outs of a working men's hostel, and of the people they encounter. Into the skilfully directed plot are interwoven various types of music ; thus in addition to Mark Hambourg we have Carroll Gibbons and his orchestra and Sandy McPherson. The concerto episode shows the pianist playing in the street while scenes of his past successes in the capitals of Europe are conjured up before his mind as he plays the stirring music of Tchaikowsky. The film was musically directed by Kennedy Russell.

Following the success of this picture and *The Great Lie*, the tuneful opening of the first movement of the concerto became very popular, resulting in a Tin Pan Alley version entitled " Concerto for Two," in which the lovely melody was " hotted-up " and completely ruined by a set of execrable words of the slushiest type. However, public opinion asserted itself in the right direction and the sales of the gramophone recordings of just the first movement as recorded by various Symphony Orchestras and concert hall pianists greatly exceeded those of the jazz version which soon died a natural death. In view of the wide range of melodic Piano Concertos, it seems rather overdoing things to have five film versions of the Tchaikowsky No. 1, but with the advent of the Rachmaninoff No. 2 in both *The Seventh Veil* and *Brief Encounter*, the film makers are at least showing some sense of proportion, and we look forward to hearing other such works skilfully woven into film plots to the advancement of the popularity of the serious composers and an extension in the artistic range of film entertainment.

12. THE YEARS 1942-1943

1942 was the most important period as regards film scoring by William Walton, for in one year we saw four films with his music on the sound track. Three were made at Ealing Studios—*The Foreman Went To France*, *Went The Day Well?* and *Next Of Kin*— and were full of very fine music. The most significant, however, was his score for the Leslie Howard production *First Of The Few*. This stirring drama of the Spitfire and its famous designer, R. J. Mitchell, ranks amongst the finest films of the war, a magnificent monument to the late Leslie Howard, a perfect example of the fictional-documentary and a notable account of one aspect of the vital days in 1940 when the R.A.F. earned that tribute from Winston Churchill which inspired the title of the film. William Walton's music ranks with *Henry V*—his two finest scores ; for the Howard picture he wrote a "Prelude and Fugue to the Spitfire", which is now available on an excellent gramophone record by the Hallé Orchestra. The Prelude is a patriotic, resounding piece of good orchestration ; simple in construction, it makes ideal film music. The later sequences of the film show how Mitchell, suffering from an incurable disease and with only one year to live unless he gives up all work, makes an irrevocable decision. He sacrifices himself and produces the prototype of the Spitfire, but just before he dies, hears that all production difficulties have been overcome. The picture ends to the roar of the Spitfires in action on September 15th, 1940, with the Battle of Britain at its height. Musically, Walton worked out a Fugue to illustrate this. For the factory scenes of the fighter aircraft in production he built up his theme for the body of the Fugue. Suddenly the urgent rushing momentum of the music halts and a second, slow, sad phrase is heard on the violin ; Mitchell is dying that the Spitfire may be born. As the sorrowful notes of the strings die away the main theme returns with renewed vigour, building up into a crashing climax as the Spitfire, now perfected at the cost of its creator's life, roars across the sky to fight the most decisive life-and-death struggle in modern history. Walton's " Spitfire Prelude and Fugue " is one of the most exciting moments in film music annals and (like *Things To Come,* " Warsaw Concerto," *Men Of Two Worlds* and *Henry V*) is strongly recommended for inclusion in your gramophone record collection.

Other scores of 1942 include Richard Addinsell's *A Day Will Dawn* ; " Tea Time Music " is the name of a published extract from it. *Thunder Rock* (Hans May) was an unusual and thoughtful film, giving the composer scope for musical expression on a big scale. William Alwyn was at his best in *They Flew Alone,* providing what was in effect a symphonic poem for the Amy Johnson England-Australia flight.

Coming to 1943, we note three scores by John Greenwood, the Sussex composer. *Nine Men,* a story of the Western Desert, incorporated the Eric Coates' march "Eighth Army" into the Greenwood music, while *San Demetrio* gave scope for plenty of drama in the scoring. *The Gentle Sex* was not so well cast musically ; the score was noisily purposeless in the worst American tradition.

The score to *Life And Death Of Colonel Blimp* offers an interesting example of what can be packed into a music track for a film of this type. Let us have a look at it in detail to see the processes that can go to make up, in this case, a balanced and efficient comment on the visuals. The music man is Allan Gray and his score was recorded by music director Charles Williams. Firstly, Gray has taken a selection of excerpts from existing music to give atmosphere in various sequences :—

" Mignon " (Thomas)
" Zampa " (Herold)
" Lohengrin ": Fate motif. (Wagner)
" Fingal's Cave " Overture (Mendelssohn)
" March of the Wooden Soldiers "
" British Grenadiers March "
and music by Offenbach.

The theme of the picture is the gradual change of Britain's attitude to war from the days of the Boer War onwards, and in addition to existing music, Gray composed further items to suit each period—ballads, waltzes, stirring marches and even modern boogie-woogie. These include :—

> " I See You Everywhere," a nostalgic foxtrot designed to express in music one of the central themes of the picture.
>
> " The Mill Goes Round and Around," a gay waltz.
>
> " Colonel Blimp March."

Then to this, he has added the " Commando Patrol," a perfect illustration of the jazz idiom in background scoring. The sequence depicts a Home Guard exercise in progress, which culminates in the capture of " Colonel Blimp " in a Turkish bath. We see the fast-moving action of the army group attacking the Home Guard boys, with messages flashing to-and-fro, orders being given and, in particular, a mobile column on the road, led by motor cyclists. A most powerful effect was obtained by the use of a hot jive tune, played in best swing style, used purely as background music to this sequence. Gray has used the technique elsewhere in his film work, usually to good effect. In this case the jazz item became popular in its own right under the title " Commando Patrol." *Life And Death Of Colonel Blimp* is an object lesson in the lighter type of background scoring.

Ralph Vaughan Williams (or " R.V.W." as he is usually referred to in musical circles) scored *The Flemish Farm* in 1943 ; part of it was played at the Proms in 1945. For *Millions Like Us*, Hubert Bath introduced a choir of Welsh singers into his score—a delightful touch. The choir, incidentally, came from a large war factory in Cardiff, and spent a busy day travelling from Wales in the morning, recording in the studio in the afternoon, broadcasting in " In Town To-night " in the evening, and filming the whole night through at the Shepherd's Bush Empire, where the stage was taken over by the film unit after the variety performance had finished. The Welshmen went back home the following day ready to get on with their engineering jobs. The conductor of this choir, Iorwerth Morgan, is a Welsh National Eisteddfod winner and an experienced broadcaster, while Tom Emerson, the solo tenor, is a miner from the Rhondda Valley and took part in the recording of the Welsh National Anthem, specially tracked for the film by Louis Levy. Which all goes to show that no expense is spared to get the right sort of music for the sound band of British films.

We note a screen appearance of the London Symphony Orchestra for the Butchers' production *I'll Walk Beside You*, musically directed by Percival Mackey. Swing fans got a rare treat in two short films made by Harry Parry and his Radio Rhythm group ; they were produced by Inspiration Pictures. Although musically colourful and interesting, technically they were about as badly made, as amateurishly handled and as plain " corny " as it is possible to make films. The band played its part well, but the photography, sound recording and general production qualities suggested that these two pictures were shot by the light of two photo-floods in a third-floor back room in Soho.

And now to continue in more detail, a survey of one or two musically outstanding items of 1942-43.

13. " THE GREAT MR. HANDEL "

In October, 1942, appeared the first product of J. Arthur Rank's new deal to bring " uplift " to the British screen. The founder of the Religious Film Society, multi-millionaire, Methodist, Rank had begun his well-planned scheme to gain financial control of the British film industry with his avowed intention to raise the moral and æsthetic value of British movies, in addition to breaking the American market on a scale never before attempted. He had the money, he had the studio space and the distribution all lined up, but he had little feature-film experience. Coming from the atmosphere of the Religious Film Society, it was natural that his first production should have religious (as well as Techni-) colour. The picture began to form along the lines that might have been anticipated. First the story came from the pen of L. du Garde Peach, beginning as a Children's Hour programme and being worked out over a period of a year (during which the author was engaged on B.B.C. work) ; there was no chance of upsetting the Censor here. The director was Norman Walker, serious-minded, stolid craftsman of such film classics as *The Turn Of The Tide*. Wilfred Lawson, Shaw and Shakespeare stage actor, star of films *Pygmalion*, *Stolen Life*, *Pastor Hall*, *The Man At The Gate* and *Jeannie*, was perfectly cast in the part of Handel. The role of Mrs. Cibber, the young prima donna, was taken by Elizabeth Allan, also a Shakespearian expert, with *David Copperfield*, *A Tale Of Two Cities*, *Camille* and *A Woman Rebels* among her film successes. So that the colourful dresses and costumes of the eighteenth century would be shown to the best advantage it was decided that the film should be produced in Technicolor ; perhaps the pastel shades of the magnificently restrained, soothing colour as photographed by Claude Friese Greene and Jack Cardiff are the outstanding achievement of *The Great Mr. Handel*. The production was supervised by Jas. B. Sloan, and made at Denham and Pinewood Studios, with Sidney Gausden in charge of the colour sets, the sound track recorded by John Cook, with the music from Handel's original scores arranged and conducted by Ernest Irving (specially loaned from Ealing Studios because of his knowledge of Handelian works), and played by the London Philharmonic Orchestra. The story was historically correct, but had plenty of dramatic possibilities. It told how, at the beginning of the eighteenth century, George Frederick Handel was the uncrowned King of Music. His operas were crowding the playhouses and he had composed and conducted music for the Coronation of George III.

Then his star began to wane. The more cynical-minded young people about the court, led by the foppish Prince of Wales, craved for frothier fare than Handel wanted to provide.

The Playhouse run by Handel and his Swiss partner, Heidegger, the " ugliest man in London," became emptier and emptier. Heidegger went to see the Prince of Wales to beg for his patronage for a new season of opera by Handel, and achieved his purpose.

The Prince and his friends attended the first performance of the new opera, but the Prince roused Handel's anger by making stupid remarks about the prima donna, Mrs. Cibber. Handel refused to conduct while the chatter went on.

The Prince and his party left the Playhouse, and as a result, fashionable distaste for Handel's operas became a feud against the man himself. Hooligans were hired to make hideous rows outside his theatre, to sling filth at this play-bills. The best of his musicians and singers were enticed away, and the theatre was rented over his head.

The only friends Handel had left were Mrs. Cibber and his Scots servant, Phineas. One after the other his enterprises failed. He became dangerously ill and although he recovered, he felt his life-work was ended. Then, however, a chance word from his servant, Phineas, evoking his deep religious faith, showed him he still had work to do.

It was then that a literary amateur, Jennens, brought him the book of an oratorio, " Messiah." Sick and sad as he was,

Handel set to work, labouring day and night. He had found inspiration in the great theme. Here was the work he had prayed for. At last, on à day some three weeks later, Handel could tell Mrs. Cibber the work was finished.

An invitation came from the Lord-Lieutenant of Ireland, inviting Handel to give a season in Dublin. In April, 1742, " Messiah " had its first triumphant performance. Its fame spread to London—everybody wanted to hear the new work. In March, 1743, it was performed at Covent Garden before the King and his Court.

Handel was restored to fame and favour. Choosing right as he saw it, and with simple reliance " on truth, on virtue, and on God," his triumph was inevitable. He had shown himself to be the Great Mr. Handel.

The story was interesting, factual, with scope for spectacle, emotion and fine music ; it should have been equally as successful as the Chopin film which followed three years later from Holly-wood—*A Song To Remember*. A great deal of work went into the music score ; here is music director Ernest Irving giving his own account of how he did the job :—

" Nearly all the music is Handel's. With so much of Tweedle-dum, there must be a little of Tweedledee, and so I have inserted a little tune of Buononcini, and there are some traditional street cries of the period. One of these is based on a motet by Orlando Gibbons. But with these small exceptions, the music is entirely Handel's.

" Some of the score is precisely as Handel wrote it. For instance, in the Fireworks music (played in Vauxhall Gardens) I have removed the extraneous timpans and trombone parts thus bringing to light Handel's cunning device of using the violas as a sort of bass trumpet, a tromba marina, in fact. Not a note has been altered or added to Handel, but in the orchestration I have given to the wind instruments chords or progressions which may well have formed part of Handel's improvisation on his own figure-bass.

" In the scoring I have not used clarinets as Handel seldom employed them. The London Philharmonic Orchestra, who recorded the music under my direction, were kind enough to remove all the metal junk with which modern orchestral string-instruments are bedizened and to substitute gut, as used in the days of our forefathers.

" It was a great task to find gut strings for this adventure, but we were able to run to earth a little hoard in a fiddle-maker's shop. The difference in the tone is, to my mind, like that between silk and fustian. I borrowed two Kirkman harpsichords, one from Morley, the harp maker, and the other from the Chaplin sisters, famous for their association with the 'Beggar's Opera'.

" A good deal of the action takes place about 1738, when Handel was rehearsing Serse (Xerxes) at Covent Garden, and several quotations are made from its score. Incidentally, it seems extraordinary to me that this work, which was a comic opera, should have failed so disastrously as it did, as it is full of the most beautiful music. The opening song, for instance, is ' Ombra mai fu ' —the celebrated Largo.

" Mrs. Cibber in *The Great Mr. Handel*, is heard in 'Ombra mai fu ' and ' Non so sesia la speme ' from Serse, as well as in ' He was Despised ' from ' Messiah,' ' Where'er you Walk ' and the Minuet from Berenice. Part of the Water music and other famous best-sellers of the great master are heard either in the foreground or the background.

" The climax of the film is the composition of ' Messiah,' for which I have made a pastiche for orchestra of six or seven of the ' numbers ' from that work. They are linked together by the leit-motiv of ' Comfort ye,' which runs like a thread all through the first part of ' Messiah.' It is impossible, of course, to quote the work in extenso, and I do not think that this ' selection ' will give offence.

" I have had the advantage of working from a copy of the earliest published score, bought by subscription for the Wakefield Club in 1766. I have taken the liberty to disregard some remarks made in the preface to his edition by Professor Ebenezer Prout, with which, in all respects, I disagree. I think, for instance, that if Handel wanted a demi-semi-quaver he knew how to write one, and that the clash of rhythms in 'Surely He hath borne our griefs' was intentional, and directed to a particular effect.

" The whole work of arranging the music was congenial and refreshing. What a grand fellow Handel was, even apart from his music . . . generous and kind of heart, and an indomitable fighter. This age could do with men of high character and undeviating integrity of thinking and living, like George Frederic Handel."

The music was ingeniously employed in every phase of construction. For example, director Norman Walker was puzzled how to denote lapses of time in the story, which covers a period of sixteen years. Ernest Irving suggested that nothing could be more appropriate than the traditional street cries of the period. His suggestion was adopted, and so the cries of the Cherry, Primrose and Mackerel sellers, and also those of the Milkmaid and Scissor Grinder, are heard in the finished picture.

The result of this careful preparation was a film of supreme artistry which was premiered amid great ballyhoo at the Leicester Square Theatre before an audience of musical notabilities late in September, 1942. The flawless recording was given a special boost by a loudspeaker system of unique design installed in the cinema, and the gala premiere was a great success. The trade press was enthusiastic ; "beautiful, restful Technicolor photography, its lovely period background, its panorama of bewigged lords and their crinolined ladies, and its dominating central study of a world-famous personality make the entertainment arresting even on these counts alone. But it is the distinguished Handel music which puts the picture in a class by itself." ...... "Artistic direction, compelling leading portrayal, strong support, beautiful production qualities. Delightful treat for music-lovers, with outstanding title pull." ("The Cinema"). Said the British Film Institute "the film is eminently sincere." As a music-lover's film, as a film connoisseur's classic, *The Great Mr. Handel* was an outstanding film event of the year, but in all the welter of music, period atmosphere, costumes and uplift, the director made one fatal mistake. The film was slow. A motion picture must move, and for long periods this one did not move. The popular press critics took this up like a shot, and there was plenty of adverse criticism. Long before it was shown, the "Sunday Pictorial" attacked Arthur Rank for his "uplift" plans ; they were able to rub it in after *Mr. Handel*, though they have long since revoked their old argument, and heartily encouraged subsequent Rank productions. The result was that this fine film, made with the very best intentions, was not the success that had been hoped for ; had it not been for a fairly good overseas distribution, it would have failed at the box office. It only ran for a week or so at the Leicester Square Theatre, and did only modest business on its main Odeon circuit release ; it has never been re-issued and is rarely, if ever, seen to-day. Ironically, at the same time as this musical masterpiece was playing to ever-decreasing houses at Leicester Square, a hundred yards away the musically worthless but slickly made American film *My Gal Sal* (Rita Hayworth, Victor Mature) was doing a roaring trade at the Odeon, where it ran for weeks. Oddly enough, *The Great Mr. Handel* did very well in Australia and Canada, while in America it was very well received in many quarters, and whatever shortcomings it had, we may well consider this review from an American film music magazine as a final word on a picture that had everything, yet just failed to become an outstanding success, for which only the director can take the responsibility, although he may read with rare satisfaction these remarks from America :—

"The great music is given a reverent and inspirational interpretation. It is never tedious and plays an integral part in the development of the story, characterized throughout by a sturdy sincerity, nobility and structural feeling. As the story holds to its climax, we are swept onward by the majestic strains of the 'Messiah' and during this music, scenes interpreting the various numbers are shown fleetingly as visions to the composer while he writes. These have a great emotional uplift and are especially good in that they help persons not familiar with the text of the Oratorio to visualize its progression, while to musicians and singers they add beauty to the well-loved words. An exceedingly capable cast lends dignity and authority to the whole and it was a happy idea to weave the London street cries into the story. Conception and composition throughout have the lovely color and depth of prints of the period and costumes and settings are authentic and lovely to the smallest detail. In these days of barren musical ideas and facile arrangements it is well to have the throes of creative genius so superbly brought to our attention. *The Great Mr. Handel* is a picture for all to see." (Hollywood, California, October, 1944).

14. THE YEAR 1944

Apart from the special item which we shall examine under section 16, 1944 saw a number of interesting photoplays. Two composers chose this year to make their only contribution to the feature cinema. Lennox Berkeley wrote music for *Hotel Reserve* ; the music was better than the picture, and emerged to receive a number of broadcasts. Particularly charming is the sequence " On the Beach," from which the B.B.C. excerpt was taken.

Tawny Pipit was the only film scored by Noel Mewton-Wood, the young concert pianist. The music was lyrical and unobtrusive, but failed to grasp the unusual opportunities offered by the long passages of silence in the bird-watching sequences.

For Michael Powell's *Canterbury Tale*, Allan Gray repeated the success of the *Colonel Blimp* score. Again there was a "jive" tune in the style of "Commando Patrol," but towards the end of the picture we were given a rare musical treat in the form of a sizeable extract from Bach's Toccata and Fugue in D Minor, played during the cathedral scene.

Hans May scored *2000 Women* for Gainsborough; it contained one of the musical tricks that come off better in a film score than in the concert hall. During a scene of the women internees gathered in the main hall of their internment camp, word is received that the R.A.F. men, "on the run" from a crashed bomber, are hiding in one of the rooms. Quickly the word is passed round, and May showed considerable ingenuity in using the strings of his orchestra to produce musically the effect of whispered conversation.

Mischa Spoliansky is our best writer for the "Mickey Mouse" effect in comedies. Witness his *Ghost Goes West* music ; I wonder if you remember the scene ? The American rotundity, Eugene Pallette, has bought up the old Scottish castle. We see dinner being served in the great hall, to the accompaniment of "Annie Laurie " on the bagpipes. Later on, the castle is shipped (complete with ghost) to the United States, but Pallette is determined to retain the old Scottish atmosphere. Dinner is again being served in the great hall and suddenly the air is filled with music as a hot negro band, led by a raucous trumpeter, "gives out " with a jazz version of the traditional Highland air. In these days of swing arrangements of Chopin Nocturnes and Beethoven Sonatas, a dance music version of "Annie Laurie " may seem commonplace, but when Spoliansky did it in 1936 the effect was highly amusing. To come back to 1944, there was some added fun from the music track in *Don't Take It To Heart* as Edward Rigby, the old butler, proceeds, terpsichorean fashion, along the winding corridors of the ancient homestead to the accompaniment of "puff puff " music by Mischa. Whether he is doing cartoons, drama or comedy, Spoliansky never fails to seize the vantage points from the visuals in order to give his scoring the strongest possible significance.

The action of *They Came To A City*, based on the play by J. B. Priestley, only demands the construction of one major setting. Due to the high degree of financial risk involved in producing such a thoughtful work, only by reducing studio cost was it made possible at all. Economy was the keynote on a picture that could obviously have only a limited box office appeal, and the figures in the Ealing Studios' accounts department showed that they were right in expecting a modest cash return from Priestley profundity. Even the music department was affected. Ernest Irving, music director to the picture, could not follow the usual expensive procedure of commissioning a score from one of his composers. Instead he used existing music. Normally undesirable in drama, he underlined the action with a work by a writer who had never seen the film and hàd not composed it for the screen. Yet Irving knew his music and *They Came To A City* is a rare case of the successful insertion of a symphonic concert hall item into a serious movie. Few people know the " Divine Poem " by Scriabin ; the average cinemagoer has never heard of him. It was this music that Irving took and he is to be congratulated on the neat manner in which he edited it into a fine background score.

Lastly, *Halfway House* is worth a mention for the Lord Berners music ; it gave the spine tingles to a weird account of a group of people given their last chance to solve life's problems in unique circumstances.

15. " LOVE STORY "

The task of writing a " second Warsaw Concerto " fell to veteran composer Hubert Bath, the Gaumont-British music expert, who had done consistently good work with scores to most of the Alfred Hitchcock films made by Gainsborough, as well as *Rhodes Of Africa*, *Tudor Rose*, *A Yank At Oxford* and *Dear Octopus*. Producer Harold Huth commissioned Leslie Arliss to direct a film which, though not a musical film by any means, was to use music in a way that would enhance and accentuate the feelings of the characters in the story, as " Warsaw Concerto " had done in *Dangerous Moonlight*. The music was again to become not so much a quiet, pleasant background, as an integral part of the development of the characters themselves. Lissa (Margaret Lockwood) a pianist, goes to Cornwall on holiday and with what she supposes to be only one year of life before her, meets an emotional experience of such strength that she is inspired to write a piano concerto into which her love for Kit (Stewart Granger), her feeling of freedom underneath the Cornish skies, the emotion inspired in her by the grandeur of the rocky coast and the sea, the sadness that her life may be ended just as she has found love, are all poured. Hubert Bath, aged 60, wrote as a result, " Cornish Rhapsody " for this film which was called *Love Story*. The sequence in which the concert performance of this work takes place was filmed in the Royal Albert Hall. With its upper galleries studded with arc lamps and cables trailing the corridors, the Gaumont-British technicians moved in for a few days to shoot the big concert finale. Hundreds of spectators filled the great bowl of the hall, whilst on the wide platform, flanked by the National Symphony Orchestra, under conductor Sydney Beer, Margaret Lockwood as the star pianist of the story, played the solo pianoforte for the Rhapsody. For three days the strains of the music filled the Albert Hall as the cameraman, Bernard Knowles, filmed long shots and close-ups from galleries and stage. The actual sound track, however, was later fitted in (with Harriet Cohen doubling for Margaret Lockwood on the piano), along with the rest of the music score, all written by Hubert Bath. Special sound tracks were recorded in Cornwall of the noise of the sea and the gulls, which helped the composer to obtain certain musical effects in the Rhapsody. A gramophone record played by the London Symphony Orchestra conducted by Hubert Bath with Harriet Cohen (pianoforte) was issued on Columbia at the same time as the picture was issued. When both the film and the music were at the height of their popularity, the composer, aged 62, died at his home in London.

16.   THE YEAR 1945

In examining month by month the film output of 1945 one gets the impression that every five years the British film industry reaches a significant phase in its development. 1930 saw the final establishment of the talking picture in British studios after two years of panic and indecision. 1935 saw the first of the great film music advances, with Arthur Bliss and *Things To Come* consolidating the position of Muir Mathieson as our foremost music director. 1940 saw the end of the slump, the end of quota quickies and Hollywood imitation. The film industry in this country was at last forced to stand on its own feet or disappear for good. It was in 1940 that we turned the corner into an avenue of a new type of national cinema—real, intense, intelligent cinema. It was also about this time that J. Arthur Rank, millionaire industrialist, first took stock of the position and eventually came in to help in the recovery of the industry. 1945 saw the culmination of all our efforts. For five years we had been building up a powerful tradition of fine films and in the last year of the war it blossomed forth into a great cavalcade of pictures that were to become famous throughout the world. *Henry V, Caesar And Cleopatra, Western Approaches, Blithe Spirit, The Way To The Stars, Perfect Strangers, The Seventh Veil, Dead Of Night, Burma Victory, Waterloo Road, They Were Sisters, I Know Where I'm Going, The Rake's Progress*—what a tremendous climax to five tough years ! And what of the next five years ? There are those who say we are already slipping back to the old ways ; the inspiration that carried us through five momentous years has gone. There is a different atmosphere in the studios, they will tell you. Hollywood's evil influences are creeping back, pinching our potential stars, setting up American production units in England to the inevitable loss of this country's workmanship and national film standards. Or there are those who claim that in 1950, we shall have secured a great world market for British pictures, that our industry will be a thriving concern destined to shatter, once and for all, the domination of Hollywood over the cinemas of the world. What do I think ? In anything so erratic and crazy as the film industry I would not dare to risk a prophesy for all the money in the world !

Musically, 1945 was important too. Certain special items we shall deal with separately, but the general line-up is impressive. Ealing Studios, with its music department led by Ernest Irving, again provided two unusual items. *Pink String And Sealing Wax* was scored by Norman Demuth, a contemporary composer well-known in musical circles, writing for his first picture. It was a pleasing score and kept the pace of the film on a better level than did the interpolation of songs by Handel, John Gay, James Hook and Sir Henry Bishop. For the magnificent thriller *Dead Of Night*, Irving commissioned a score by Georges Auric, famous French composer, music critic, ballet expert and film music writer. The music was written in Paris and sent over to Irving who conducted and supervised the recording at the H.M.V. Recording Theatre in St. John's Wood. The problem of synchronising music and picture presented some headaches, working with a score written in Paris, recorded in London, and filmed at Ealing, especially on sequences like the golfing scenes, featuring Basil Radford and Naughton Wayne, in which the music has to fit closely shots of a wavering golf ball in a ghost-hindered drive off the first tee.

Hubert Bath died in 1945, but his music was heard in a number of films during the year. Apart from *Love Story*, he scored *A Place*

Of One's Own and *They Were Sisters*, while only a day before he died, it is said that he was still at work, making rough sketches for the music to *The Wicked Lady*. His later years were spent in great work to ensure that the standard of British film music was maintained and, despite constant bad health, he worked continuously during the war years, often with little recognition for his labour. The music for *The Wicked Lady* was later done by Hans May and from the score came the pleasing song " Love Steals Your Heart," published by Chappells; May's song "Rosanna" from *Madonna Of The Seven Moons* was also published.

Richard Addinsell wrote one of his finest scores to the Noel Coward film *Blithe Spirit*. This witty, beautifully orchestrated music is a perfect case of the most successful type of light score ; the Prelude and Waltz are both available on a gramophone record and the Waltz is frequently heard on the air and at light music concerts. As pure film scoring, many consider that Addinsell's *Blithe Spirit* is a greater achievement than the " Warsaw Concerto," being more characteristic of the composer's true style.

Another hit of the year was Nicholas Brodszky's music for *The Way To The Stars* ; two outstanding themes were made available on a gramophone record. The film also includes a pleasing song hit called "How Long?" Brodszky's scores have always been extremely tuneful ; he has the gift of securing strong, individual themes for his film characters which register quickly and effectively. In this he is well served by the team of orchestrators with whom he has collaborated at various times, and in the case of *The Way To The Stars*, by his music director, Charles Williams.

I Live In Grosvenor Square had music to meet all tastes in an assembly of no less than five orchestras. In view of the fact that this Herbert Wilcox production featuring Anna Neagle and Rex Harrison is not a musical picture by any means, that is a lot of music. Anthony Collins wrote the background score ; he is a famous Hollywood composer, familiar over there as conductor on the Orson Welles radio programme sponsored by Lockheed Aviation and as founder of the Mozart Symphony Orchestra of Los Angeles. The score was recorded by the London Symphony and the R.A.F. Orchestras conducted by Muir Mathieson. Additional music was also written for the film and played by Carroll Gibbons and his Savoy

EILEEN JOYCE. The film star of the sound track. Her films include *The Seventh Veil, A Girl in a Million* and *Men of Two Worlds*, as well as *Battle for Music* and *Brief Encounter*.

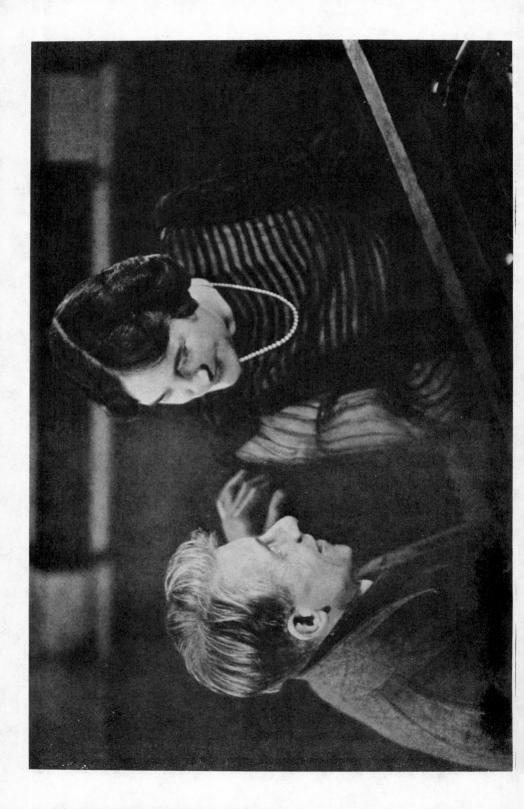

Orchestra. Irene Manning, accompanied by the R.A.F. Band (Canadian Section) conducted by Captain Farnon, introduces the main theme song of the film entitled "Home" and Sergeant Viccart and his G.I. Band are responsible for the swing numbers and jitterbug sequences in "Rainbow Corner," all of which amounts to a feast of featured and background scoring in the best Hollywood tradition.

Two films made by Butchers contained notable musical inserts. First is *For You Alone* featuring the London Symphony Orchestra with the famous singer, Heddle Nash, well-known in operatic circles. In the same picture are numbers recorded by Albert Sandler and his Palm Court Orchestra of radio fame. He accompanies the singer, Helen Hill, in one of the musical interludes. The musical programme includes :—

> Overture : " Merry Wives of Windsor " (Nicolai)
> " For You Alone " (O'Reilly and Geehl)
> " At Dawning " (Cadman and Eberhart)
> " Fascination " (Marchetti)
> " Flight of the Bumble Bee " (Rimsky-Korsakov).
> " Tales from the Vienna Woods " (Strauss)
> " Bless This House " (Brahe and Taylor)
> " Early One Morning " (Trad.)

Musical direction was by Harry Bidgood. The other film is *Home Sweet Home*, a Frank Randle epic, which introduces as guest artists, Rawicz and Landauer, the famous pianists. Helen Hill is seen also as a soloist. The film was made at the Riverside Studios in Hammersmith, being musically directed by Percival Mackey. In recent years the modest productions of Butchers Film Company have shown a considerable improvement in their general standard of entertainment, while musically they have followed a policy of frequent screen appearances by the London Symphony Orchestra in the lighter type of semi-classical music.

Other scores of note in 1945 include Alwyn's grand music to the Rex Harrison comedy *The Rake's Progress*, Clifton Parker's writing for *Perfect Strangers*, and the delicious musical effect achieved by Allan Gray in the Michael Powell picture of the Scottish Isles called *I Know Where I'm Going*.

DIARY FOR TIMOTHY. The director of the film Humphrey Jennings discusses a scene with Dame Myra Hess during the shooting of the National Gallery sequence.

17. " HENRY V "

The film *Henry V* was largely a one-man venture, for Laurence Olivier appeared in the lead as well as producing and directing this magnificent British " prestige " work of art. In a picture backed by the strongest team of expert technicians it was possible to muster, the music score, nevertheless, shone forth in a manner rarely witnessed before. The trade and popular press are normally immune to this question of background film music, and rarely, if ever, does the music get a line in any write-up. *Henry V* was an exception. In papers such as the " Daily Telegraph," " Daily Express " and " News Chronicle," the critics commented on the powerful score written by William Walton, conducted by Muir Mathieson with the London Symphony Orchestra and recorded by John Dennis and Desmond Dew at Denham Studios. In America, the picture received a most cordial welcome from the critics, and the hard-boiled film section of the magazine " Time " devoted three pages to a very complimentary write-up which included a note on the music. William Walton was very enthusiastic about the production of this Shakespeare play and took a great deal of trouble over the music, which, as a concert suite, was performed at the Promenade Concerts in 1945 and has received a number of other public interpretations in addition to the very complete set of records specially made by the B.B.C. Northern Orchestra, which includes the " Globe Playhouse " Overture, Passacaglia and the Agincourt Song and Battle Music.

But for a full survey of this most important score, here is Hubert Clifford, himself a composer, giving his own impressions of the film :—

" Walton has written much fine music in this score, and I cannot but believe that he has enjoyed doing it, and that he thinks highly of it. Judged by purely musical standards the best in this score nears comparison with Walton's own output for the concert platform. Judged as film music, it is one of the most distinguished and effective scores in recent times. The form of the film posed an awkward problem for the composer—the conflict between three periods. With the resources of 1944 (for the ears of 1944), the composer had to encompass a musical atmosphere of the days of Queen Elizabeth and those of Henry V. Walton's solution of the problem was as satisfactory as any stylistic compromise of this kind could be. Apart from the use in certain sequences of plain-song and organum and of the Agincourt Song, Walton's method was to divide the dramatic atmosphere and express it in terms of his own musical mind. The result was a happy absence of the ersatz, or the musical equivalent of Wardour Street Tudor. I had never previously been aware of the essential Englishness of Walton, but in *Henry V* there was an authentic English musical voice, just as English in its own way as that of Elgar or Vaughan Williams. More than that, Walton's music attained a virility and a dramatic range greater than that displayed by any other contemporary British composer.

" For me, the musical 'high-spot' was the Passacaglia which accompanies the interpolated scene of the death-bed of Falstaff (George Robey as the dying Falstaff achieved an almost unbelievable effect of poignancy). This music moves with a simple dignity and a restrained pathos, and adds to the scene something which will make it remain long in the memory. For sheer excitement—excitement which provoked the sophisticated press-showing audience to an ovation—the crescendo of the French cavalry charge which commenced the Battle of Agincourt would be hard to surpass. I suspect the audience did not realise that they were applauding 't'other side'—but no matter. The gathering momentum of the charge was enhanced by the cunningly mixed sound-track. A long 'crossfade' brought the music to the foreground, interchanging in prominence with the harness and armour-clanking sound effects as the charge gathered its impetus. The director very wisely suppressed the effects and allowed the music its full head as the climax was approached. The result was a tour-de-force which, with the action and the strident primary colours of the banners and surcoats of the knights, drew a burst of spontaneous applause from the audience. Another point of special musical interest was the choral and orchestral version of the Agincourt Song. The duration of this was all too brief, but one had the impression that Walton had made a fine setting. The tempo appeared to have been speeded up to meet the dramatic exigencies of the sequence, and the result was that the tune lost some of its sturdiness and acquired an urgency which was foreign to its original characterization.

" Two other particularly happy pieces of writing stay in one's mind—the 'title music' at the opening, when the roulades of a solo flute accompany the swirling of a wind-tossed fragment of paper which is to emerge as a playbill of the Globe Theatre, and the theatre overture in the Globe itself. Walton creates a musical atmosphere here by very simple means. He might have tried to produce a replica of the theatre music of Elizabethan times, but wisely refrained from doing so. The result was quaint, charming and convincing. Almost as successful was the music for the French Court scene during Henry's wooing of Katharine.

" The standard of performance by the London Symphony Orchestra, under Muir Mathieson, is consistently high throughout the film. Unfortunately, though, the recorded sound as reproduced in the Carlton Theatre was slightly distorted. The tone had an unpleasant edge and an exaggerated upper frequency range which affected both speech and music. I am loth to believe that this existed on the original recording, but whatever the cause, there is no justification for having anything but first-class sound to a film as important as *Henry V*.

" The film itself leaves one with mixed reactions, but mostly of enthusiastic admiration. There are fundamental difficulties in adapting a stage play for the screen, and they are increased if the play be a literary classic which demands an inviolability of dialogue. The director has solved some of these problems in an ingenious fashion. Another question, too, is whether the cinema-going public will readily accept the convention of stylised models photographed in Technicolor—they are rather reminiscent of Disney.

" Nevertheless, the total impression which the film gives is one of magnificent achievement. Anyone who values fine language, fine acting and fine music must retain from it many unforgettable moments, and feel a sense of gratitude to Laurence Olivier and his collaborators, seen and unseen.

" This appeared to be the general reaction of the audience when I saw *Henry V*, but what was especially significant for musicians was the round of applause which greeted the name of William Walton in the ' credits ' at the end of the film."

Extracts from Walton's *Henry V* were performed at the Promenade Concerts in 1945, and " Death of Falstaff " with " Touch Her Sweet Lips and Part " (two small scenes) appeared in the H.M.V. record catalogue in January, 1946, recorded by the Philharmonia String Orchestra conducted by the composer.

Incidentally, we had a glimpse of the economic side of film music from the producers of *Henry V*, who boldly published a " statement of account," which gives the cost of sound, shooting, editing, the orchestra and music with recording sessions as £25,104.

18. " THE SEVENTH VEIL "

In October, 1945, appeared the finest featured film music production so far made in England. . At the time when a lot was being talked about vastly expensive " prestige productions " on the British screens, a quickly-made, medium-budget picture, produced by Sydney Box and directed by Compton Bennett with James Mason and Ann Todd, made an unheralded entrance, came out in front of all the American films for the month of November, and ended up the 1945 Box Office Biggest Winner in the year's " Box Office Stakes " organised by " Kine Weekly," who voted it the best British film of 1945. It was called *The Seventh Veil*. Based on an original story by Muriel and Sydney Box, *The Seventh Veil* derives its title from the simile of Dr. Larsen, the psychiatrist in the film : " The human mind is rather like Salome at the beginning of her dance—concealed from the outside world by veil after veil of reserve. With friends and intimates the average person will drop two or three veils—with a lover five or six. But in all normal human contacts, the mind still retains one veil, the ultimate protection against the nakedness of its most intimate thoughts. This veil—the seventh veil—only a psychiatrist can tear down." Francesca Cunningham (Ann Todd) is a celebrated pianist whose hands have been burned in a car accident and who is suffering from acute depression. She attempts suicide, and afterwards becomes silent and lifeless. A psychiatrist, Dr. Larsen (Herbert Lom), places her under narco-hypnosis, during which she reveals the truth of her past life, stage by stage. First, she is at school, late for classes, and is caned on the eve of an important musical examination, which she fails as a result of her hands being swollen. Next as an orphan, Francesca goes to live with Nicholas (James Mason) a distant cousin of her father, who encourages her to continue with music and sends her to the music academy. There follows two love affairs, interspersed by an Albert Hall appearance and other concerts. While eloping with Maxwell Leyden (Albert Leiven), a famous artist, their car crashes and Francesca burns her hands in freeing him from the blaze. Her injuries are superficial, but she believes she will never play again. Larsen manages to cure her fixation and unites her to the man she really loves, Nicholas.

Into this tale of psychiatry and personality is introduced a series of concert works with such skill that they never clash with the plot, which continues to develop smoothly despite the interpolation of the music. Similar attempts have often failed, but *The Seventh Veil* is an outstanding success in bringing music to a wider audience in an artistically satisfying, technically pleasing (even box office gratifying) manner. The musical programme contains these items :—

> Chopin Prelude No. 7
> Mozart Sonata in C Major
> Overture " Merry Wives of Windsor " (Nicolai)
> Grieg Piano Concerto in A Minor
> Rachmaninoff Piano Concerto in C Minor
> Beethoven Pathetique Sonata
> Seventh Veil Waltz (Ben Frankel)

Ann Todd plays the part of the pianist on the screen and Eileen Joyce doubles for her on the sound track, supported by the London Symphony Orchestra. Benjamin Frankel, dance music expert, provides an excellent background score which includes the specially composed " Seventh Veil Waltz." The orchestra makes a full screen appearance with such familiar concert hall figures as John Moore and George Stratton (leader of the London Symphony Orchestra) well in the foreground. Arnold Goldsborough, well-known concert hall conductor, dons a beard in the role of the Italian conductor, while that notable British film music expert, Muir Mathieson makes his first screen appearance, after ten years in the studios as a " Number One backroom boy " with about 200 films to his credit. The music was recorded by George Burgess on a specially redesigned stage at Riverside Studios, Hammersmith, using the most modern principles of acoustics and microphone technique.

After its highly successful run in London, it was pleasing to note the warm reception accorded to *The Seventh Veil* in America. " English film czar J. Arthur Rank, now reaching full stride in a drive for U.S. movie markets, has his most likely American winner to date in *The Seventh Veil*," was the comment of the American popular magazine " Look." They continued : " A forerunner of his 6,000,000 dollar *Caesar And Cleopatra*, this British film offers two formidable personalities, James Mason and Ann Todd, in a constantly engrossing case history of a lady pianist's mental ills. Coinciding with current screen vogues for psychiatry and classical music (seven concert selections are superbly played by pianist Eileen Joyce and the London Symphony), it promises a profitable American future for Rank and its two stars." With typical American high spirits, " Look " goes on to quote a comment on the performance by James Mason " indicated by the violent reaction of a New York bobby-soxer : ' He's so handsome and so mean ! Gee ! ' " A pity we didn't get the bobby-soxer's reaction to the music !

This review is taken from the official journal of the National Film Music Council of America :—

" By far the best of the psychological pictures presented thus far, this one tells an interesting and absorbing story, well written and acted by a fine cast under superb direction. The title is subtly developed by playbacks, settings and photography are noteworthy and the recording is the best of any British film to date. Moreover, the use of classical music beautifully cued in and performed, adds further distinction to a dignified and distinguished production. The piano playing of the concerto (by Eileen Joyce, noted English concert pianist) has real virtuoso feeling, a plus rarely conveyed in a picture. There is nothing artificial either about the entrances—a delightful rapport is established when the Mozart Sonata is played—the drudgery of the practice is cleverly suggested—the waltz which Francesca associates with Peter is charming—then comes the gradual change to the bravura type of work. The montage of the continental study required for a concert artist is marvellously conceived and executed. There is a feeling of being present backstage, of experiencing the Grieg, the Rachmaninoff. With the playing of the Beethoven Pathetique Sonata the story enters another phase and at the end we share in the suspense of the four men as they await Francesca's verdict."

This film is one of the great achievements of the rejuvenated British industry. It is not a mighty million-dollar epic, but an ordinary, medium-budget, thoroughly competent picture with an intriguing and human story, good acting, neat dialogue, and noble music, which provided good cinema, good box office and an unusual success in the American field at a time when it was badly needed.

19. " CAESAR AND CLEOPATRA "

Was there ever such a film? It is the story of one man and his picture—Gabriel Pascal, producer and director of the screen version of *Caesar And Cleopatra*, the man who called on Bernard Shaw, persuaded him to let him produce *Pygmalion* and lend him

£1 for lunch. It was " Gaby's " picture down to the last detail ; the production was completely under his supervision from the colour of a flower to period atmosphere. No one knows just exactly how much it all cost. The rumours were plenty. We heard stories of £30,000 just for transport costs at the studios, of eight millions dollars spent on the most wastefully expensive picture of all times. *Gone With The Wind* was cheap by comparison. We heard of a full-sized sphinx that was shipped to Egypt ; someone said they shipped a load of sand as well (by mistake). " Gaby " was bitten by a camel. The film split the critics wide open and it was hard to say whether the cost, the director or the film was most frequently attacked. For all this, the George Bernard Shaw play had been faithfully reproduced on the screen against a lavish background of ancient Egypt. There is spectacle and wit, magnificent acting and plenty of entertainment in *Caesar*, though a weakness in bringing all these threads together is a fault that can only rest with the director, Gabriel Pascal, who tried to do the impossible.

Even the music has a story to it in this case. It was originally announced that Arthur Bliss was to score the film, but this was subsequently cancelled. Both Benjamin Britten and William Walton were approached, but they were too busy to take on the job ; Prokoviev was unable to come from the Soviet Union to write the music, as Pascal had at one time hoped. Finally, it was decided to call in a French composer, and Georges Auric was the choice. He is one of the most famous of French contemporary writers, and the man responsible for a number of important Continental scores, including Rene Clair's *A Nous La Liberte*, the experimental pictures by Jean Cocteau and the music to the Ealing film *Dead Of Night*, written in Paris and sent across to be recorded here by Ernest Irving. A member of the French music group known as "Les Six," Auric came to England to consult with Pascal and Shaw, being formally introduced to the English press by Benjamin Britten on his arrival in London. Then he went to work on the *Caesar And Cleopatra* music, described in detail by Marjorie Deans in her book " Meeting at the Sphinx " :—

" A big, loosely-built, rather indolent-looking man, Auric composes with an absent air, sitting humped up over the piano with a cigarette dangling from his lips, under frowning, half-closed eyes, and plays his own melodies apologetically—' Je ne suis pas pianiste, vous savez!'—with hands that look curiously large and inexpert on the keys. Can he really do this film job, one wonders ? Can he compose with the precision and accuracy demanded by this most exacting musical medium ? He looks too relaxed and easy-going to be capable of so much strain and concentration.

" But he takes it all so easily, it presently appears, because it is so easy to him. So many feet of film, so many bars of music— ' Bien, Bien ! Entendu ! ' He nods his head, and smokes, and strums a little ; and very soon there it all is, graceful and effortless, the Cleopatra motif, the Caesarean theme, weaving in and out of the lovely dreaming music of the Sphinx, the battle-music of the Roman legions, the young Queen's lullaby, the languorous background of the royal banquet, till finally, with the urgent swell and beat of newly-spread sails, it carries Caesar's galley away from Egypt on its journey back to Rome.

" ' When that boat sails away,' said Bernard Shaw, the music critic, ' Auric's music touches greatness. It is almost Handelian.' " Coming from G.B.S., there could scarcely be higher praise. Handel is one of his gods."

The music is excellent though there is something of the detached modernist about it that does not always fit the visuals very closely. The National Symphony Orchestra had a hectic time at the recording session as Pascal kept a very keen eye on all that went on. Part of the score involved the use of an anvil. The usual type of mobile orchestral imitation anvil was installed in No. 1 Recording Theatre at Denham for Desmond Dew, the sound engineer, to make the sound-track of the music. " Gaby," however, did not approve of the set of small steel bars that served to conjure up the vision of metallic resonance associated with the blacksmith. It was removed and a bigger one was obtained. Still it was no good, so yet another was brought in and set up amid the orchestra. Then Pascal spotted the real trouble ; " play it with *feeling*," he commanded the anvil expert. The anvil was duly sounded " with feeling," and director of music Muir Mathieson again continued with the recording of Auric's music.

Whatever the final verdict of the public, the studios will long remember the making of *Caesar And Cleopatra* ; no film ever told such an excitingly original, tragi-comic tale as the story that unfolded itself for two long years in the sandy wastes of Egypt and on Gabriel Pascal's Sphinx-infested stages down at Denham.

81

20. "BRIEF ENCOUNTER"

The famous concert pianist Eileen Joyce has, in the last two years, become a film star of the sound track. In *The Seventh Veil*, she gave a splendid performance with such atmosphere and punch as to contribute very strongly to the emotional success of the picture. For *Men Of Two Worlds* we have a masterly performance of the Arthur Bliss score and an eloquent playing of the César Franck Symphonic Variations in *Girl In A Million*, in which she makes a screen appearance. *Brief Encounter* was a very fine British film, homely and real, moving and effective, but I think it was a mistake to use the Rachmaninoff Piano Concerto No. 2 in this particular case. I like the Rachmaninoff No. 2 far too well to be able to follow a first-class film at the same time which is largely unrelated in any way to the music. *Brief Encounter* is solid screen entertainment with Coward wit, homely Celia Johnson, and an outstanding lighting camera job by Bob Krasker. Add to this feast a world-famous concerto and intellectual indigestion results.

One of the loveliest railway shots ever is amplified by those first eight chords of the No. 2 Concerto and as we swing into the main theme, up comes the titling. However, as soon as the story begins to unfold we are continually distracted from the fascinating plot to listen to Eileen Joyce, with Muir Mathieson and the National Symphony Orchestra, in a brilliant rendering of a work which, despite many hearings, still requires my full attention. It cannot be done. Either you listen to Rachmaninoff or Coward, but they have so little in common that you cannot listen to both. Either your attention is directed to this fine story of suburban life or to the work of the Russian composer. If one wants to introduce serious music to the public via the screen (an excellent idea) there are plenty of methods of doing it so that the music will work with the story as in *The Seventh Veil* and *The Common Touch*. It is an old problem, this business of using well-known music as a background for films, and it is very often, as in this case, unsatisfactory.

All of which does not detract from the technical quality of the recording, the clear-cut orchestra, and the fine piano music, but I had to go to the cinema once to see Noel Coward's film and once to listen to the Rachmaninoff Concerto, both of which constituted two separate entertainments, a thing which should not happen to any " background music."

21. THE YEAR 1946

The early months of 1946 saw a number of films of considerable musical interest. *The Captive Heart* was a remarkable examination of the life in a German prisoner-of-war camp, with sincere studies of the personal experiences of a representative group taken from the many thousands who endured the demoralising process of weary months behind barbed wire enclosures. Alan Rawsthorne was the composer and it was his first film after leaving the army. " The excellent music by Alan Rawsthorne," writes the British Film Institute reviewer, " endorses the policy of using the finest of our younger composers for the scoring of our more important films." His music director, Ernest Irving, gives a good account of the score : " Alan Rawsthorne, whose music for *The Captive Heart* scored such a success, makes no concessions whatever to the ' low-brow.' He possesses a keen eye for the dramatic points of a film, and has shown that music which can follow the outlines dictated by the ' visuals ' of a film need not be without form or void of content. His score is lean and spare, Brahmsian in its economy of colour, devoid of embellishment and completely without superfluity of any kind. He has no orchestral ' tricks,' his ' effects ' are all simple and direct, relying upon the structure of the music for its appeal both to the intelligence and the sub-consciousness.

" He has an easy technique in symphonic development with all kinds of contrapuntal device well under control, used in sympathy with the action and never running away with the job in hand : the weary march of the Dunkirk prisoners is a two-part canon, which matches the dragging broken rhythm of the tired and dispirited prisoners to a nicety. I doubt whether Rawsthorne said anything about canon form to his directors, and I hope they will not think any the worse of the music now the secret is out.

" There are one or two rather ' sloppy ' love scenes in the film, but Rawsthorne's slightly acidulated accompaniments go far towards making them bearable. The music is beautifully played by the Philharmonia Orchestra, making, I believe, its first appearance in ' motion-pictures.' There is some very nice horn-playing and the wood-wind and brass show exceptional quality. Rawsthorne is now completing a violin concerto begun before the war ; and is finding that a certain amount of reconstruction is necessary to replace material outgrown during his years of military service. The music to *The Captive Heart* was broadcast by the B.B.C. Orchestra, so that some millions of listeners will have heard it before the film came round to their local cinema. This is a splendid thing both for the composer and his public, very much better, in my opinion, than gate-crashing into a concert programme where, by its nature, it must be out of place."

Mischa Spoliansky scored a hit in *Wanted For Murder* (Eric Portman) : his song "Voice in the Night" and background score were major elements in the film's success. For the Stewart Granger vehicle, *Caravan*, Louis Levy got Walford Hyden to write just the sort of pseudo-Spanish music to give vitality to this melodrama of dusky dancers and elegant villains. In *I'll Turn To You*, a timely account of "resettlement" problems for an R.A.F. Flight-Sergeant getting demobbed and settling down somewhat awkwardly in civvy street, the musical setting designed by Harry Bidgood included interpolated scenes of the London Symphony Orchestra with John McHugh as solo singer ; also some items by Albert Sandler and his Palm Court Orchestra.

Sydney Box, producer of *The Seventh Veil*, once again gave us a musical treat in his picture *Girl In A Million*. This time we saw Eileen Joyce in her first screen appearance for Box, instead of just hearing her on the sound track. She played the pianoforte for César Franck's Symphonic Variations in a stirring seaside pier sequence, in which a breakaway mine explodes against the pier supports, but not, I am glad to say, before Muir Mathieson has concluded the performance of the rousing finale to the César Franck music.

22. " MEN OF TWO WORLDS "

Kisenga, a negro scholar and pianist, is giving his last concert performance in the National Gallery before returning to his native Tanganyika at the request of the British Government. Flying back to Africa with Kisenga is Randall, the District Commissioner, to fight a threatened plague of sleeping sickness. Kathleen Munroe, a clear-headed, if over-zealous, young woman doctor, is the resident medical officer. She and Randall instruct Kisenga to go to his own village and persuade the Litu, his tribe, to move to their resettlement area in a place untouched by the tsetse fly, carrier of the germ. He is greeted with joy by his family, but Magole, local witch doctor, is hostile to Kisenga and, after deliberately bringing about the death of Kisenga's old father, cunningly attributes the sad event to the wrath of the native gods. The villagers are scared and refuse to budge. Randall then challenges the witch doctor to cause his death, but is told that there can be no power held by a black man over a white. Kisenga then takes up the challenge. Magole bleeds him and tells him that he will die before the moon is full. By now Kisenga is fast losing faith in himself, realising that he is a "man of two worlds," with ten years of European training battling with ten thousand years of African tradition within him. As a result, he becomes mentally sick and suffers violent hallucinations, but with the help of Randall and Kathleen he recovers in time to break the witch doctor's spell, and he leads his people to the healthier zone.

A unit under the director, Thorold Dickinson, spent about eighteen months in Africa filming the location material. Returning to Denham studios, the picture went on the floor early in 1945. A reconstruction of the Litu village on Stage 5 was the largest set ever built in England at that time. Everything on it was authentic. Cooking utensils, farm implements, weapons and even the dead leafage and bamboo splinters on the dusty ground came from Africa. If you are interested in Technicolor photography, the picture contains some extremely difficult " zip-pan " shots, taken with a 35 mm. lens, notably in the village sequences. For shots of the District Commissioner driving through the night to visit Kisenga, a very low platform was slung on to the chassis of a V.8, so that the camera could be placed to show the driver's viewpoint. Two 250 amp. arcs took the place of the headlights. Tracking shots of up to 75 feet were carried out frequently during production. A scene shows Kisenga relating to the District Commissioner an ominous visit by Magole to his hut, and the camera is recording a flash-back to the actual occurrence. Working with a 50 mm. lens in 800 feet candle-power lighting, the camera started with Magole's face out of focus in the centre screen. As he begins to speak the camera tracks back a distance of only three feet. The face has to be in focus in this short space, with Kisenga's profile appearing at the side showing his reactions. The follow-focus assistant had to turn his salsen apparatus madly from the word " action " in order to make sixteen revolutions by the time the camera had tracked the short three feet, to ensure Magole being successfully in focus. Then, to put Magole out of focus again, the whole process had to be followed in reverse. The lighting cameraman was Desmond Dickinson and the camera operator was Ray Sturgess. In the same way as maximum attention was given to photography, so every section of the film's construction received the careful consideration of the director.

While on location in Africa, recordings were made of every variety of native music. Returning to England, the records were sent to Arthur Bliss. They were "rough-and-ready" discs of folk songs and drum beats, quite useless for use on the finished sound track, but invaluable for giving Bliss his. atmosphere material in preparing a score.

The picture opens with a fanfare based on an elaborate drum rhythm which features strongly throughout the music. During the credit titles, we hear a solo voice interpreting an African folk song. Then we see the National Gallery in Trafalgar Square, and simultaneously is heard the " Baraza " music, which constitutes the background of the sequence inside the National Gallery.

" Baraza " is a Swahili word meaning a discussion in council between an African chief and his headman. It is the title given to the minature piano concerto, consisting of three short movements and piano cadenza, which is heard in the picture. It has been written (in the film story) by Kisenga, an African native who has studied music in Europe for a number of years. Thus Bliss has attempted to translate African rhythms and colour to a Western style. It is a concert piece for orchestra, piano and male chorus as the composer imagined Kisenga would have written it. It is bold, brazen, strident film scoring at its very best, a superb piece of movie music.

The next sequence shows Kisenga and Randall flying to Tanganyika. Travel scenes offer little scope to a composer ; most pictures are content with some sort of " hurry " music or a passage of negative content. Bliss asked Thorold Dickinson how he should score the flight scene to capture the dominant factor of the visuals. Dickinson did not know what to say off-hand, but he and Bliss went into the theatre and were shown the part in question. It was just an aircraft flying over Africa, jungle scenery, matter-of-fact discussion between Kisenga and the D.C. Then there was a scene of a snow-capped mountain, majestically dominating the surrounding countryside. " That," said Bliss, " is the emotional peg on which the sequence rests." Instead of a musical imitation of aircraft noise or an impression of speed, the music is sweeping, slow, and conveys the grandeur of Kilima Njaro, the snow-capped mountain.

Kisenga returns to his village, and is greeted joyfully by his mother and father. The scene was filmed at Denham, but the two elderly natives were not professional actors and could not put the necessary emotion into the scene. Thorold Dickinson tried in vain to achieve the joyous effect required. He suggested to Bliss that perhaps the music might supply the missing emotion. By the use of strings and woodwind, the score secures an over-all rejoicing above the dramatic content of the scene itself.

Kisenga, in his capacity as schoolmaster, teaches the children of the village to sing one of his own works. It is the music they sing when he is in danger of dying. Bliss took two African folk songs from the recordings made in Tanganyika and used them as a basis for the children's song.

Horror music was required for Magole's evil-doing as he attempts to bring about the death of Kisenga by witchcraft. Drum rhythms figure prominently here, culminating in the hallucination scenes during which a battle is fought between the " Baraza " themes, the children's song and the drum patterns of Magole in one magnificent mass of weaving sound and music.

The score written by Arthur Bliss for *Men Of Two Worlds* was recorded by John Dennis with the National Symphony Orchestra conducted by Muir Mathieson. The music for the " Baraza " sequence in the National Gallery was written and recorded before the film was shot, so that the visuals were made to fit the score and not the other way round as is often the case. All the drumming sound tracks were made in the studios at Denham, including the tom-toms for the feast sequence, and were played by members of the orchestra in most cases. No location sound is heard in the film. The piano part is played by Eileen Joyce.

" Baraza " was published and recorded independently by the Decca Gramophone Company at the Kingsway Hall, London. Eileen Joyce was again the soloist, with the National Symphony Orchestra conducted by Muir Mathieson. It was issued in May, 1946, as the first of a series " Incidental Music from British Films," and offers the chance to examine in detail one of the finest film music works ever written.

The instrumentation of the " Baraza " is :—

Flauto
Piccolo
Oboe
2 Clarinetti
2 Fagotti
2 Corni
2 Trombe
3 Tromboni
Timpani
Xylophone
Tamburo rullante ⎱
Tamburo piccolo ⎰ } 1 Player
Violini I, II
Viole
Violoncelli
Contra Bassi

As heard on the gramophone record, it opens with a discussion between piano and trumpet, with skilful balance securing a delightful reverberation for the brass. The full orchestra enters with the main theme, followed shortly afterwards by the male chorus. The tempo instructions read : " Maestoso ma non troppo lento." This leads into " Tempo primo," and on to the piano cadenza, brilliantly executed by Eileen Joyce. The drumming theme appears most effectively on the piano, with the African colour in combination with Western lay-out. Side 2 introduces the " Larghetto " and the voices return, singing the Swahili words. With a wild cry from the brass, the " Vivace " leads quickly to a mounting blaze of sound from the chorus, piano and orchestra as the work ends.

23. " THE MAGIC BOW "

During 1945 a film based on the life of Paganini was launched at Shepherd's Bush Studios with Stewart Granger as the composer and violinist. Maurice Ostrer, Gainsborough's executive producer, was fortunate enough to secure Yehudi Menuhin, the world-famous violinist, to come across from America to record the sound track. Menuhin, who commenced violin lessons at the

LOVE STORY. The Royal Albert Hall becomes a film set during the making of the picture. The Orchestra is the National Symphony, conducted by Sidney Beer.

age of three, made his first public appearance at seven, and became world-renowned as a sensational child prodigy, is an ardent admirer of Paganini's music and co-operated enthusiastically with Gainsborough by cabling regularly from America with suggestions on the musical selections to be used and their treatment in the film. Concluding a recital to the San Francisco Conference delegates, the virtuoso of the violin came to London in May, 1945. The musical programme recorded included :—

Campanella (Paganini)
The Devil's Trill (Brazzini)
Violin Concerto No. 1 (Paganini)
Caprice No. 20 (Paganini)
Concerto Opus 1 (Paganini)
Beethoven's Violin Concerto : Last movement

In addition, a special work designed for the film was played. It is the " Romance " by Phil Green, based on a theme from the first movement of the Paganini E Minor Concerto.

The tracks were made at the H.M.V. Studios at Abbey Road and at Kingsway Hall. The National Symphony Orchestra, conducted by Basil Cameron, was used ; on one of the recording days, Cameron was unable to attend and his place was taken by Eric Cundell. The soloist was, of course, Menuhin, who was recording music for films for the first time. B. C. Sewell, the sound recordist, used an entirely re-designed channel for these recordings in addition to an improved type of microphone and a recording camera of new design to ensure first-rate quality sound. After Menuhin had left the country, the work of shooting the picture went ahead. Stewart Granger could not play the violin at all, so David McCullum, first violinist of the London Philharmonic Orchestra, was brought to the studios to coach Granger in his film part of Paganini for which Yehudi Menuhin had already supplied the sound tracks. During the shooting of the Concert Hall scene, the producer, director and stars all had gramophone record copies of Menuhin's music, which they could study privately in order to help them work out the action and atmosphere of the plot. Louis Levy, supervising music director to the production, was very impressed by Stewart Granger's performance. A film was made of Menuhin, David McCullum

YEHUDI MENUHIN recording violin music for the film *The Magic Bow* in the great H.M.V. recording studio at Abbey Road, St. John's Wood. The orchestra is the National Symphony.

and Granger playing the violin separately ; these three films were examined afterwards and Louis Levy said that Granger's performance was, perhaps, the most realistic on the screen, although he had never played before. Naturally, there were some problems in synchronisation, especially as all the sound had been done before the film was shot, but director Bernard Knowles had previously photographed Margaret Lockwood in her screen role as a concert pianist (with Harriet Cohen on the sound track) in *Love Story*. However, *The Magic Bow* is the first time that this process has been applied to a violinist, with all the added complications of fingering and bowing, and Gainsborough are to be congratulated on the experiment in bringing us such fine music and such a unique film.

24. THE BRITISH MUSICAL

Ever since the coming of sound the American film industry has turned out a continuous stream of musical films. Beginning with Al Jolson, we find an unbroken record of large-scale productions in which music has been a dominant feature—*King Of Jazz, Broadway Melody, Goldwyn Follies, Roberta, Footlight Parade, George White Scandals, The Gay Divorce* and *100 Men And A Girl* through a long series of Deanna Durbin, Bing Crosby, Betty Grable, Alice Faye and Frank Sinatra films up to the present day, when we have as many musicals as ever coming across from Hollywood in a great flood of Technicolored Tin Pan Alley triumphs. Of course, many people are sick of them. The same old plot of mistaken identity, of struggle-for-success rewarded by ultimate triumph, and a tremendous song and dance finale, of mushy, slushy lyrics, interspersed with hot jive and novelty numbers, the luxurious apartments, the swanky night clubs, the back-stage settings—we know it all so well. It is customary nowadays for the better type of film critic to dismiss them airily with a few well-chosen words—" every time I go to see a Hollywood musical, I am sure that it can't possibly be worse than the last one I saw, and every time it is." Even the trade press gets weary of writing " Excellent musical fare for the masses."

Nevertheless, the Hollywood musical is a successful commercial factor in America cinema, like the Western ; musicals make money. And they entertain. The many thousands of men and women who have sat in a draughty Nissen hut on an east coast gun site, sweated in a jungle clearing in Burma or squeezed into a converted mess-deck on a troopship know the value of the musical film. What does it matter if the projector breaks down ; there is no real story to follow. What if the sound is bad ; the jive is noisy enough anyway. Light, bright, cheerful music, nothing to think about, luxurious beds, furs and fine foods, beautiful women and handsome, useless men. The high-faluting critic, sitting in the little private cinema on a cosy-cushioned seat, having had a morning coffee and sweet biscuits, knowing he will get a steak and chips in that small Soho restaurant when the film is over, happily dismisses the furs, the luxury and the jive as vulgar escapism. The army bloke, sitting on a N.A.A.F.I. table in the Nissen hut or the troopship mess-deck, after a hectic day on the assault course or a seasick afternoon on deck-watch, has a greater respect for an hour's " vulgar escapism." Another thing about musicals is that you don't have to bother about getting in to see the film from the beginning. If you are shopping in the afternoon, or you have been to the ice rink and feel like dropping in at the pictures later on, it is much easier to go in at the middle of a musical than it is in a serious drama. (And it would be interesting to discover just what percentage of cinemagoers go to see a film from the start compared with those who just drop in casually.) There is a very strong basis of fact for dismissing the average Hollywood musical as " vulgar escapism " and judged by critical æsthetic standards, it is just that ; but at the same time, as long as the cinema remains the mass entertainment system it is to-day we cannot afford to ignore it.

Britain has not had very much to do with the evolution of the big scale musical. Although it is claimed that the theme song idea originated over here, it was America that developed it during the first few years of talkies—and how they developed it ! For a time, we went on steadily turning out modest but quite good pictures, occasionally incorporating musical numbers, rarely designed on the Hollywood pattern. Then came the big upheaval from about 1935 to the beginning of World War II. Hopes suddenly ran high (based largely on the success in America of one British film *Private Life Of Henry VIII*), and money poured into production schedules planned to capture the American market. Great experiments were undertaken, ambitious productions were worked out, but few resulted in success. Alexander Korda continued to make good pictures, while Gaumont maintained a steady flow of reasonable films, both emerging from the fray in which many new companies sprang up overnight, backed by finance born of wild rumours hinting at vast profit which circulated in the " City " with amazing alacrity. Operas were to be filmed, ballets, big spectacles, musicals, everything. The American market would be captured wholesale ; British films would lead the world.

The bubble burst with a big bang at the box office ! The fact was that the British film industry was not yet sufficiently advanced technically or artistically to blossom forth ; it proved conclusively that money alone was not enough. The Americans clamped down on the home market and we just could not get a look-in anywhere. Far more significant was the failure even to capture our own market ; people found our films slow and technically inferior, a state of affairs which the " quota quickie " helped to create, thus prejudicing the chances of the films that were well-made. The test of time is a good guide to the success of a film (as it is to any art form) ; check on the re-issues and you gain an excellent idea of how successful a picture has been in the past. However, it does happen that an artistically good film may fail at the box office (which, of course, is the guiding factor in commercial re-issues), but there are thousands of film societies which screen pictures without any reference to box office considerations. Thus, by sifting the joint evidence of commercial re-issue and film society shows, it is possible to obtain a fair estimation of true values in pictures of the past.

During the period up to World War II almost every big dance band in this country made a film, but you will not find these pictures shown to-day. Our stage comedians, radio singers and variety stars were all making pictures, but the prints lie rotting in Wardour Street vaults or have long since been scrapped. At the time when Hollywood was giving us Bing Crosby, Deanna Durbin, Leopold Stokowski and Louis Armstrong in a series of musicals that are still enjoyable and have received full scale circuit re-issue, our musicals, with a few exceptions, were playing second-feature to American successes. Unfortunately, this is a branch of film production which has consistently failed in this country. We had the bands—Jack Hylton, Harry Roy, Ambrose, Henry Hall—and we had the stars—Jessie Matthews, Jack Hulbert, George Formby, Max Miller, Jack Buchanan, Gracie Fields—but it seemed that the British film industry was permanently cursed with a fundamental inability on the part of all the studios to get any life or spectacle into our musicals. Always they were technically inferior in every way to the Americans ; in star build-up, in general publicity values, in direction, in photography, in sound, in editing and in music. Of course, that is true to-day ; we have not the right temperament for the " all-singing, all-dancing " stuff and now we have realised our weakness, we avoid them. We can't do big Hollywood musicals and we don't try. We couldn't do them between 1935 and 1939, but unfortunately we kept on trying. Perhaps you remember a few of them—*Radio Parade Of 1935, She Shall Have Music, Everything Is Rhythm* or *Music Hath Charms.*

Out of it came one or two better attempts. I remember some of the Jack Hulbert films, Jessie Matthews in *First A Girl* and *Evergreen*, and an occasional Gracie Fields film, but in the main I recall Bing Crosby in *Pennies From Heaven*, the mighty *Ziegfeld Girl* or Deanna Durbin in *Three Smart Girls* far more clearly and enthusiastically. Then came the war and with it a true British cinema—new, vital, realistic, eminently successful. No more imitation Hollywood musicals, no more " quota quickies " ; " show the world what Britain was like," show reality on the screen, not idle, " phoney " fiction. Naturally dance music disappeared for a while and for the first four years there was little except a series of semi-musicals adapted from popular radio programmes—*Band Wagon, Hi! Gang, I Thank You, It's That Man Again* and *Happidrome*—none of which were true " song and dance " as such. Butchers turned out a series of pictures which introduced musical items such as Alfredo Campoli, Rawicz and Landauer, Heddle Nash and the London Symphony Orchestra, and have continued with them up to the present date ; occasionally these modest little films have been good. Vera Lynn, radio singer, made two pictures, both extremely bad.

By 1944, our fictional-documentary technique had been developed to such an extent that the time came to try it out on a musical, and it fell to Ealing Studios to carry out the experiment. Within a month of each other appeared two pictures by documentary directors with an entirely different approach to their usual style of picture. One featured Tommy Trinder, Frances Day and Sonnie Hale, with Harry Watt of *Target For To-night* fame as the director. Entitled *Fiddlers Three*, it was a flop. The other was more fortunate. Starring Tommy Trinder and Stanley Holloway, *Champagne Charlie* was a story set in the music halls of the 1860's, dealing with the rivalry between two singers, George Leybourne and the Great Vance, culminating in a battle of drinking songs, an attempted duel, and a final reconciliation after a move by the theatre proprietors to close the music halls. A notable feature was the complete capture of the period atmosphere by Cavalcanti, another documentary director and one-time head of the G.P.O. Film Unit. All the musical resources of Ealing were turned on this job, as music director Ernest Irving took original songs by Alfred Lee and George Leybourne, plus a series of specially composed items such as " Rum, Rum, Rum," " I Do Like a Drop of Gin " and " Ale, Old Ale." Lord Berners, Billy Mayerl, Noel Gay and Una Bart are amongst the writers who joined forces with Irving in assembling the vigorous score. Here then was one of the very few steps so far taken to evolve a true style of British musical. Not entirely successful because of a certain slowness in parts, nevertheless *Champagne Charlie* did show what could be done when documentary met musical in an English studio.

The year 1945 produced two musical films of some consequence. First, *Flight From Folly*, a bright musical claimed by Warner Bros., as " Britain's first major effort in the realms of sophisticated, high-polished crazy film comedy, a challenge to the best in the comedy-with-music class America's film colony could produce." Pat Kirkwood is seen as a demure miss who, in order to impress play-wright Clinton Clay (played by Hugh Sinclair) poses as a nurse who will look after him while he is mentally dazed. He has been deserted by his wife. Hilarity is the keynote of the early sequences, until music and spectacle take the scene in a grand " Majorca " song-and-dance finale. Apart from being a great personal triumph for Pat Kirkwood (ending in a Hollywood contract), *Flight From Folly* was definitely good of its kind. Among the people who collaborated on it were comedian Sydney Howard, dance experts Buddy Bradley, Halama and Konarski, composer of hit tunes Michael Carr, and two West End orchestras, Edmundo Ros and his band from the Bagatelle and Don Marino Barreto and his band from the Embassy. The picture was only just finished when a flying bomb fell on the studio, practically destroying the whole plant, and killing A. M. Salomon, the studio manager. The film itself was saved and the music sessions were held in a garage among the wrecked buildings. Into this small space an orchestra of thirty-five and a choir were fitted with great difficulty. The garage was found unsuitable acoustically, but by the use of wire and canvas this fault was overcome. Several hundred yards of emergency cable were laid for power, sound and inter-communication between recording theatre and garage. An old van became the projection platform outside the garage, and threw the film on to a screen inside. The choir was used for the dream sequence, when Hugh Sinclair and Pat Kirkwood go through a series of fantastic adventures which finally unites them. The picture part of this sequence was one of the last shot at Teddington before the studios were destroyed and it was particularly important to have the music exactly synchronised with the intricate movements of the ballet. This goes on record as one of the toughest music sessions ever held !

Then there was Gainsborough's *I'll Be Your Sweetheart*, with Margaret Lockwood and Vic Oliver. Dedicated to " the great melody-writers of yesterday who lived a strange life in the heart of London, a life of struggle and adventure as memorable as their own songs," this was again claimed as " the most spectacular British musical film." The story deals with the struggles of the early twentieth century song writers against the music pirates of the time, who sold their songs for 2d. a copy, putting them out of business and often causing them to die in poverty, though their songs were the musical hits of their day. The music in the film includes " I'll Be Your Sweetheart " (Harry Dacre), " Oh, Mr. Porter," " Honeysuckle and the Bee " and " Liza Johnson," as well as three specially written items by Manning Sherwin and Val Guest. Spectacular dance scenes were devised by London stage experts Robert Nesbitt and Wendy Toye, with Louis Levy in the joint capacity of associate producer and music director. Orchestrations were done by Bob Busby and Ben Frankel. The result was a competent, neat, well-handled musical, thoroughly entertaining. Margaret Lockwood is excellent, Vic Oliver keeps the pace cracking and Michael Rennie provides an adequate love interest. The old-time songs are put across with vigour and interest. Looking back over the war years, we may say that *Champagne Charlie* was the best original British-style musical, *Flight From Folly* the best crazy comedy with music, and *I'll Be Your Sweetheart* the best Hollywood-style musical.

Nothing seemed more out-of-place during the British Film Festival at the Leicester Square Theatre in 1946 than the appearance of George Formby with his song " Get Cracking." Although Formby has turned out a steady stream of films every year, despite the fact that he has often been Britain's Number One comedian of the screen in numerous nation-wide polls, yet to many London cinemagoers he is little more than a name. Very rarely are his films given a West End showing, and often not even a general release. *Bell Bottom George, He Snoops To Conquer, George In Civvy Street, I Didn't Do It, Let George Do It, Come On George, Get Cracking* and so on, have, nevertheless, played their part in the general comedy-with-music pattern. Like Gene Autry, Formby is a small-town star, a great hit up North and in the country cinemas where his infectious, irrepressible style has won for him a considerable following. His work in providing entertainment to such audiences makes him a unique figure in British cinema for which he provides two pictures annually with absolute consistency.

In 1945 the British National group at Elstree embarked on an ambitious programme of British musicals. Titles issued include *Waltz Time, Lisbon Story, Meet The Navy, Laughing Lady* and *Spring Song*. These are in the American style and have proved moderately successful. *Waltz Time* is a story of Old Vienna, a musical romance of court life in the best stage tradition, and once again is " the finest British musical ever produced." It features Carol Raye, Patricia Medina, Peter Graves, Webster Booth, Ann Ziegler, George Robey, Albert Sandler, Harry Welchman and Richard Tauber—a powerful line-up of stars. The music was composed and directed by Hans May, with direction by Paul Stein. Said the British Film Institute : " The whole production is on a lavish scale . . . all the principals are well suited to the parts they play, and the whole thing is garnished with tuneful music." It had a reasonably good general release, though it seems to have made a bigger hit in America than it did here, if this report from the Los Angeles " Examiner " is typical : " *Waltz Time* is probably one of the most elaborate and costly films to be imported from Britain."

This was followed by a film version of the Harold Purcell-Harry Parr-Davies stage hit *Lisbon Story*. Once again here was a competent, moderately-proportioned, tuneful picture, starring Patricia Burke, David Farrar, Walter Rilla and Richard Tauber, but not up to Hollywood standards of production. Now well into 1946, producer Louis H. Jackson followed through with *Meet The Navy*, a screen version of a Canadian Navy show. The picture was distributed by M.G.M. and was good, solid stuff, making its West End bow at the Empire in Leicester Square. Encouraged by these successes, British National went on to make *Laughing Lady*, an all-Technicolor production with Ann Zeigler and Webster Booth, followed by Carol Raye, Leni Lynn and Peter Graves in *Spring Song*. At Elstree then we now have a team of British musical makers who already have shown that they can "make a go" of this style of motion picture that has so far eluded us and we shall follow their future closely.

London Town is another " greatest British musical ever made." Yet it is hardly a British picture at all. Back in 1945, when the war was still on, came Wesley Ruggles to make a U.S.-type story with Hollywood music, routine and set designs, but to be shot in Britain. He ran into some problems. When the unit moved into Sound City it began work with aircraft being repaired on two of the stages. The whole studio was released by the Government at the beginning of 1946. Equipment—especially lights— had to be borrowed from other studios : a crane from Pinewood, arcs from Denham, and so on. The settings were designed in Hollywood and erected at Sound City, often with great difficulty as the Hollywood man had not even the details of the stages before him in designing his sets. A switch of dance directors during production was a further snag.

Another thing not exactly " Hollywood " was the recording of the music. Stage 2 at Sound City was taken over and turned into a recording stage, as Ruggles was very insistent on a good track, though we had no recording system available in this country that could compete with the " brilliance " of the average Hollywood sound band. However, they rigged up a sound stage " within a stage," built of plaster and supported by steel tubes ; the whole room was shaped like a giant loudspeaker horn. A screen was fitted at the narrowest end, with a movable felt curtain hung in the centre and the area behind this was lined with felt. The sound quality could now be mechanically adjusted and the curtain opened and closed or moved nearer the screen end of the studio (closing in the orchestra), or further away. Traps in the roof were adjustable to let out sound in any quantity ; the orchestra could be positioned in any number of ways. This special stage allowed for multi-channel recording. Soloists and choir were housed in ante-chambers and were able to look into the main theatre through control-panel windows. The R.C.A. equipment gave full multi-channel recording, but there were many delays to be overcome when this stage was built. The Government refused a quota of three-ply wood, so it had to be made in plaster, and because of the shortage of studio plasterers the sections had to be built by a London firm and sent to the studio by road.

It has always been doubtful whether American-sponsored production in this country is desirable ; such a system once gave us the worst possible variety of " quota quickie." It remains to be seen how far such schemes as *London Town* can be developed in the future. The film by the way featured Sid Field, Tessie O'Shea and Claude Hulbert ; it was directed by Wesley Ruggles, famous Hollywood musical man, with special American orchestrations by " Toots " Camarata.

Another production sponsored by a company whose head office is in the States was *Gaiety George*, directed by George King and starring Richard Greene and Ann Todd. This proved a competent British musical nicely handled with a reasonable story and some good music by George Posford, but in the technical qualities it again was hardly in the Hollywood class.

Of course, it is questionable whether we even want to rival Hollywood in this type of production. We have evolved our own strong line and have no real need to enter this foreign field. But it is possible that eventually we shall evolve our own special type of musical, as they have in Russia and in France, and that then there will be the Hollywood musical and the Denham musical— two entirely different forms of cinema.

As regards true jazz in British pictures, distinct from ordinary commercial musicals, the prominent swing and jazz expert Peter Noble has adequately covered the subject in his excellent book on " Transatlantic Jazz," in which he says :—

" In England swing has not yet come to mean much as a commercial proposition or as a popular favourite. In this respect we still seem to lag a good deal behind America, for in this country popular commercial, sweet music and the orchestras who dispense it are still number one with the British public. The type of orchestra popularised by Jack Hylton and continued by Jack Payne, Henry Hall, Maurice Winnick, Joe Loss, Geraldo and many others is still what the public wants in this country. There is a very small number of orchestras who not only play jazz, but are able to make a living from it as well. Among these may be numbered Harry Parry and his Radio Sextet, Johnnie Claes and his Clae-pigeons, Art Thompson and his Band, Carl Barriteau and his Orchestra, Frank Weir and his Sextet, Lew Stone and his Band, Leslie Hutchinson's All-Coloured Orchestra and one or two other groups. As far as films and jazz are concerned in this country, here is, perhaps, the place to point out that of the above both Harry Parry and Johnnie Claes have made appearances in films. Claes especially has been extremely successful and has been able to play good jazz in a number of small independent films made in London. But the English film on the whole is not conducive to the playing of real jazz. In any case musicals (in which most jazz may be heard deliberately or accidentally) are not very often made in this country. And as we have no jazz tradition, therefore, there is no possible chance of films being made around the story of British jazz such as were made in Hollywood. Commercial jazz in England has made great strides and features largely in films, on radio and records while of course it is a huge industry out of which many thousands of pounds are made from each one of its facets. But an examination of real jazz in British films could not occupy more than a paragraph simply because it hardly exists ! ''

CHAPTER III

MUSIC FOR THE DOCUMENTARY FILM

"*Music can serve one of its most satisfactory and useful purposes in the cinema in connection with the Documentary film.*"

MUIR MATHIESON.

(A). THE G.P.O. FILM UNIT

Stirling, in Scotland, is a town that seems to specialise in great men of the film world. Muir Mathieson was born there. So was John Grierson, the man who was responsible for the British school of documentary film makers. In 1929, he bought a film camera, and made a movie of the North Sea herring fleet called *Drifters*. Produced for the Empire Marketing Board of London, it was the beginning of a small group of documentarians known as the Empire Marketing Film Unit. In 1933, the E.M.B. was wound up and the film unit transferred to the Post Office, to become known as the G.P.O. Film Unit. Upon this small group of men and women was thrown the task of founding the great tradition of documentary films that have become famous throughout the world. Led by the directors trained by John Grierson, the G.P.O. Unit continued its work up to the coming of war, when they eventually reorganised under the title of the Crown Film Unit. To-day, they remain with us as " Crown "—vigorous, progressive, industrious film makers as ever.

Such was the financial state of the early days of the E.M.B. Film Unit that they were not able to make sound films at all and only on conversion to the G.P.O. do we find a complete transfer to talkies. Their first musician was Walter Leigh, a talented, serious composer who had the gift of writing light music of an excellence hardly attained by any other contemporary composer. Partnered by V. C. Clinton Baddeley and Scobie Mackenzie as librettists, Leigh composed " The Pride of the Regiment " and " Jolly Roger "—two light operas of which the latter proved that there is a large public for intelligence, as well as gaiety, in light music. One of his earliest films was the Harry—"*Overlanders*"—Watt production *Six-Thirty Collection* (G.P.O. Unit, 1934). In 1935, the film *Song Of Ceylon* won the first prize for documentary productions at the Brussels International Film Competition. Directed by Basil Wright and produced by John Grierson, *Song Of Ceylon* was a dialectic film of old and new Ceylon, showing the influence of Western civilisation on native life. Without Walter Leigh's music, it might have passed off as an ordinary, competent travelogue. Many innovations were used by Leigh for this film. The music was written first, and then the picture was cut—unheard-of at that time. The sound track sometimes involved seven channels, as Leigh worked solidly for over three weeks on a long series of recording studio experiments—again a technique many years in front of its time. The native music was made with a troupe of Cingalese dancers and drummers, who were brought over from Ceylon for the greatest single musical experiment in the history of early documentary. Kurt London, in his book on Film Music pays this tribute to Leigh's work :—

" Leigh has realised that the sound-film, a new art, requires a new musical technique. His music departs from tradition, not only in its form but in connection with the tonality of the whole film ; his instrumentation also displays in its transparent economy a striking understanding of the special requirements of the microphone. Wind, above all wood-wind, dominate in delicate contrapuntal sound-texture, even in combination with strings, used solo. The score of *Song Of Ceylon* points the path which real film music has to follow."

Walter Leigh was connected with documentary up to the time of his death in the summer of 1942.

For a number of years, the now famous composer of the English opera " Peter Grimes " was connected with the G.P.O. Unit. Benjamin Britten joined the unit shortly after Leigh, and Kurt London said of these two composers that they had, even as early as 1936, already " proved themselves real experts in forming the musical elements of a film into universal representations of sound. Their film music transcends the score of musical notes and absorbs within itself the sound of real life (in a stylised form), whether it be of single voices, of choruses, or of natural noises, by turning it to music and giving it rhythm." In 1936, Britten wrote two outstanding scores. First, *Night Mail*, film impression of the Post Office train sorting offices in action, full of fine photography and remembered for an unusual sound track involving much natural sound, poetry by W. H. Auden and music by Benjamin Britten, a fascinating mixture of music and noise in a closely-knit pattern.

Secondly, there was *Coal Face*, another G.P.O. Film Unit production of 1936. It was made by similar means and with the same technical crew as *Night Mail*. Of Britten's music, Kurt London wrote : " In the G.P.O. film *Coal Face*, an exceedingly searching pictorial survey of Great Britain's most important industry, he formed a unity of music, words spoken in chorus, and stylised noises. It is astonishing to observe how, with the most scanty material, using only a piano and a speaking chorus, he can make us dispense gladly with realistic sounds. This stylisation makes a much stronger impression than a normal musical accompaniment. The commentator's explanations are cut to extreme brevity and limited to such information as by its context may knit the connection between the sound-groups still more closely together. The atmosphere of the dark world of the work in the mines, the grim monotony of the miner's hard life, but, notwithstanding, the vital importance of that work, exclude any lyrical feeling. The rhythms of this life are hard ; hard likewise is the music and its interweaving with the speaking choruses. The general atmosphere of the film is dark, and its music neither makes it brighter nor does it underline the shadows superfluously. In a word, the power-ratio between picture and music is always most ideally balanced."

All Britten's work for the G.P.O. Unit was on this high level as we recall some of his many scores—*Sixpenny Telegram*, *The Savings of Bill Blewitt*, *Calendar of the Year*, the silhouette fantasy *The Tocher* and *Line to Tschierva Hut*. Always Britten showed complete mastery of his medium; this young composer must have learnt much of life and music that was later to be of value, as he worked with this group of film realists. No wonder Ernest Irving regretfully remarked in 1946 : " Britten has not yet condescended to the commercial screen. He could, of course, write magnificent picture-music and possibly it is his knowledge of this latent power that has restrained him." Actually Britten has scored one commercial feature—*Love From A Stranger*, directed by Rowland V. Lee in 1937, but (although he has received many offers) he has since concentrated on other forms of composition, apart from the recent short film for the Crown Unit on the instruments of the orchestra.

Ernst Meyer was another G.P.O. Unit discovery. Director Cavalcanti introduced him to films with *Roadways* in 1937. He, too, studied the use of natural sound in films, and produced an orchestrated sound track of car noises and screeching brakes for *Roadways*, in addition to fitting various passages of background music. For the famous G.P.O. film *North Sea* (1938), Meyer went to sea with the trawler fleet to get the correct atmosphere before writing his score—a rather drastic process for any composer !

At one time the G.P.O. Unit invited French composers to score one or two films, especially at the time when Cavalcanti, the French director, was working for them. Thus, in 1937, Maurice Jaubert scored *We Live In Two Worlds*, while *The Islanders* had music by Darius Milhaud, and *Forty-Million People* was handled by Francois Gaillard. It was this distinguished trio who started a pioneer movement that later affected the feature film world when Honegger and Auric began writing for British pictures.

We cannot leave the Post Office people without two other references to their amazing array of musical talent. Brian Easdale, another young contemporary, scored a number of later productions, including *Big Money* (1937), *Job In A Million* (1937) and *Men In Danger* (1939). Composer Alan Rawsthorne also made his film debut with the G.P.O. Unit for *The City*, produced in 1939 and fitted with what the British Film Institute described as " particularly successful " music.

Most books that deal in any detail with the work of British film men contain a section on the G.P.O. Film Unit, recalling to the reader such pictures as I have listed here. Yet I often wonder how many of the readers have actually seen these specialised productions. I remember myself the difficulty of tracking them down to some small exhibition cinema, a remote film society screening or to the little picture house in the Imperial Institute at South Kensington. True, the Unit claimed a very large non-theatrical audience for their productions, but all the same, it was not until the war that the average film-goer saw much documentary.

However, for those of you who have not seen many of the old Post Office pictures, I do recommend you to follow up any chance screenings that may come your way, for there will you find the work of the composers who wanted freedom to develop and express their own ideas, free from the restrictions of the commercial cinema. There can be no doubt that the G.P.O. Unit (and incidentally, the present Crown Unit) offer unique examples of experiment in picture music, and that the work of the early documentary musicians paved the way for our present day successes in other fields.

(B). OTHER DOCUMENTARIES UP TO 1939

Although the E.M.B. and G.P.O. Units were the main organisations specialising in that essentially British contribution to the cinema world which we rather vaguely call " documentary," their influence spread and other units were formed to make factual films. From the large collection of such pictures, let us examine a few representative cases.

Strand, Realist and Rotha Films are three units that arose out of the school founded by Grierson, and by 1936 Strand, for example, were turning out a regular series of films for the commercial cinemas, as well as special jobs for trade organisations and industries like the Gas Association or the Southern Railway. And in 1936 came William Alwyn, a Professor of Composition and Fellow of the Royal Academy of Music, to embark on a film music career that was to put him in the forefront of our documentary musicians. His first picture was called *The Future's In The Air*, written in collaboration with Raymond Bennell ; there followed a long series of such films and to-day Alwyn looks after the music for as many documentaries as his heavy commitments in the feature film studios will permit, for, in 1941, he began writing for big pictures, starting with *Penn Of Pennsylvania*.

When we claim that almost every important composer and musician in the country has at some time or other been connected with films, it is no idle boast. Who, for example, would expect to find such an eminent and revered name as that of Sir Henry J. Wood turning up in the credit titles simply as " Musical Adviser " ? In 1937, Widgey R. Newman directed a set of four films under the auspices of none other than that startling buttress of British journalism, the " News of the World." They were called *The Heritage Of The Soil*, *Heritage Of The Sea*, *Heritage Of The Land* and *Heritage Of Defence*, a quartet of patriotic panegyrics. The main work of the musical adviser was to provide stirring themes suitable for scenes of the Navy at sea, Imperial Airways in action and the busy life on a farm. Incidentally, the late Sir Henry Wood made a screen appearance in 1936 for a film story set against a gramophone factory background ; it was entitled *Calling The Tune*.

The organisation known as G.B.I. (Gaumont-British Instructional Films) did much to cultivate the popularity of the interest and factual film. Per-

FIRST OF THE FEW. Leslie Howard, David Niven and Anne Firth learn something of the Nazi plans for world domination. Music by William Walton.

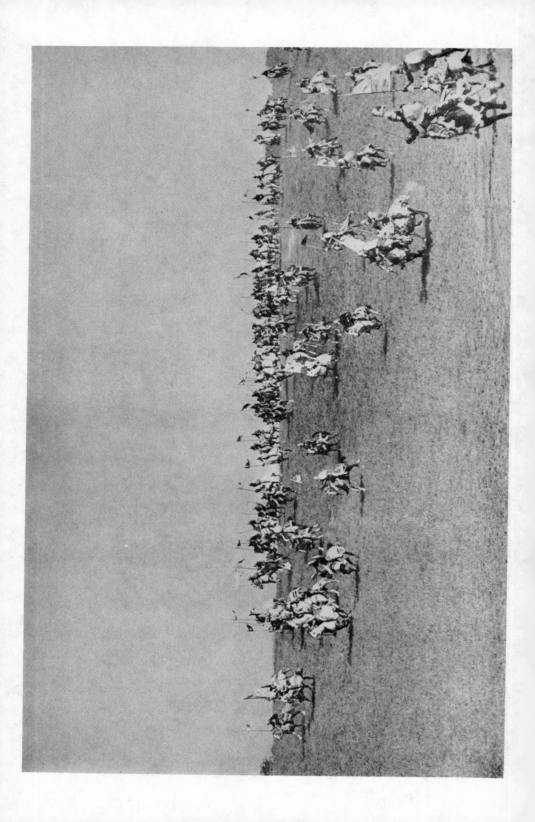

haps their most familiar product is the *Secrets Of Nature* and *Secrets Of Life* series. The fascination of watching a common or garden runner bean live up to its name as it nips smartly up a stick before our very eyes is, despite Betty Grable and Mickey Mouse, an interesting screen novelty in any cinema programme. The delightful background music to the series has been provided by Jack Beaver from 1934 to 1946 without a break ; over twelve years as composer to one series. of shorts must surely be quite an achievement.

When the commercial feature film companies saw the success of documentary in its specialised sphere, they too wanted to try it. One of the earliest experiments was made by Gaumont-British ; in 1933 they sponsored and distributed *Man Of Aran*, a lyrical film made by the great documentarian Robert Flaherty. Music was most effectively provided by John Greenwood, who also scored *Elephant Boy*, in which Flaherty went in with Zoltan Korda and the London Film Company (1937). Greenwood is an excellent composer of lyrical, broad scores with plenty of atmosphere and romance ; other neat jobs of his include *The Drum, East Meets West* and *San Demetrio*. The Brighton composer's music to *Elephant Boy* was broadcast in one of Muir Mathieson's early film music programmes.

In 1934, London Films had carried out their original trial documentary, making *Wharves And Strays*, a film account of the Thames dockland area. It was shot by cameraman Bernard Brown as a spare time task, being musically handled for him by Arthur Benjamin, an Australian composer now living in Canada. *Wharves And Strays* was released in 1935 ; in the same year Benjamin scored *The Turn Of The Tide* for G.-B., another commercial feature showing a strong documentary influence, as did their *Wings Over Everest* (music by Hubert Bath), made a year or so before. Michael —"*Matter-of-Life-and-Death*"—Powell used the Glasgow Orpheus Choir most pleasingly in his semi-documentary of the Scottish Isles called *The Edge Of The World*. It was a remarkable film, made doubly interesting by the singing. Powell did not forget this ; when he came North some eight years later to make *I Know Where I'm Going*, he again used the Orpheus Choir in his glorious sequence. of the Highland Ceilidh (pronounced as only the Scots can — " Kayley ").

HENRY V. An impression of the charge sequence made so impressive by the music of William Walton in combination with an outstanding tracking shot.

So it was that the documentary influence, expressed as a desire for realism and fact, began to exert its influence soon after John Grierson's boys got going, but up to the time of the war, it was only a very mild and occasional influence. World War II was the turning point, however, for documentary as a major factor in British feature cinema, but it must be remembered that *Target For To-night*, *Western Approaches*, *Desert Victory* and *The True Glory* would not have been possible without the spadework of the G.P.O. and other documentary units between 1929 and 1939.

(C). THE CROWN FILM UNIT

Although the name was not altered until some months after the outbreak of World War II, the G.P.O. Unit became in effect the Crown Film Unit a few hours after Premier Neville Chamberlain had announced the fateful news that Britain was at war. Here was a first-class documentary unit with years of experience behind them ready to take on the job of recording the war on film, and overnight their field of activity was extended from the specialised productions of Post Office affairs to the full arena of a country at war. As Cabinet Ministers came and went in Downing Street and as the first sirens sounded, Crown Film Unit went to work on their picture *The First Days*, produced by Cavalcanti, which showed that this famous documentary group, led by its founder, John Grierson, was still as keenly efficient as ever. After a short spell as chairman of Crown, Grierson departed to Canada to take over the National Film Board there, and the M.O.I. Director of Films, Jack Beddington, accepted the job of keeping the group together and forming them into an experienced team of war documentarians of the highest order. Everyone who goes to the cinema will have seen some of their work, either in short single-reelers like *Britain At Bay*, or in features like *Target For To-night*, *Western Approaches* and *Coastal Command*. C.F.U. went everywhere and saw everything of the war ; wherever a good story was to be found, there were Crown Unit cameramen—in the London raids, on an Atlantic convoy, in a submarine off Norway, in a factory canteen. Always their approach was realistic and human ; never did they thrust propaganda down our throats, but rather did they allow the facts to emerge naturally and smoothly from their film stories.

The G.P.O. Unit had already become famous for their use of the best type of music and many young composers had approached films through them, finding an outlet for experiment and initiative not possible under the restrictions of commercial cinema. Crown maintained the tradition. With Muir Mathieson as their resident music director, Pinewood, new requisitioned home of C.F.U., always had the best possible music for their productions. Some of the outstanding films from a musical viewpoint include :—

Squadron 992

(Director : Harry Watt. Music by Walter Leigh. 1940).

This was the last film score by Walter Leigh, who had done so much to raise the standard of film music in documentary films. He was killed in action with the Tank Corps during the Libyan campaign in the summer of 1942. *Squadron 992* has a delightful score, notably in the gay march to the sequence of the balloon convoy on the move and in the realistic music to the scenes of a barrage balloon being brought out of its hangar. As it gives a lurch in mid-air, so the music follows it to give the impression of some clumsy elephant dancing. Said the magazine " Documentary News Letter " : " Here is not only the best film which has been made about the war ; it is a film which sets a new high spot in documentary, by achieving a perfect combination of fact, humour and dramatic story. . . . The music of this film is as good as everything else about it."

Men Of The Lightship

(Director : David MacDonald. Music by Richard Addinsell. 1940).

The film that really put Crown on the front page (though at this time they were still officially called the G.P.O. Film Unit). Every now and then the world of pure documentary, non-commercial cinema produces a picture that has powerful repercussions in the feature film world ; *Men Of The Lightship* was among these. Said the " Cinema " (trade press) : " This three-reeler demands a place in any cinema's programme. The exhibitor can forget completely the propaganda angle or that it was made under the ægis of the Ministry of Information. Rely on it rather as an absolutely first-class job of work, as the reconstruction of a despicable act done with such grim realism and actual backgrounds that it lacks only the seven dead men who failed to come out of the ordeal . . . a front page film . . . will stir the stoniest heart . . . a credit to everyone concerned in its production." These comments by a tough trade press critic, frequently hostile to documentary, are testimony of the film's success, and they were amply borne out by the general press : " Grim, tense, exciting . . . this is the best British documentary film I have yet seen " (" Daily Express.") " A brilliant little film " (" Evening News.") The music by Richard Addinsell was excellent and gave a tremendous dramatic impact to the visuals. For example, in the sequence where the lightship men are rowing in an open boat after their vessel has been sunk by German bombers, the music conveys not merely the actual rhythm of the rowing, but some of the thoughts of the men—the horror and endurance of being shot up, lost at sea in fog, without hope of survival. The final scenes of the seven dead bodies lying on the shore were exceptionally dramatic due to the moving, tragic music that accompanies them.

Merchant Seamen

(Director : J. B. Holmes. Music by Constant Lambert. 1941).

This was another outstanding success in the early days of C.F.U. It is a magnificent short film of stark realism, the Battle of the Atlantic brought home to twenty million people during its extensive release on the British screens in 1941. The score was written by Constant Lambert, the composer who, in 1936, wrote the foreword to Kurt London's book on Film Music, and a very excellent score it was. The stirring march, the powerful attack music, the opening title music, all are preserved to-day in a fine concert suite taken from the film and especially arranged by Constant Lambert. The suite has received many performances, being first presented in its full version by the London Philharmonic Orchestra in Bristol in October, 1943. For the film it was played by the Sadler's Wells Orchestra and recorded by Ken Cameron at the National Studios, Elstree. In 1944 the suite was recorded by the B.B.C. Symphony Orchestra conducted by the composer, while it was a marked success at the 1945 Promenade Concerts. Here then is a case of a documentary background score of the highest order providing music that can stand on its own in the concert hall yet fitting perfectly into the picture for which it was originally written. Crown can be specially proud of this score ; it is the only film for which Constant Lambert has written music.

Christmas Under Fire

(Crown Film Unit, 1940).

This was the short film that went with *Britain Can Take It*, both with commentary by Quentin Reynolds and both designed for American audiences in the first instance. The dynamic effect of the quietly disturbing voice of " Colliers Weekly " journalist, Quentin Reynolds, was combined in this case with the voices of the choir of King's College, Cambridge. Very effective were the scenes of Christmas celebrations by the tube shelterers in London's Underground stations with a fine shot, photographed from a moving escalator as it descends to platform level, to show the pile of pitiful bundles of bedding and the women and children gathered at the foot of the shaft, all to the accompaniment of the choir singing " Come All Ye Faithful."

The Heart Of Britain
(Director : Humphrey Jennings. 1941).

A moving and successful account of Britain at war designed for American audiences. A visit is made to blitzed areas in the industrial Midlands and North to talk to a fire watcher, a Coventry W.V.S. official about tea, and to see an air raid shelter where Lancashire mill girls show how to pass the time during a raid. There follow two excellent featured music sequences. The first presents the Hallé Orchestra playing Beethoven's Fifth Symphony, excellently recorded on the spot by Ken Cameron in the Odeon Cinema, Manchester. He also recorded the second sequence— the " Hallelujah Chorus " from " Messiah," sung by the Leeds Choral Society and taken in the Huddersfield Methodist Church.

Target For To-night
(Director : Harry Watt. Music by Leighton Lucas. 1941).

The film is a detailed account of a bombing raid on Germany at the time of those critical months when Britain stood alone. It starts with the discovery of a new oil storage depot by means of reconnaissance photographs and follows through with the manner in which a raid is prepared, the crews are briefed and the attack is pressed home in face of fierce flak. The aircraft is damaged, but struggles back to base with the wireless out of action and the operator wounded. Once again we have realism and drama in a pioneer production that influenced many subsequent air films. Great credit belongs to Harry Watt for this star picture by Crown, notably in his magnificent handling of real-life characters, outdoing the most experienced professional acting. The music to *Target For To-night* was written by A.C.2 Leighton Lucas, who had just joined the R.A.F. after a number of years' work conducting ballet and composing. He had been over three years in Louis Levy's music department at Shepherd's Bush before 1937, but had done little film work since then. Wing-Commander R. P. O'Donnell sent for A.C. Lucas, a complete "sprog" to the R.A.F. at that time, and asked him to write music for this film. Lucas saw the film and went to work, writing the score in a barrack room at Uxbridge. A recording session was held at the Warner Brothers sound stage in Teddington where Aircraftman Lucas handed over his score to Sgt. John Hollingsworth of the R.A.F., who conducted the R.A.F. Central Band. The music is grand, and the march theme has been played many times since by R.A.F. bands. Notable amongst a series of well orchestrated passages is the memorable full screen shot of a Wellington bomber flying just above a cloud-bank to the accompaniment of the powerful Lucas music.

Ferry Pilot

(Director : Pat Jackson. Music by Brian Easdale. 1941).

An account of the Air Transport Auxiliary. A neat music score.

Wavell's 30,000

(Director : John Monck. Music by John Greenwood. 1942).

The first decisive victory for the security of Egypt with Wavell's success over a huge Italian army.

Listen To Britain

(Director : Humphrey Jennings. Music recorded by Ken Cameron. 1942).

The music of a people at war. The sound of life in Britain by night and day in the period of recovery and maximum effort that eventually carried us through. The film records the roar of Spitfires and tanks, the noise of furnaces and factories, the march of miners and soldiers, music and songs in trains, dance halls, canteens and in the National Gallery. For the National Gallery sequence, we have a recording of Dame Myra Hess with a section of the R.A.F. Orchestra playing the Mozart Concerto in G Major (K.453).

Coastal Command

(Director : J. B. Holmes. Music by Ralph Vaughan Williams. 1942).

The story of Coastal Command operations with emphasis on experiences of the crew of a Sunderland flying boat in protecting a convoy and shadowing a surface raider for attack by Beauforts and Hudson bombers. The music was written by Ralph Vaughan Williams and dedicated to Coastal Command. It was his second film score and a tremendously stirring one. The Sunderland, T for Tommy, is detailed to accompany a convoy until the hour she is relieved by a Catalina, and the crew deplore the fact that the night has been so lacking in excitement They dodge a Focke Wulf and rejoice when the Catalina scores a direct hit on a U-boat. News is received of a surface raider that has left Bergen harbour and the Sunderland goes off to relieve a Catalina which has been damaged and is on the way home. Hudsons take off from Iceland to bomb the surface raider (a very effective music passage here), while Beaufighters attack with torpedoes. The Sunderland then goes in close to inspect the damage (once again a very neat piece of scoring by Vaughan Williams), is hit by flak and then attacked by J.U.88's, but eventually gets back to base, the job completed. Said the British Film Institute, the music has been used " skilfully in conjunction with natural sound to heighten the dramatic effect." Said the film reviewer of the " Documentary News Letter " : " Vaughan Williams has done a magnificent score, but it suffers from the fact that while it tries to overplay the action, the director is endeavouring to underplay it." Ken Cameron, the man who recorded the music, gives the opinion of the Crown Unit people themselves to the Vaughan Williams score for *Coastal Command*. " When we heard the music," he says, " we knew that here was something great, something, indeed, finer and more alive than any music we had ever had before. Nor did we waste. On the rare occasions when the music was slightly too long or too short to match the existing picture, then it was the visual material which suffered the mutilation. The music for · *Coastal Command* is as V.W. composed it. It is, in fact, the picture."

We Sail At Midnight

(Director : Julien Spiro. Music by Richard Addinsell. 1942).

The story of how urgent tools were rushed to England from America through the operation of Lease-Lend. A new tank has been passed on test, but can only go into full-scale production when certain gear-cutting machinery has been obtained from the U.S.A. Priority for this is arranged in Washington by the Lease-Lend authorities, and the machines are rushed to the New York docks in lorries, cross the Atlantic and are successfully delivered on time. This film is distinguished by remarkably fine photography

111

from Chick Fowle and by one of Addinsell's best scores. The music is of an unusually dynamic type, and especially notable is the scoring to the sequence in which the transport convoy sets off from the factory, through the country, down Broadway and finally into New York Harbour. Much ingenious orchestration is used to mark the urgency of the trucks mingled with the jazz theme of Broadway and the triumphant note of the arrival at the docks. "Documentary News Letter" commented: "A very original score by Richard Addinsell gives many of the sequences a lot of value." This is an under-statement; the music at times carried the whole emotional success of the story. As with all the Crown Unit films listed here, the recording was by Ken Cameron and the musical director was Muir Mathieson.

Malta G.C.

(Produced by the Army, R.A.F. and Crown Film Units. Music by Arnold Bax; played by the R.A.F. Orchestra and recorded at the H.M.V. Studios, St. John's Wood. 1943).

The story of Malta's suffering and triumph, made up from newsreel and official material, photographed with great skill during the extensive bombing of the "George Cross Island." Whatever Arnold Bax thought of the way in which the film people went about the handling of his first score for pictures, this was good solid stuff. It was again something of a personal triumph for Mathieson in introducing Bax to the cinema, and the result was magnificent music. Hubert Clifford wrote:— "Arnold Bax's music for *Malta G.C.* is of the highest distinction and ranges from the epic to the naively human in parallel with the exciting subject matter of the film." It immediately became a successful concert hall suite, being broadcast even before the film was released, and is recorded in the special music section of the B.B.C. Recorded Programmes Library. Details of the suite will be found in the Index Section, page 237.

Fires Were Started

(Director: Humphrey Jennings. Music by William Alwyn. 1943).

A powerful, human and realistic documentary on the work of the Auxiliary Fire Service during the great fire raids of 1940-1941, with a typical and stirring score by William Alwyn. Evelyn Russell, reviewing the film for the British Film Institute, commented: "I was much impressed by William Alwyn's music to

Fires Were Started, the Crown Film Unit's full-length documentary made by Humphrey Jennings. . . . The music is so closely knit with the shape of the film that one would be incomplete without the other."

Close Quarters

(Director : Jack Lee.   Music by Gordon Jacob.   1943).

Before The Raid

(Director : Jiri Weiss.   Music by Gordon Jacob.   1943).

These subjects were the first two film scores by Gordon Jacob. As Hubert Clifford nicely says it, the first occasion on which he " turned his craftsmanship and consummate sense of style to the advantage of film music." The occupied-Europe story (*Before The Raid*) is neatly scored without being overwhelming, as are so many war-time movies of this type, while the submarine picture *Close Quarters* combines with the Ealing Studio production about the Air-Sea Rescue Service of R.A.F. *For Those In Peril* in presenting two excellent examples of " sea music " in pictures, both the work of Jacob.

The True Story Of Lili Marlene

(Director :   Humphrey Jennings.   Music score by Dennis Blood.   1944).

Among the many excellent productions of the Crown Film Unit, there appeared in 1944 a perfect gem of a musical short film, based on a simple tune that had a colourful story behind it, a song captured by the Eighth Army from the Afrika Korps, symbolic of a victorious campaign by the Allies. Film poet Humphrey Jennings directed this reconstruction documentary, with musical scoring by Dennis Blood, and recorded by sound engineer Ken Cameron with Muir Mathieson as music director. The words of " Lili Marlene " were written in Hamburg in 1923 by a poet and painter, Hans Leip. Fifteen years later one of Goebbels' "Tin Pan Alley" boys set the words to music, and it was sung by a Swedish cabaret girl, Lala Andersen, in a Berlin night club. When the Germans marched into Belgrade, their propaganda unit brought with them some records and all but one were broken—the one of Lala Andersen singing " Lili Marlene," the song of the sentry thinking of his girl waiting at the barrack gates. Throughout the time that " Lili Marlene " was on the air to the men of the Afrika Korps our men of the Eighth Army listened too. Every night they used to sit in the dusk and quietly hum and whistle the song until it became so familiar with them that they adopted it as their own. It was when the Eighth Army paused before the assault on Sicily that someone wrote new words for the song and turned it from a tango into a march ; this became the battle song of the Eighth Army. Marius Goring, famous for his B.B.C. part as Hitler, and his wife, Lucie Mannheim, provided the narration and featured in the film. The simple song was given a dynamic treatment on the sound track, and although a number of commercial recordings were made, they all fell very far short of the original film recording with its orchestration and colourful presentation of the captured tune.

Western Approaches

(Director : Pat Jackson. Music by Clifton Parker. 1944).

Twenty-four merchant seamen from a torpedoed ship are sailing a lifeboat in the Atlantic. After two weeks at sea in an open boat, they see the smoke of a lone merchantman and send up distress rockets, but simultaneously they sight a U-boat periscope and realise they are being used as a decoy. A desperate attempt to warn their rescuers fails and she is struck by two torpedoes. The captain orders the men to the boats, but remains behind with a small party of men. The U-boat surfaces to finish off the vessel they believe to be abandoned, only to be sunk itself by the guns that the few who had remained behind now operate. The men in the lifeboat are rescued after their grim experience and anxious moments as onlookers to the fight.

This was one of Crown's best. Shot in Technicolor, realistic, exciting and dramatic, *Western Approaches* had music by Clifton Parker. Hubert Clifford wrote in the magazine " Tempo " : " The film is full of magnificent sequences, true and convincing, and provides the composer, Clifton Parker, with many opportunities of contributing to it even within the scope of the naturalistic drama. This is, I believe, Clifton Parker's most important score to date. It is highly effective and is always apt, and it reveals quite a new side of a composer who has previously been known— and far less known than the quality of his music merited—only as a composer of light music. To his task in *Western Approaches* Parker brought a fine sense of orchestral colour, plus skill and taste in handling his medium. Although it seemed that his music broke little new ground, it, nevertheless, was always vital and significant."

The Broad Fourteens

(Director : R. Q. McNaughton. Music by Benjamin Frankel. 1945).

South Africa
New Zealand

(Crown Unit productions. Music by Victor Hely-Hutchinson. 1944-45).

Neat scoring by the B.B.C. director of music, though the music to *New Zealand* was badly fitted in its relation to the commentary.

The Channel Islands

(Director : George Bryant. Music by Christian Darnton. 1945).

Highly modernistic score by a comparatively recent film music writer.

The Last Shot

(Director : John Ferno. Music by Guy Warrack. 1945).

Excellent writing by a B.B.C. musician and well-known conductor.

Two Fathers

(Crown Unit. Music by Clifton Parker. 1945).

A Harbour Goes To France

(Crown Unit. Music by Christian Darnton. 1945).

A Diary For Timothy

(Director : Humphrey Jennings. Music by Richard Addinsell. 1946).

Timothy was born on the fifth anniversary of the war, and this film gives an account of the last part of the war—Arnhem, flying bombs, rockets, the final defeat of Germany, and the transition to peace. It is a faithful and moving record of the reality of life in this country set down as only Crown can record it. Included is a sequence of Dame Myra Hess playing at a Royal Academy lunch-hour concert, reminiscent of Jennings' earlier film *Listen To Britain*.

Myra Hess

(Crown Unit. 1946).

This film runs for eleven minutes and is made up of material shot by Humphrey Jennings for *A Diary For Timothy*. It features Myra Hess playing the whole of one movement of Beethoven's Appassionata Sonata, thus providing a valuable film record of considerable interest to concert-goers. It is neatly edited, with good camerawork (although the famous pianist appears troubled by the lighting at times, reminiscent of Paderewski in *Moonlight Sonata*) and perfect sound recording by Ken Cameron.

A Defeated People

(Director : Humphrey Jennings. Music by Guy Warrack. 1946).

Germany in its hour of defeat.

Children On Trial

(Director : Jack Lee. Music by Clifton Parker. 1946).

Instruments Of The Orchestra

(Director : Muir Mathieson. Music by Benjamin Britten, played by the London Symphony Orchestra, conducted by Malcolm Sargent. 1946).

Designed originally as a twenty minute short film for schools, it is a demonstration in picture and sound of the instruments and sections that go to make up a modern symphony orchestra. Benjamin Britten took a theme by Purcell and worked out a Fugue which clearly illustrates the use of the various instruments first individually and finally in concert. The music was recorded at Wembley Town Hall and the picture shot to " playback " at Pinewood, with a commentary by Malcolm Sargent, who conducted the orchestra and collaborated closely with director Muir Mathieson throughout the production.

(D). THE FORCES FILM UNITS

1. THE ARMY FILM UNIT

During the course of World War II, the film played a large part as a medium of instruction and entertainment. For entertainment, the three fighting services formed a system of mobile cinemas, camp theatres and what is called " sub-standard distribution " to enable ordinary feature films to be shown to our troops in all parts of the world. In addition, they set up film production units that the civilian population of this and other countries might see what our forces were doing at every stage of the fighting. Never before was a war so fully reported to those at home. For instructional purposes, the services called on the already-existing organisations to make their training films, but they also established units, staffed by Army personnel, to deal with specialised teaching requirements. In the case of the Army, Navy and R.A.F. Film Units, we have the two types of production to consider—instruction for internal use, and information for public consumption.

The Army film organisation was more complex than in the Navy or the Air Force, and involved three divisions known as " The Army Film Unit " (A.F.U.), " The Army Kinematography Services " (A.K.S.) and " The Department of Army Kinematography " (D.A.K.). These were largely divisions of internal planning, but the A.K.S. was responsible for training films, while the A.F.U. dealt with most of the publicly-shown Army films. First, then, let us consider the training pictures. These began to make an appearance about 1941, the early ones being scored by Richard Addinsell. Addinsell had already done good work on Government-sponsored films like *Men Of The Lightship* and *The Lion Has Wings*, so he was accustomed to this type of material. Among the Army training films for which he wrote music were *Camouflage* and *The New Lot* (a Carol Reed picture designed to combat that " browned off " feeling so readily felt during the first few weeks in the Services). Speaking personally, I found that Addinsell's bright music did a lot to improve those rather grim, early days of drill and " basic training."

Addinsell was followed by a series of feature film composers who contributed music intermittently to A.K.S. productions, among whom were Clifton Parker and Alan Rawsthorne. By far the most important of the Army training music men, however, is John Bath. Son of the famous composer Hubert Bath (who died in 1945), John joined the A.K.S. as a musician and film cutter in 1944, and quickly showed himself to be a composer of merit. His first film score was for *According To Our Records*, and the music was recorded at Pinewood by the R.A.F. Orchestra. During the next two years, he scored many of those training shorts with such uninviting titles as *You Too Can Get Malaria* and *A Day In The Line* ; in addition, he did the *Letter From Home* series, *The Story Of D.D.T.*, and one or two cartoon sequences for the Army. John Bath has many amusing stories to tell of the problems of Army music sessions, often working as he was with " scratch " orchestras who had never been in a film studio before. He recalls the time when one of

117

his scores required a harp ; eventually, an A.T.S. girl was located and arrangements were made for her to be detached to the studio for the recording session. After numerous Orderly Room procedures had been complied with in the best Army tradition, the A.T.S.-harpist arrived at the studio twenty minutes before zero hour, but without a harp. One was finally procured from the H.M.V. studio and the session got under-way twelve hours late. Bath is at present musical director at Merton Park Studios, and he already has quite a reputation as a film musician. He remained with the Army until the end of the war, where we find him due to record the music for a film *Japanese Soldier* on VJ Day. The picture was scrapped and so was the music. One of his more unusual jobs recently was dubbing new music to the Korda film *The Thief Of Baghdad.* A Hindustani version was being prepared for release in India, and Bath found it something of a major task in view of the fact that he did not know a word of that complex language. The B.B.C. television service later presented a special programme to show how the Hindustani transcription had been made.

Next, we come to the work of the Army Film Unit on pictures intended for general release, to show the housewife what life was like for her husband in Ceylon, or the factory worker how his Bren gun stood up to it in the field. In 1940, there were two cameramen in the British Army ; the film record of Dunkirk was made by a single newsreel operator working with the Navy. By the end of 1941 there were over one hundred cameramen in the Army Film Unit, with studios at Wembley, Merton Park, Pinewood and Marylebone at their disposal, and in 1941 their pictures began to appear. At first these were only " shorts," but even so they often " stole the show " with a realism and human interest not apparent in the fiction part of the programme. As with the training films, Addinsell was one of the first composers in the field, and for the earlier period we find his name frequently on the credit titles of A.F.U. productions. Other names appearing later include Hubert Clifford and Alan Rawsthorne, one picture by Ralph Vaughan Williams, and a group of Canadian Army short films fitted with polished, modernistic scores by Christian Darnton.

By far the most significant work done by the A.F.U., however, is the group of four full-length features issued between 1943 and 1945. Three had music by William Alwyn. *Desert Victory* (1943) showed the start of the Libyan campaign, taking up the story from two previous " shorts " *The Siege Of Tobruk* and *Wavell's 30,000*. From Alwyn's magnificent score to *Desert Victory* came the march of the same name to establish itself as a popular hit, with a gramophone record issued by Columbia, and a special performance at the British Film Festival of 1946. A year later the British and American Service film units joined forces with *Tunisian Victory*, again continuing the story, this time to its successful conclusion. William Alwyn supplied the British music and Dimitri Tiomkin wrote the American contribution to a joint Anglo-American production. In 1945, Alwyn completed a trio of perfectly scored films with music for *The True Glory*. British and American film technicians combined their efforts once more, just as American and British soldiers had done in the field to make the picture a reality. The reviewer of the magazine " Documentary News Letter," describes Alwyn's music as a " very great score." In fact, it is on this set of three pictures that he brought to a climax many years of fine writing for documentaries dating back to 1936.

Burma Victory, issued rather belatedly in 1945, is the fourth high-light of the Army Film Unit's career. It tells in graphic and inspiring manner the story of the men who had sweated and fought in the jungle ; a S.E.A.C. Army corporal told me that every shot was accurate. Direction was by Roy Boulting, whose brother John was simultaneously making the R.A.F. Unit picture *Journey Together*, when Roy was compiling his material at Pinewood. The *Burma Victory* music was written by Alan Rawsthorne and recorded by the London Symphony Orchestra under John Hollingsworth's direction. It is a good score, but has suffered at the hands of the sound department, who have faded the best passages almost to the point of extinction. In all four films, a good deal of material was contributed by the Crown and the R.A.F. Units.

At the instigation of the Directorate of Army Kinematography, by far the most important " outside job " for military training was put into operation in the early days of the war. Security is always a headache for a country like Britain in war-time, and it was agreed that a major picture should be devoted to the subject and shown to all members of the Armed Forces. At the time there was no Service film unit capable of handling such a venture, so the studios at Ealing were given the task of producing a forceful lesson in " keeping your mouth shut." Ealing Studios set up a military organisation within their grounds : barbed wire, armed guards, strict secrecy and special passes became the order of the day as Thorold Dickinson, the director, began work on *Next Of Kin*. The results were in excess of all expectations. An almost overwhelming urgency was injected into this story of spies and invasion, which proved not only instructional, but entertaining as well. Late one afternoon on the R.A.F. site where I happened to be at the time, we had just finished a busy watch on the radio transmitter in Flying Control and I was preparing for a night out at the local hostelry. In the act of closing down the wireless cabin, I and my fellow operators were informed by the camp loudspeaker system that all (they meant all) personnel were to parade at 18.30 hours for a compulsory talk on Security. Feeling very fed up, I went on the parade, whence we were all herded into the camp cinema for what we thought would be a " binding " lecture on " Keeping it under your hat." I was pleasantly surprised to see instead the film *Next Of Kin*, and so was everyone else. In addition to Security, we had a preview on a new and vital type of British photoplay which showed immense possibilities for the film industry in this country. I was even more impressed to find that the music was by that most eminent of modern composers William Walton. I am afraid that most of the fellows thought I was mad when I went again the following night to a repeat performance, but then it takes more than one viewing of a William Walton picture to get the full enjoyment out of his scores. *Next Of Kin* was such a hit with the troops that it was eventually agreed to give it a general release on the commercial circuits. It set a standard in film realism that helped in no small way to bring about the sudden improvement which swept away the cobwebs of pre-war quota quickies and replaced them by the high quality fictional-documentary that became the guiding principle of the reborn British cinema.

Returning to the actual productions of the Army Film Unit itself, here are a few of their films which received screenings at the ordinary cinemas :—

Special Despatch (1941). Music by Richard Addinsell.

A.T.S. (1942). Music by Richard Addinsell.

The Siege Of Tobruk (1942). Music by Richard Addinsell

Troopship (1942). Music by Richard Addinsell.

THE OVERLANDERS. A scene from the Harry Watt documentary photographed in Australia. The music was composed by John Ireland and directed by Ernest Irving.

Street Fighting (1942). Music by Alan Rawsthorne.
Desert Victory (1943). Music by William Alwyn.
Left Of The Line (1944). Music by Hubert Clifford.
The Story Of D.D.T. (1944). Music by John Bath.
Tunisian Victory (1944). Music by William Alwyn and
   Dimitri Tiomkin.
The True Glory (1945). Music by William Alwyn.
You Can't Kill A City (1945). Music by Christian Darnton.
The Antwerp Story (1945). Music by Christian Darnton.
Burma Victory (1945). Music by Alan Rawsthorne.
Stricken Peninsula (1945). Music by Ralph Vaughan
   Williams.

2. THE ROYAL NAVAL FILM UNIT

The Navy Film Unit was small and only engaged in films for training purposes. Film stories of the Navy for public showing were always done by commercial documentary units and by detailing newsreel cameramen to various ships of the Fleet. In the field of instruction excellent " shorts " were produced to which music (on the rare occasions when a special score was needed) was provided by individual arrangement. Thus, for example, Ken Cameron made trips to Portsmouth in order to hold recording sessions at H.M.S. Collingwood for Naval training pictures ; the music in this case was by William Alwyn. For feature productions dealing with the work of the Navy made by external organisations, full collaboration was always accorded. Crown Film Unit produced *Close Quarters*, a film record of Britain's submarine service. The music was written by Gordon Jacob and recorded under the direction of Muir Mathieson with the orchestra of the Royal Marines, Chatham Division—only one example of Naval co-operation for films made about their own work.

3. THE ROYAL AIR FORCE FILM UNIT

The R.A.F. Film Unit was not formed until the end of 1941. Its main purpose was " to provide a film record of the part played by the R.A.F. in the war, but it was also to provide material and films for outside concerns, to

CHAMPAGNE CHARLIE. Tommy Trinder, Stanley Holloway and Betty Warren as they appeared in the film ; musical direction was by Ernest Irving.

film technical developments that could only, for reasons of security, be shot by R.A.F. personnel, and to make training films for internal consumption." In other words, it was similar in scope to the Army set-up, but was more centralised and operated from a single large studio—Pinewood. Its productions fall into two main categories—training and public information. A great many training films were made, including one of eight reels that was shown to one audience and then destroyed. It was a complete sound and visual briefing for the pilots of the great Ploesti oil plant raid, and was prepared at Pinewood in seven days of almost continuous work, and then flown out to the Middle East. It is not recorded whether there was any background music involved !

Muir Mathieson was the resident music director to the Unit, while the Air Force had its own Symphony Orchestra available for recording sessions. From this pool of musicians controlled by Wing-Commander R. P. O'Donnell, the R.A.F. Symphony Orchestra was formed.

Perhaps the best musically-served newsreel ever made was to be found in the R.A.F.'s own film magazine *The Gen*. Produced at Pinewood, it was distributed to Air Force Station cinemas all over the world, and had music tracks written by no less than ten first-rate film composers (although they never received credit on the screen). They include William Alwyn, Dennis Blood, Christian Darnton, Norman Del Mar, David Moule Evans, Ben Frankel, Norman Fulton, John Gough, Victor Hely-Hutchinson and Leonard Isaacs. As you can see, we have here a B.B.C. musical director, symphonic, operatic and light music composers of every type, and the foremost documentary writers of the country. Thus *The Gen* was always packed with musical interest in addition to the excellent pictorial matter that made it an item of unusual note at any R.A.F. film show.

From the public viewpoint, the R.A.F. Film Unit kept everyone well-informed on what it was doing to make a complete account of all branches of the Air Force. Looking at the various " Commands " which constitute the R.A.F. organisation, we find a picture devoted to them all, made either by the R.A.F. Unit or by feature film producers. Thus, Bomber Command was effectively covered by Crown's *Target For To-night*, Coastal by *Coastal Command*, also a Crown item. Fighter Command, although not the subject of a specific documentary, received its full measure of public recognition in R.A.F. material supplied to numerous newsreel editions and to such features as *Dangerous Moonlight* and *First Of The Few*. Seeing this, the R.A.F. Unit went to work on the less spectacular but equally important Balloon Command (*Operational Height*), Maintenance Command (*The Big Pack*) and Training Command (*Journey Together*). This last-named film marked the end of the R.A.F. Unit's career; it was undoubtedly one of their best and featured Richard Attenborough and Edward G. Robinson. To complete the story, Ealing Studios, off their own bat, made *For Those In Peril* (1944), virtually a documentary account of the work of the R.A.F. Air-Sea Rescue Service, although it had a fiction plot added on. Gordon Jacob wrote the music.

The detachments that went into the field from Pinewood brought back a comprehensive record of the R.A.F., a record not obtained without casualties, for thirteen members of the unit lost their lives and seven were taken prisoner during the filming of operations. The Army Film Unit also suffered casualties in the field in order to secure a film history of six eventful years in that mixture of savage destruction and barbaric cruelty, comradeship and courage, that constitutes modern war.

Here are the music credits for the main productions of the R.A.F. Film Unit ; music direction in all cases is by Muir Mathieson :—

> *Operational Height* (1943). Music by Hubert Bath.
> *Maintenance Command* (1944). Music by Gordon Jacob.
> *The Big Pack* (1944). Music by Gordon Jacob.
> *Ship Busters* (1945). Music by Leighton Lucas.
> *Journey Together* (1945). Music by Gordon Jacob.

(E). 1940-1946 : OTHER DOCUMENTARIES

In addition to the factual films produced by the Crown and Service Film Units, the war saw a number of other fine documentaries turned out by the vast number of excellent groups which sprang up to fulfil the government demand for instruction and propaganda brought about by the six-year struggle. These films will, for the most part, be found under the individual composers listed in the index of this book. From this large group are three representative pictures of special musical interest :—

C.E.M.A. (Strand, 1942).

The aim of the Council for the Encouragement of Music and the Arts was " to bring the best to as many people as possible to cheer them on to better times." A film record of the work of C.E.M.A. was made by Strand in 1942 and showed first of all a harp trio playing Vaughan Williams' arrangement of " Greensleeves " in a village church. This was a beautifully handled sequence, making full use of the visual possibilities ; the recording however (on the film copy that I saw) was poor. The second sequence showed an industrial town seeing its first exhibition of paintings by living artists. Thirdly, the Old Vic company are seen on tour presenting " The Merry Wives Of Windsor " in a provincial theatre. The final sequence shows the Jacques Symphony Orchestra playing the first movement of Tchaikowsky's Piano Concerto No. 1 in B Flat Minor to a factory canteen audience. The recording was again poor, but the presentation was excellent. We see first the orchestra and soloist, then the faces of the audience and general views of the canteen. Finally, the music forms a background to a series of impressionistic shots of the factory at work, turning out munitions. A nicely balanced, competent short film with unusual music interest.

Conquest Of The Air. (London Films, 1940).

This picture, many years in production and undergoing re-editing, made a final appearance in June, 1940. It is a scrappy, documentary reconstruction of the development of aviation with extracts from newsreels giving a background of fact. Among its most interesting aspects is a music score written by Arthur Bliss, three or four years before, which is still heard on occasions as a concert suite of considerable merit.

Battle For Music. (Strand, 1944).

One of the most notable documentaries of recent years from a music point of view made its appearance in February, 1944. Three years before, the original idea of making a film about the colourful history of the London Philharmonic Orchestra had been conceived, but there were many hold-ups and set-backs before the job was finally completed. The film *Battle For Music* is an orchestral biography, a simple story of war-time vicissitudes and eventual triumph.

In the years that preceded the war, the L.P.O., as the London Philharmonic Orchestra is universally known, built itself up under world-famous conductors to the perfection that made its playing a byword amongst music lovers. But many of these people could only hear the orchestra on records, or on the radio, and see them at infrequent intervals. It is at Covent Garden Opera House at what was to be the last performance of " Tristan and Isolde," that the picture opens. No one believed war was imminent. The usual glittering crowd, the tiaras, the jewels, the ermine. The applause as the last notes die away and the curtain falls.

Then the orchestra. Talk of holidays. The ballet season they were to start afterwards . . . and then over beaches and seaside resorts, over a country at play came the news of war. But worse—the news that London was being evacuated. And suddenly the L.P.O. —eighty men trained for years—found themselves facing bankruptcy —the backers had left, music was finished.

Even then, amidst this chaos and disaster, the men found that this could be an opportunity—the one they had hoped would come in a very different form—the chance to give their music not to a select few, but to all people in every walk of life. The creditors of the company wished to wind it up. " You have no money. The theatres are shut. Give up, get jobs—be sensible."

But headed by Tom Russell, viola, Gregory and Bradley, French horn players, Morley, 1st violin, and Stead of the trombones, the committee faced creditors and company solicitors. Formed their own company and looked for work. Share and share alike was the rule. But during the weary weeks of rehearsal to keep their spirits up there was nothing to share, except the conviction that when the sudden shock of war subsided, the nation would need music and the arts and entertainment as much as munitions of war.

It wasn't easy all this. Wives and sweethearts don't like to see their men in such straits. Musicians must eat, and only by pooling and helping each other were they tided over till the first date at a Cardiff cinema was obtained.

Constant Lambert conducted " Romeo and Juliet," and only a few overdrafts and pawn tickets told of how they managed to get there. Their reception was terrific and the rest of the short tour an enormous success in everything but money. The houses were small ; fares and food left little over. Bedrooms were an unknown luxury to these men of the Royal Opera House.

Then Russell's idea to link up with the French in a series of Anglo-French concerts. His trip to Paris. His escape just ahead of the Germans. His miserable return to the orchestra rehearsing under Warwick Braithwaite, waiting and hoping.

Then a miracle happened. A call from Jack Hylton—now impresario, theatre owner. Jack would take a chance. Their spirit infected him. He would back them in a tour of provincial music halls.

The spell had broken. With Dr. Malcolm Sargent, Warwick Braithwaite and Constant Lambert conducting, with Eileen Joyce and Moiseiwitsch at the piano, they toured the country. In air raid, death and destruction, they played and through the infernos the people came.

But at this peak, the air raids became deadly. The theatres empty. Money again short. It was now that J. B. Priestley came to their aid. Alone, he arranged what he insisted on calling a Musical Manifesto at the Queens Hall. The people that he wished to attract came under the joint stimulus of his and the L.P.O.'s name . . . the same people who had left them to their fate in those early days of war. But J.B. in his own inimitable manner, took their cheques from them, Sir Adrian Boult and others conducted and the day was saved.

They had ideas of taking a theatre of their own—a home of music. Tom found one, the Orpheum at Golders Green. The owners agreed to a convenient lease. At last they could put into practice all they preached.

During that night's blitz, the Queens Hall burned to the ground. Nearly all their instruments were lost in the fire. This was the cruellest blow.

But this time fate stepped in to help them. The B.B.C. broadcast their misfortune and from homes of rich and poor, from every county town and hamlet in the country, came the response. Some amusing relics, some pathetic, but the orchestra was re-equipped, the theatre re-taken and the people came and that tumultuous reception repaid all they had suffered in their battle for music. . . .

All the original personalities took part in the film version, including the conductors Sir Adrian Boult, Constant Lambert, Warwick Braithwaite and Dr. Malcolm Sargent, with Moiseiwitsch,

Eileen Joyce, Jack Hylton, J. B. Priestley, Brian Michie, Thomas Russell, and members of the orchestra committee. The film was directed by Donald Taylor at the National Studios, Elstree ; Al Rhind and Edgar Law were responsible for the sound recording on Western Electric. But it cannot be called a successful film. The reason for its failure as a large-scale, first-class production is deep-rooted ; it is basically connected with production difficulties, differences of opinion as to methods of story-telling, and an over-extended time factor. The story of the L.P.O. had magnificent film possibilities that called for a " Hollywood " approach to convert it into a fine fictional-documentary and could have added greatly to the prestige of British musical cinema. Instead, it became an unco-ordinated mix-up at each stage of its production resulting in failure to emerge either as a good feature or a good documentary. What did result was a very pleasant series of well-recorded concert hall works, interspersed by naive interludes of real people trying in vain to act convincingly their ordinary everyday lives. However, let it be said that this record of the London Philharmonic Orchestra is an invaluable piece of film music history and a very worthy project ; the complaint is not against the excellent basic principle of *Battle For Music*, but only the failure to develop the tremendous possibilities that remain untouched in the half-hearted presentation of this intriguing narration. One of the outcomes of this was that the picture failed to secure a decent release and only with great difficulty could it be tracked down to some little independent cinema, though it has had one or two odd bookings during the last year or so when music lovers have trekked many miles to some small repertory or " classic " cinema to see it.

The critics were all very fair about it. First from the film trade comes these comments :—

" Unassuming direction, artless leading portrayal, upholstered at times by professional cameos, spectacular concert-hall settings complete with acclaiming audiences. Clear-cut attraction for musical devotees." The British Film Institute, representing the more serious approach to films, realised the underlying excellence of *Battle For Music* and said : " The film has been sympathetically directed and in every case justice has been done to the brilliance of execution by the high technical qualities in the recording and photography. An unusual and pleasing film." Finally, we get the views of Otis L. Guernsey, Jr., writing in the " New York Herald Tribune " : " An unusual motion picture. . . . Between renditions of Grieg, Mozart, Rachmaninoff and Beethoven, the members of this orchestra double as actors playing themselves in the face of financial difficulties. Their story is repetitive, and as actors the musicians are just barely convincing ; but the action is of importance only as a musical ' book ' to hold the interludes of classical music together . . . *Battle For Music* is designed for those who would like to hear the London Philharmonic Orchestra play these works through the medium of the motion picture."

The L.P.O. are to be congratulated on their enthusiastic collaboration in making this piece of film history and as an occasion to hear good music on the screen in large quantities *Battle For Music* has rarely been equalled, but we hope that further attempts will be made for a large-scale production of such a story as this, without the limitations that prevented Donald Taylor's film from becoming the achievement that it might have been.

CHAPTER IV

THE INDUSTRIAL, CARTOON AND NEWSREEL FILM

" Why kid ourselves ? Film music is utilitarian first. It may be ' cultural ' after that."

M. ZALSTEIN, Philadelphia Symphony Orchestra.

(A). THE INDUSTRIAL FILM

The margin between the Documentary and the Industrial film is often a narrow one. Many of our finest documentaries were sponsored by commercial companies for commercial purposes, yet they emerged to comply with Paul Rotha's complicated definition of documentary : " . . . beyond the simple descriptive terms of the teaching film, more imaginative and expressive than the specific publicity picture, deeper in meaning and more skilful in style than the newsreel, wider in observation than the travel picture or lecture film, more profound in implication and reference than the plain ' interest ' picture . . . " For example, Paul Rotha himself made two films in 1933 ; one was for Imperial Airways, Ltd., and the other for the Empire Trade Board. *Contact* told of the ground organisation and flying of the Empire air routes and the importance of air communication, while the other dealt with Southampton Docks. Industrial films ? Yes, but they went beyond pure commerce into the realms of documentary, especially with the addition of two of the earliest of original British film scores, written by Clarence Raybould, a well-known orchestral figure to-day and at that time a young composer straight from the Guildhall School of Music.

However, there are a number of films which are purely industrial in their design, but nevertheless have music that may be of interest. A recent example is Clifton Parker's lovely, neat, compact score for *Steam*, a picture made in 1945 for Babcock & Wilcox, or perhaps, *Steel*, also shown in 1945, with a restrained, pointed track by Hubert Clifford. Going back a bit, there was, I remember, a set of publicity films made for Cadbury Bros. ; one of them called *Workaday* (1937) had a number of delightful music passages by

129

E

the late Walter Leigh. Then there was a Shell-Mex picture *Oil From The Earth* (1938), with a rather unusual quality of composition, from Ernst Meyer. A remarkable interlaced effect had been obtained so that music merged into the clatter of pipeline construction and derrick erection with a fine facility of interplay between natural sound and music. In 1946, I saw a film on the optical industry with music by Norman Fulton. Called *Optics*, it was full of bizarre, quaint effects in which the composer showed great musical talent, though it must be said that, clever as it was, a lot of the music was entirely inappropriate to the subject matter.

Almost a specialist in industrial films is Francis Chagrin. In two advertising films *Carnival In The Cupboard* and *Fable Of The Fabrics*, he showed a distinct aptitude for this type of work. So much so that Hubert Clifford wrote a review in his film music critique, published in the magazine " Tempo," discussing Chagrin's work in another industrial film : " Francis Chagrin's score for *Castings*, a technical film, sponsored by High-Duty Alloys, seizes the few opportunities the film provides. Stylised music of this type ' comes off ' admirably when associated with shots of engineering and industrial processes." A little-known aspect of the film music world, the industrial picture should not be ignored by movie music fans any more than they can afford to ignore the productions which, if one went no further than the banality of their official title, might cause them to overlook the remarkable work of the General Post Office Film Unit.

(B). CARTOON FILMS

The cartoon film as developed in Hollywood by Walt Disney and his many imitators offers the closest combination of music and film that it is possible to achieve. In making cartoons no broad approach is allowed as in, say, a documentary film. The music score for a cartoon must be planned to fit the visuals, frame by frame and bar by bar, and Walt Disney has shown us just what can be done. He has experimented with everything from Bach's Toccata and Fugue in D Minor to " Pop Goes the Weasel " in planning the musical side of his magnificent pictures, producing an entirely new cinema art, providing a major factor in screen entertainment and giving us a film form that is refreshingly independent of jungle love, passion, and the other ingredients of oversophistication so frequently associated with the American cinema. In recent years Paramount Pictures have presented a series of puppet films by George Pal. Filmed in Technicolor and made by a technique similar to the cartoon animation but substituting brightly painted wooden models for drawings, these " Puppetoons " have likewise offered considerable scope for the music department at Paramount.

In Britain we have no large-scale cartoon or puppet film facilities ; yet oddly enough many of the early experiments in both types of film were made here and on the Continent, to be adopted and exploited later by Hollywood, as was the theme song idea. Some of the earliest silent cartoons were made in Britain, but Walt Disney's arrival in Hollywood at the beginning of talkies soon put the American output in the lead. Anson Dyer has made a series of cartoons in this country over a number of years, though they have never achieved widespread popularity. In 1935 Mischa Spoliansky scored *The Fox Hunt*, an early British cartoon, but the experiment was not repeated. Also in 1935, Len Lye was making puppet and cartoon shorts for various organisations like the G.P.O. Film Unit and Shell Lubrication. George Pal, now doing so well in the States, did a series of his puppet films for Horlick's Malted Milk and Phillips Radio between 1936 and 1939 ; the music for the Malted Milk pictures was handled by dance band expert Debroy Somers. In 1938, Benjamin Britten scored *The Tocher*, a silhouette fantasy on a Scottish theme, made by Lotte Reiniger for the G.P.O. Film Unit to popularise the Post Office Savings Bank. It is true that cartoons and puppet films were being made in this country, but many were not shown in the commercial cinemas, while others were marred by the advertising that was their life-blood in many cases. During the war years the cartoon technique was applied to national requirements ; there were cartoon trailers on salvage and savings, with animated diagrams by the Isotype Institute and "food flashes" on cabbages and carrots. Musically two men have done the most notable work in this direction—Matyas Seiber and Ernst Meyer. Both have been closely associated with the Halas-Batchelor Unit, a small Soho studio specialising in cartoon trailers and shorts. Matyas Seiber, well-known London musicologist, scored a dozen or more for them. Ernst Meyer, composer, film editor and sound effects expert who has been associated with the G.P.O. Unit, Paul Rotha and most of the leading documentarians, is at present working with the Halas-Batchelor group on a Technicolor cartoon called *The Magic Canvas* for which Matyas Seiber composed the music (recorded by the Blech String Orchestra). A special system has been applied to this particular film. With the music already recorded the artists have prepared a special gramophone record in which every bar of music is played separately and numerically announced by a person speaking the bar number before the music is played. From this the artists drew up a unique shooting script. Each instrument of the orchestra is represented by a different coloured crayon on a graph which is marked out in frame numbers, bar numbers and musical pitch. After drawing in all the instruments on this chart, every musical movement comes before you as a rising or descending, a fading or an intensifying colour scheme from which the story and visuals are worked out. Musically and artistically *The Magic Canvas* offers the possibility of something that has hardly existed at all in this country so far—a good colour cartoon.

The work of the Isotype unit has been to provide animated diagrams for the purpose of getting facts and figures across in a lively and interesting manner. A notable example of their work was to be seen in the Paul Rotha housing film *Land Of Promise*. In one or two war-time salvage films, Ernst Meyer collaborated in providing some unique experiments in " orchestrated sound effects." Cymbal crashes, tom-toms, car engines, tin cans, bells—all manner of sounds are recorded by Meyer and then assembled into tracks for the panorama of diagrams and figures that juggle themselves to-and-fro across the screen in such films as *A Few Ounces A Day*. By applying the cartoon cutting method to ordinary film material, Meyer similarly produced those fascinating manœuvres of cardboard boxes and sardine tins that seemingly march down the street on their own and jump into the salvage bins, to the accompaniment of a march rhythm scored for two dustbins, four mangles and a sheet of corrugated iron.

In 1940, Ealing Studios made a few commercial cartoons, but by far the most significant move in this direction occurred in 1945, when the Rank organization set up a cartoon section and brought in a Walt Disney right-hand man, David Hand, to supervise production of the various departments connected with this work. So far we have not seen any major circuit releases of any British cartoons, but it takes a long time to get such a unit going. However, the Children's Cinema Clubs are being catered for in this respect, while Ernest Irving, music director of Ealing Studios, recently scored a puppet film called *The Good Samaritan*, over which he was very enthusiastic. This lovely little picture was designed for the

Children's Cinemas, as was the Halas-Batchelor song cartoon *Heave Away My Johnnies*, musically handled by Leslie Woodgate.

Finally, comes news of a full-length feature cartoon, also the work of the Halas-Batchelor Unit, with music by their full group of composers, including Ernst Meyer, Matyas Seiber and Francis Chagrin (who has done a number of cartoon trailers for them) with the possible inclusion of Ben Frankel and Benjamin Britten. So far, Britain has had little say in the world of the cartoon for commercial distribution, but to-day there are strong signs both in and out of the Rank organization that the time may come when we too will have a firmly established group of artists and technicians specialising in that ever-popular item of the cinema programme—the colour cartoon.

(C). THE NEWSREELS

The newsreel companies are engaged in a high-speed, competitive form of film making which does not permit the use of specially composed music. The work of fitting a musical background to the twice weekly issues of the newsreel organizations is usually done by the film editor or the recordist, and there are no musical directors pure and simple in this type of work. Instead they rely on library music. Each newsreel company builds up a collection of film track music in a similar way to the old " compilations " of the silent days, except that in this case the music is in the form of a film (and not a sheet music) library. Various sources are tapped to enable each company to build up its own library to suit its own purposes. For example, Gaumont-British News use a lot of music composed and recorded by Louis Levy, music director of the feature film department of the Gaumont-British organisation at Lime Grove, Shepherd's Bush. Boosey & Hawkes, the London music publishers, founded a special " Sound Tracks " department in 1943 and undertook to arrange special recording sessions at which a supply of music orchestrated to suit newsreel work was recorded on film and made available to the short film producers and the newsreels. Thus, most of the newsreels use this celluloid music ready " canned and labelled " to facilitate speed in compiling the latest reel. Other companies specialising in this type of work include firms like Chappells or the Bosworth Company.

Taking one company as typical, we follow the course of the latest issue of British Movietone News. Stan Wicken is the supervising sound recordist and film editor, and he has a library of over a million feet of music comprising material for every conceivable occasion, recorded either in British studios, at the special recording sessions held by Boosey & Hawkes, which Stan Wicken frequently attends himself, or in the States as originally used by Movietone News over there for their American reels. As soon as a " rough cut " of the current newsreel has been made up from the material sent in by Movietone cameramen all over the world, it is screened in the tiny studio cinema and viewed by the music man. Instinctively music suggests itself to a particular sequence, for the arranger must know his music intimately, even down to short phrases of only ten or twenty seconds' duration. From a card index giving the name of the piece, film length in feet, composer and copyright details, in addition to a list of newsreels for which it has been used, the music director-editor gathers together a collection of short lengths of celluloid. On an " Editola " or " Moviola " the music is checked on a small loudspeaker and the work of compilation begun. .Sound is added, the commentary recorded and given the " O.K." and the music arranged, when, after the finished job has received the approval of the newsreel chiefs, the work of printing the finished copy begins.

The music man of a newsreel is primarily a technician, not a musician. Yet he must know his library so thoroughly that he can assemble his score (with sound effects) in, say, two hours. There is little room for æsthetics, for the producers require a good story with sound and music, ready for the laboratories to print as quickly as possible. His job is to obtain a score from existing music supplies, to provide appropriate music that will consolidate and exploit the cutter's story to the full. He must fit music to current world news. Stan Wicken, of Movietone, is in charge of the sound editing as well as the music, while at Gaumont-British, Roy Drew, the chief cutter, selects the music. In the Wardour Street cutting rooms of Pathé Gazette, W. S. Bland, chief sound engineer, is responsible for the music library; music selection is carried out by Derek Coldman. The music librarian for Paramount is J. W. Hall. Occasionally, a special story may be built up around a certain piece of music. Pathé had a good example of this in their El Alamein Anniversary story, for which they used the El Alamein Concerto composed by Albert Arlen, while in the Soviet newsreel production *The Defeat*

Of The Germans Near Moscow, a " Fanfare for Heroes " by Arthur Bliss was used. Although this form of musical background is technically a throwback to the silent days, in the hands of a good technician it can, nevertheless, add greatly to the impact behind a newsreel story, and British newsreels have maintained a high standard in the use of library music which, considering the time factor involved, has been used with restraint and good taste to combine with smooth editing and first class camerawork in producing a consistently satisfactory item in our motion picture entertainment.

At the British Film Festival of 1946, a number of extracts from wartime newsreels were shown and the two outstanding items were those in which music had been used rather cleverly. The first was based on the popular song " I Can't Give You Anything but Love, Baby," and the tune was fitted to a newsreel sequence of a Hitler-Mussolini meeting. Originally designed by British Movietone for a Ministry of Information picture, the rapid development of the war suddenly put this item out-of-date and the Ministry abandoned the project. Newsreel chief, Gerald Sanger, however, bought back the Hitler-Mussolini bit from the M.O.I. and put it into the film vaults ; when the British Film Festival was convened, it was brought out and given its premiere showing at the Leicester Square Theatre and was a great success. Coupled with it was the *Panzer Ballet*, another Movietone speciality. In the dark days of 1940 a newsreel of German troops doing the goose-step in triumphant style was taken from a Nazi eleven-reel documentary and to it was added the music of " The Lambeth Walk." The individual frames of the German newsreel were reversed and advanced in cartoon fashion and the finished effect on the screen was one of the biggest laughs I have ever experienced in newsreel work. To the lilting tune of Noel Gay's " Lambeth Walk " the stern body of Nazi goose-steppers go dancing through the streets like robots on the spree in a highly amusing manner. Out of Hitler's grim documentary studios had come this record of the triumph of power and destruction that was to herald in the world domination of the Nordic race as represented by the Nazi régime, a film designed to show the decadent democracies and the numbed neutrals that resistance to the German mechanised hordes was useless. Through various channels, a copy of the film came to England ; from England it went out again to every country in the world as the *Panzer Ballet*, answering Germany with a weapon that they did not possess in their military organisation—a sense of humour. Eventually the German newsreel men got their film back, complete with the " Lambeth Walk," and in a private cinema in Berlin at the Goebbel's Ministry of Propaganda, Hitler and his chiefs sat down to watch a British newsreel that, even in those days of Nazi triumph at its peak, must have given them something to think about.

Both these items were the work of Charles Ridley, an independent music and story editor still working for Movietone News ; the music tracks were synchronised and recorded by Norman Leevers.

I'LL BE YOUR SWEET-HEART. Margaret Lockwood as she appears in a major musical sequence from the film. Musical direction was by Louis Levy.

CHAPTER V

RECORDING FILM MUSIC

◆

" To record a piece of music successfully, the first and most important factor is to know the piece of music."

HAROLD KING,
(Sound Supervisor, British National Studios).

At present, most film scores are written after the film is completed, except in the case of a musical or instances where the music has some special significance. For these exceptions the music is written and recorded, usually on gramophone records, which can be " played back " (i.e., performed over a loudspeaker like an ordinary gramophone record) in the studio whilst the film is being shot. As a general rule music is never recorded on the set or on location during the making of the picture ; it is easier and better to handle all of it after the completion of the " floor " work and the filming of exterior shots.

Having assembled a " rough cut " or outline version of the film in the cutting room, the picture is screened with dialogue and a little sound, but without full sound effects and without music. It is still very much the director's and the film editor's picture, but they eventually decide on a more or less finished version. Then the composer and music director get to work. The music director already knows from the script and by seeing the rushes or the " rough cut " what type of film he is handling. From this he can decide which composer would best suit the job in hand. Maybe the composer is already under contract or maybe he is a free-lance and will have to be approached to take on the music writing. Having fixed up with the composer, the music director then arranges for him to see the film in what is supposed to be its final, irrevocable version, but which in practise it rarely is. The composer then confers with the musical director and often with the film director to decide how much and what sort of music is required. A date is fixed for recording the music and the composer departs to write his score. Meanwhile the music director arranges for the recording session—the orchestra to be booked (or "called"

THE GREAT MR. HANDEL. Wilfred Lawson as Handel, Elizabeth Allan as Mrs. Cibber and Hay Petrie as Phineas.

E*

as they say in studio parlance), the projection of the film during the session to be organised, and so on. In this country it is often necessary to book an outside hall for the music recording; in this case the music director must arrange, through the normal studio channels, for a mobile sound unit to be laid on at the outside hall to make the " music tracks " as they are called.

To record a musical score for a film may take a day, a week or a month; usually it takes four or five days for the average feature film. On the days previously arranged, the composer arrives with his manuscript score. To produce this, the composer may have done a full orchestral score himself, with copyists to produce all the parts for each member of the orchestra; he may have written an outline or piano score and had it orchestrated by someone else; he may have written it partly on his own and partly with some assistance; or he may have whistled a little theme, had it written down, orchestrated, arranged and copied by a veritable army of musical assistants. Whatever his method it must be remembered that almost always he will be working against time. A week, three weeks, a month; he is very lucky if he has much more than that in which to prepare his score.

The orchestra varies greatly. It may consist of 10 players in a little private theatre attached to some small documentary studio, 35 players in a moderate studio recording stage or an assembly of 80 plus choir, soloists, and additional percussion in one of the largest of London's public concert halls. Recording sessions are usually informal affairs. The conductor (who is normally the music director, sometimes the composer) is in shirt sleeves and has frequent conferences with the composer (when the composer is not the conductor as well), talks with the director, discusses with the orchestral players and debates with the sound recordists. The music is rehearsed, checked, altered. " The eighth bar, is it a C Sharp or a C Natural? " asks the second trumpet; the conductor and composer go into a huddle. " Should be a C Sharp," says the music director. " George," says the music director, " that cymbal roll in the fifth bar before the end has got to come in right smack on the moment of the kiss, so come in at the beginning of the sixth from the end. O.K.? Right, settle down, please. We'll take it this time. O.K. for a take? " He signals to the sound recordist's booth. " Right, turn 'em over. Stand by. Speed up." The sound recording machine is now running, the music director beats out the time, and the music gets under-way. Thus the music is " shot," piece by piece, inside a film studio or in an outside hall, more or less in the same way as the picture itself is made.

For many films it is desirable to see the actual scenes on the screen at the same time as the music is played. This is not normally practicable in the outside halls, but in a studio recording theatre, a screen and a projection room are part of the standard equipment. In this case the music director can see the picture on the screen and will follow it closely while the music is played and recorded, permitting close and accurate synchronisation between music and film. The film appears in silence on the screen, though the music director may listen to the dialogue on headphones. Alongside the projected picture appears a footage or second indicator, which gives an illuminated figure continuously announcing the number of feet of celluloid film passing through the projector, or the passage of time, measured in seconds. Thus the recording equipment for the music starts running and the music director watches the indicator for the figures " 00 " to appear on the screen. At this point, the scene requiring the music begins and the orchestra starts to play it. In the meantime, the numbers advance— " 01," " 02," " 03 "—in either seconds of time or in feet of film in the manner of a car mileage indicator. Where the music is recorded in a theatre or concert hall away from the studio, it is necessary to take stop-watch timings in order to synchronise music and picture later on when the music recordings are taken back to the studio.

The music being played in the recording theatre or concert hall is picked up by microphones placed at various positions in and around the orchestra. Much depends on the acoustics of the hall and on the individual approach of the sound recordist, also on the type of effect the composer and music director want in their finished sound track. The question of " balance " is always an important feature of any recording session ; that is, the adjustment of microphones and orchestral players in such a way as to obtain an effective sound track on which the instruments of the orchestra will be correctly inter-related, clearly recorded and set out in the pattern of sound conceived by the composer and music director. And as the recording session may extend over a week, it is essential to make sure that the " balance " is correct each morning when you start work, or an uneven music track will result. One music director has a special composition, designed to exploit the instruments of any particular orchestra with which he is working so that he can go into the recording room, listen over a loudspeaker while the orchestra in the theatre plays his special piece, and, by his familiarity with the music, immediately tell if the balance and recording level are correct. A predominance of, say, the strings at the expense of wood-wind is quickly revealed by this special " balance " composition.

The music then is picked up by microphones and passes to the sound supervisor, who listens either on a loudspeaker or on headphones, and he controls the amount of sound going to the actual recording machines. Usually he will listen on loudspeakers in preference to headphones so that he can hear the music as it will sound in a cinema later on when the finished film is shown. Passing on from the volume controls of the supervisor, the music goes by cable to the actual recording machines, housed either in a mobile truck or in a special room belonging to the studio sound department. Here the music is photographed on to film, and it is well to remember that music and sound are photographed in very much the same way as the picture is photographed on to a moving strip of light-sensitive emulsion-coated celluloid. They even call it a " sound camera," to emphasize the fact that film sound bears no relation whatsoever to a gramophone record, but is basically an electro-photographic process. There is no need to describe a microphone or loudspeaker, as these are fairly familiar objects ; a sound camera is about the size of a large table model radio set, and incorporates an electric motor to draw the film through the " light cell," which is the heart of the sound recorder (it involves a very small ray of light which is made to flicker in time with the frequency impulses of electric current, produced by the microphone in response to air vibrations set up by the musical instruments, and amplified through large banks of radio valves and their associated electrical circuits). All this may sound very complicated to those of you who are not familiar with radio theory, but it would take a large size text-book to explain in full. The sound camera is fed with reels of 35 millimetre film in just the same way as a motion picture camera. Apart from these machines, the recording truck or room will be surrounded by banks of amplifiers, knobs, switches and meters which are concerned with the boosting-up of the weak microphone signals in preparation for their delicate task of actuating the little ray of light in the sound camera itself.

The studio recording theatres are designed for the job and produce good results within the limits of their acoustic capacities. At Denham, for example, there is a fine recording theatre, designed by sound chief A. W. Watkins and suitable for orchestras of up to about 50 players. In addition, they now have a large music stage which will take up to 120. The sound stage at the G.B. studios in Lime Grove, Shepherd's Bush on the other hand, will only handle orchestras of up to 20, so they do a good deal of outside work. Ealing Studios have no facilities for a big orchestra and they go to the H.M.V. Gramophone Recording Studios in St. Johns Wood quite a lot. Pinewood and Elstree again are without proper full-size music recording stages as is the Riverside plant at Hammersmith. Thus there is keen competition to find acoustically suitable theatres and concert halls in and around London in which to record film music. The Crown Film Unit sound expert Ken Cameron was the first to discover the excellent facilities of Watford Town Hall as a music recording theatre ; since then many other studios have got to hear about Watford and Ken Cameron will tell you with some vehemence that it is as much as he can do to book up a music session there nowadays, so keen is the competition. Wembley Town Hall is another favourite with music directors ; Muir Mathieson is keen on it and says " it makes an orchestra of thirty sound like one of a hundred." Places like the Kingsway Hall, Central Hall, Westminster, the Scala and the Cambridge Theatres are also used, and at the end of this section is a list of some typical British pictures, showing where the music for them was recorded. A good stand-by for all the studios, by the way, is the mighty H.M.V. Recording Theatre at Abbey Road, St. Johns Wood, where the orchestral platform is reputed to accommodate 250 players, with room for an audience of 1,000 in the main hall.

The music emerges as a separate entity of its own : a straightforward musical sound track. This is then handed over to the people who prepare the final film, bringing picture, dialogue, sound effects and music together in completed form. The process of making up the finished sound track is known as " dubbing " and " re-recording," whereby the separate tracks carrying music, sound effects and dialogue are " laid out " and brought together by the dubbing man, who mixes the three ingredients into the final pie. This is also known as " heartbreak house " for the composer, who may find that it has been necessary to fade down

141

his music to almost nil at just the point where he planned his musical climax. In any case it is desirable that the music director should be in attendance during the dubbing and to-day, with good music planning, the " heartbreaks " are less frequent.

/ Here at the recording and dubbing sessions the mechanical side of film composition reaches its final stage. First, we have our composer, working in his study at home, setting down his themes, planning the timing of the music, creating his score. He may know little or nothing of the technicalities of the film industry, so his music goes on to the music director. He is the liaison between the pure artist (the composer) and the technician (the sound recordist). It is he who assembles the orchestra and understands music and film problems alike. He also acts as the music casting director. Then come the pure technicians, the sound supervisor and the recordists ; finally, on to the dubbing expert and the finished film. It is a debatable question as to how much inter-change should exist between each section of specialists. Obviously it is invaluable to have a composer who understands microphone technique, a sound recordist who is a musician, and a dubbing expert who knows the principles of musical composition. The director too, who is musically minded, can help with suggestions for the type of music and where it should appear. On the other hand, most composers and music directors have had the experience of being pestered with useless hints and suggested alterations to music which they know by their specialist knowledge to be correct, but which some director with that little knowledge which is such a dangerous thing, insists on giving out to the detriment of the recording session in progress. Music, like every single section of the intricate process of film production, is and must be a matter for complete co-operation, plenty of give-and-take, and the ability of a group of specialists to work together in harmony.

This section includes two articles in which first a music director, and secondly, a sound recordist outline some of their problems and explain their work. Louis Levy, music director of Gaumont-British Studios, discusses some of the new developments in film music recording and puts out a few indications of the future, while George Burgess, head of the Sound Department at Hammersmith, comments on to-day's problems and gives his idea of the ideal music recording stage. In addition, an orchestral player gives a realistic description of a film recording session.

142

WHERE THE MUSIC IS RECORDED FOR FILMS

Things To Come	Scala Theatre.
Target For To-night ..	Warner Bros. Studio, Teddington.
Coastal Command	H.M.V. Studio, St. Johns Wood.
Caesar And Cleopatra ..	Denham Recording Theatre.
Caravan	Watford Town Hall.
Battle Of The Books ..	Marylebone Studio.
The Four Feathers.. ..	Denham Recording Theatre.
The Seventh Veil	Stage 2, Riverside Studio, Hammersmith.
The Islanders	King George V Hall, London.
Heart Of Britain	Huddersfield Methodist Church and the Odeon Cinema, Manchester.
The Magic Bow	Kingsway Hall, H.M.V. Studio, St. Johns Wood and Watford Town Hall.
Goodbye, Mr. Chips ..	Denham Recording Theatre.
The Overlanders	H.M.V. Studio, St. Johns Wood.
Total War in Britain ..	Scala Theatre.
Land Of Promise	Watford Town Hall.
Dead Of Night	H.M.V. Studio, St. Johns Wood.
Meet The Navy	National Studio, Elstree.
Flying With Prudence ..	Merton Park Studio.
London Town	Stage 2, Sound City, Shepperton.
Carnival	Denham Recording Theatre.
Close Quarters	Central Hall, Westminster.
Fires Were Started.. ..	Pinewood Recording Theatre.
Instruments Of The Orchestra	H.M.V. Studio, St. Johns Wood.
Merchant Seamen	National Studio, Elstree.
Lisbon Story	National Studio, Elstree.
A Girl In A Million ..	Riverside Studio, Hammersmith.
Diary For Timothy ..	Watford Town Hall.
Stricken Peninsula ..	Kingsway Hall, London.
The Voice Within	Walton-on-Thames Studio.
Meet Me At Dawn ..	Stage 1, Music Theatre, Denham.
Green For Danger.. ..	Stage 1, Music Theatre, Denham.
Odd Man Out	Stage 1, Music Theatre, Denham.
Great Expectations	Stage 1, Music Theatre, Denham.
World Of Plenty	National Studio, Elstree.
Forty-Million People ..	B.B.C. Studios, Manchester.

The Drum	Denham Recording Theatre.
Listen To Britain	National Gallery, London.
One Of Our Aircraft Is Missing	Denham Recording Theatre.
Flight From Folly	Warner Bros. Studio, Teddington.
The Story Of D.D.T. ..	Wembley Town Hall.
Burma Victory	Watford Town Hall.
Squadron 992	National Studio, Elstree.
Malta G.C.	H.M.V. Studio, St. Johns Wood.
The Channel Islands ..	Pinewood Recording Theatre.

THE IDEAL MUSIC RECORDING STAGE

by GEORGE BURGESS

The sound engineer who recorded the music for " The Seventh Veil" and " Girl In A Million" describes the basic principles of ideal sound recording conditions.

Before the war the standard of music recording was very low in British studios. Little or no attempt had been made to provide suitable stages for music recording purposes. Since the war, a small amount has been done, but at the present time there does not exist in Great Britain any stage which can be termed ideal for a music session of any magnitude. This lack is to an extent due to commercial considerations ; it is somewhat difficult to convince " the Powers that be," who are naturally primarily concerned in the monetary returns from the studio floor, that it is worth while setting aside 400,000 cubic feet of space to be used principally for music recording—which at any rate cannot be used for set building and dialogue shooting—yet how else to improve the quality of recorded music ?

There are at the moment two ways of approaching the problem of good music recording, both subject to the criticism that they are not ideal.

1. Recording on dialogue stages that happen to be free at the moment. The results are invariably bad, since it is generally accepted that a stage damped down for dialogue recording is completely unsuitable for music. The lack of reverberation gives a very dead effect to the resultant recording, the absorption characteristic of the damping (usually rock-wool) makes it impossible to obtain a good musical balance of the orchestra without the use of many auxiliary microphones with attendant troubles, and the instrumentalists feel themselves that their performance is below par. This factor of reverberation is well illustrated by the age-old effect of the inducement to sing in the bath because of the improved resonance and quality of one's singing due to the acoustic sharpness of most bathrooms. Improvement can only be brought about in studio music recording by altering the acoustics of a dialogue stage each time it is used for music, and this is the common procedure

145

in studios at the moment. The disadvantages are as follows : the large size of the sections of the " music shell " from a storage and handling point of view (roughly three sides of the walls of the stage to be treated plus a ceiling piece to cover) constitutes a major snag, made worse by the difficulty of adapting these sections to other stages. The time factor in building and striking on the stage plus the ever alternating acoustics as one changes from stage to stage are further troubles.

2. Recording in an outside hall that is known to be good acoustically for music by means of a mobile recording channel is the second method. This system often results in better recording, but again suffers from disadvantages : good monitoring conditions are difficult to obtain (there is the case of one famous recording studio in which the sound men have to sit in the gentleman's cloakroom with their gear in order to get a good sound track, surrounded as they are by frequent rushes of water, extremely cramped conditions and music and sound breaking through from the studio next door). Working outside, it is usually impossible to run synchronous picture and/or track as a guide for the conductor. Finally, most concert halls are designed to have optimum acoustics with an audience of at least two-thirds capacity, a condition that cannot be fulfilled normally at a recording session.

There is another great disadvantage inherent in both methods mentioned above when dealing with music subsequently to be used for " playback " purposes. These tracks should be as flexible as possible, for it is impossible before the picture is shot and cut to record the most suitable admixture of solo voices, orchestral accompaniment and chorus, for example. Ideally, therefore, these should be recorded on separate tracks, thus giving flexibility for altered perspective, change of vocalist, change of accompaniment, and/or change of chorus with a minimum of retakes.

Apart from the question of the multiplicity of channels with cross connected monitor amplifiers for this type of work, the most important question is the isolation of the three tracks to ensure that there is, for example, so little accompaniment on the solo vocalist's track as will permit a subsequent substitution. Attempts have been made to carry this out on one stage, but with little success, as nothing short of a portable booth for the vocalist will give the separation required, while this booth, unless of considerable size and very careful design, will only ruin the track because of its poor acoustics and discomfort.

146

Attempts have also been made to achieve the flexible results desired by recording the vocal part separately to light piano accompaniment, adding the orchestral accompaniment at a subsequent date. There is, however, no doubt that at any rate certain vocalists miss the uplift and help of a large orchestra and are quite incapable of giving the same performance with a piano accompaniment, particularly a light one. It would, therefore, seem to be important to have available facilities for shooting simultaneously at least three separate tracks of a musical number, each being virtually free of any admixture with the others.

The ideal music stage, therefore, begins to take shape. A hall of at least 400,000 cubic feet capacity with acoustics and reverberation time adjusted to the best curves available for this work, with auxiliary halls on either side, isolated acoustically from the main hall, but having large double glass windows to ensure visual contact between the conductor, vocalist and/or chorus. These two auxiliary halls are treated acoustically for optimum reverberation times, etc., and are fitted for headphone and/or directional loudspeaker injection, at controllable level, of the accompaniment. The conductor's earphones are usually matched to cover the mixture of all three outputs, but may at will cover any one only. This applies similarly to the recordist's monitor, which is itself contained in a third auxiliary room, again acoustically treated for optimum results, and again preferably fitted with double glass windows giving a full view of the main hall, in order that a check may be kept on synchronisation with the picture. Two small well illuminated panels on the picture screen itself give indications of secondage and/or footage.

It will be seen that with this type of set-up, all the disadvantages mentioned under methods 1 and 2 have been removed, while at the same time the following advantages appear : firstly, orchestral recordings with bands up to 130 players can be made under ideal conditions. Then the control of the reverberation can be readily made by means of drapes when smaller bands are to be recorded. The instrumentalists and the vocalists all give of their best, since they are performing under ideal acoustical conditions. The conductor obtains the desired musical balance between vocalist, chorus and band, since he can blend all together during the recording ; at the same time acoustical lag is absent, and the tracks, being all separate, can be subsequently mixed with all the perspective called for by the picture. Should any exception be

147

taken to any one track, it can be retaken with, if necessary, different vocalists or musicians without the necessity of calling the rest of the performers.

Thus only do we begin to bring our recording methods in this country up to the standard achieved in other parts of the world, and although great improvements have been made already in British sound and music in pictures, it is vital that, with the rapid growth of our industry as a major factor in world cinema, we may send out our films with sound tracks equal to anything anywhere.

Riverside Film Studios,
Hammersmith, 1947.

THE FUTURE OF BRITISH FILM MUSIC

by LOUIS LEVY

Louis Levy, famous musical director of Gainsborough Studios since the beginning of talkies, who has been working on film music since 1910, gives an outline of modern methods of film music recording as used in this country and in America, concluding with a few guesses at the future.

At the beginning of talkies, we soon found the snags caused by shooting the film and recording the music at the same time, and the method was very soon abandoned. The next stage was pre-recording. The pre-recording technique is very much like making a gramophone record, which means that all concentration is put into the recording of the music, without the limitations of filming at the same time. The disc is afterwards played back to the artiste on the set who mimes the words and actions, and it is in the further development of this technique that we in this country have lagged behind the Americans. It might be a good thing here to try to explain the technical methods now used in the U.S., which are also used here, but I am afraid, only with exceptions due to the recent war, which has hindered our technical progress.

The method now adopted in the U.S. is a multiple of sound channels. To simplify my explanation, let me quote as an example any up-to-date musical where one of the routines may have, let us say, a solo voice, or voices ; a specialised vocal trio, or quartette ; a full choir and a large symphony orchestra. In the first place, in the States, large well-equipped studios are available to house this young army. Such special studios are not available at present in this country. The band is put in position, also the solo singer, the specialised trio or quartette and also the vocal choir. These are separated by means of partitions, generally made of glass and wood. All these different sections are microphoned separately, and also they are all recorded into their own separate channels, therefore getting a multiple of four in one. The result is that for one number you have four negatives. The benefits resulting from this are that if any one of these negatives is not quite good enough, only that one section which is faulty need be recorded again.

Next, editing and cutting of routines becomes a practical proposition, and the most important point of all is that perfection of balance and an attempt at perspective is made possible. Also, in the finished result, if it is desired to scrap an orchestration for any particular reason, or even change the voice, such possibilities are now practical.

Recently I was responsible for the production and musical direction of the musical *I'll Be Your Sweetheart*. Multiple channels were not available to me, and so I adopted the following method :—

At the first recording I had everybody present, such as the orchestra and singers. We rehearsed in the usual way, with everybody taking their part, while I was in the listening room to judge the effect. When rehearsed, balanced and satisfied, we recorded the band only, after which we played the track back through earphones and recorded the solo artist on a separate channel. Then the same thing was done with the choir. In effect, the result of multiple channels was obtained, but the method at the best is only a makeshift, has its snags, and from an efficiency point of view, does not compete with the multiple channels being recorded at the same time.

Now, what of the future ? What progress is possible ? It's always risky to try and prophesy. Looking into the future, I find it necessary to go beyond the limits of music and include shooting scenes. My opinion is that the microphone has a direct bearing on future developments, for at present it is the microphone which limits any technical advance that we would like to make. The present-day microphone in a way is really like a man who is hard of hearing ; in order that this deaf person can hear, you have to place his ear in a certain position close enough to hear, and according to his degree of deafness, you have to shout louder. That, in a way, is my case against the mike, both for dialogue and musical recording. Directors of films are handicapped in movement, shots and angles, all due to the limitations of the mike. A lot of hearts are sometimes broken because some directors have thought out a beautiful angle for the next day's shooting, only to find that the only way to keep this shot in is by having the mike in the eye of the camera ! Referring back to music, although vast strides have been made in recording, the microphone still limits the possibilities.

I think that any future development will be towards a much wider sensitiveness, either by the use of a mike, or probably without the use of a mike—I don't know which. Maybe the time will come when wires or rays of light round the studio will make it possible for any equal part of sound coming from any particular spot in the studio to be brought within complete range of the sound camera. The same applies to music.

"A FILM MUSIC RECORDING SESSION"

by EDWARD SILVERMAN

A film music recording session is described through the eyes of EDWARD SILVERMAN, *a violinist of one of our leading national orchestras, following a visit to Denham studios*

In the centre of an enormous dimly lit barn of a building, a tiny figure stands on a small high-up platform; at his back is a chair, before him a large tilted illuminated table-top, piled with manuscript music and typewritten sheets; earphones, plugs and wires are strewn about in profusion.

Vainly he tries to be heard above the chattering voices and preluding of musical instruments.

" Gentlemen, will you please look for 7M4A."

At the studio end, facing him, a large white screen is hung, waiting to be brought to life by the projector. In front of and beneath the screen, at row upon row of heavy music stands, sit the brass section. Against the right wall sit the woodwind, and massed against the left gleam the golden reds and yellows of the strings, violins, violas, 'cellos and basses, in all the glory of their fine wood and varnish. Completing the rough semi-circle are the odd flotsam and jetsam of the percussion department; gongs, xylophone, bells, cymbals, drums, tympani, celeste, piano and, joining up with the strings, the classically beautiful harp.

Behind the string and woodwind sections massive slabs of wood, hung by heavy chains, reflect the sound. High above each section more slabs, suspended in mid-air like a canopy, focus the sound down and into the centre for the mikes to pick up, lest it should escape into the far corners of the dark vaulted roof.

At the back of the studio an open door and glass let-in wall reveal the heart of this gigantic organisation, the recording room with the projecting cabin above it.

A loud banging from the composer, who is once more trying to establish contact with his unruly men, echoes over the vast cable-strewn floor-space :

" Gentlemen, we have a lot to do. If I have to shout like this

THINGS TO COME. Raymond Massey as he appears in the H. G. Wells story. The music was composed by Arthur Bliss and directed by Muir Mathieson.

I will lose my voice. Please let's run through 7M4A."

At last we raise our instruments and read through the piece of music. We are scarcely settled on the final pause when the composer's baton cuts us off. A commotion of queries about wrong notes ; sheets of music waving in an effort to attract the composer-conductor's attention ; but he (poor man) has been too much concerned with a stop watch to attend to details of performance yet.

The commotion dies down a little. Some of the queries will still have to be made later, but it is surprising how many will be settled unobtrusively by the musicianship of the orchestra, as the rehearsing goes on.

From the door at the back comes the command : " Strings alone for balance."

We play a few bars and are stopped, as a recording engineer lowers the long skeleton microphone-arm, unplugs the delicate nerve centre, replaces it with a different type, and raises the long arm to its former position. Finally he turns a small handle at the base, twisting the tiny mike round to face the upturned sound-holes of our instruments.

Another few bars to reassure the sound people, and we can put our instruments down whilst it's : "Woodwind alone, please."

Now comes the most difficult part of the session. Some of us make or renew acquaintances, exchange confidences and anecdotes. Others occupy these periods with a surreptitious game of chess played on a pocket board which shares the place of honour with 7M4A on the stand.

" Brass and percussion alone, please."

One violinist, whose name has been a household word wherever the *Radio ·Times* is read, sits back with eyes closed in dulled re-laxation ; his one remark this morning—" This boredom is not worth it, however much they paid us." Never mind, at the end of nine hours of this dim sunless atmosphere he may be fresher than the others, perhaps.

LOVE STORY. Margaret Lock-wood plays Hubert Bath's ' Cornish Rhapsody ' with the National Symphony Orchestra. The piano record-ing on the sound track was by Harriet Cohen.

It is yet too early for the real born comedians and clowns of the orchestra to get going ; they wake up when all the others are most jaded and in need of something to keep them awake.

" Everybody playing, please."

We reach for our instruments and give a creditable performance, hoping that we are approaching the real thing at last.

Men issue forth from the door of the " holy of holies " and stand round the conductor gesticulating wildly. We are too far away to hear any details, but gather it must be still a question of balance. We are right. The musical assistant, like some squire of the past leaping into his knight's saddle, jumps on to the dais and takes up the conductor's baton, while the conductor goes into the recording room to hear for himself.

Nothing seems to have been achieved by this interruption and repeat performance, except perhaps a deterioration in the neatness of the playing.

Now the film is coming up.

" Take it easy, this is only for my benefit," yells the conductor. We were going to, anyhow ; as the screen becomes alive with light and movement, multitudes of heads strain to catch a glimpse and it is very difficult indeed to play properly whilst looking over one's shoulder, with a very occasional glance back at the music or baton.

We finish quite out of synchronisation with the film but oblivious of all save the silent drama on the screen. A vague feeling of incongruity about the silhouette of a microphone and its supporting arm against an ancient paddle steamer—and suddenly the film is cut.

Again the consultation with the stop-watch. " We'll have to repeat the two bars before letter B and hold on the last pause till I cut you off. I think that will be O.K. Let's try for a take."

At these magic words we gird up our loins with much noise and movement ; chairs scraping, bows hitting stands, the coughing and spluttering of throats being cleared. We wait, confident that intense silence has been achieved, but a loudspeaker opens up with—

"Quiet, please, less noise in the orchestra." Looks of pained denial from the musicians. Even more intense silence and "O.K., we're turning."

This time we attend to our business, playing the music at the precise spot indicated by the baton.

"7M4A, take one" says the conductor. " We'll go for a but first let's clean up one or two passages a bit."

We start to rehearse again, but the projection people have started up by mistake. Someone shouts " *Film* " as the screen lights up. We stop, bewildered, as the conductor tries desperately to catch the beginning of his sequence, fails, and throws the baton down in disgust at the unpredictable behaviour of projection room.

" Cut it." We sit moodily waiting while the film is rewound.

Once more we prepare for a take, determined, confident in our freshness, that this will see the end of 7M4A.

Dead silence ; the film flickers onto the screen ; tensely the conductor counts the ticker—" Five, six, seven, eight. . . ." We have begun to play with a perfect start, right on the opening shot of the sequence. Everything sounds O.K. Everything *is* O.K. But we don't relax until the voice declaims " 7M4A, take two."

We are lucky, later on in the day it might have been "7M4A, take five," but right now our thoughts are turning to other things.

Murmurs of "Tea, tea, tea," rise from all over the orchestra as we put down our instruments rebelliously and straighten up for a dash to the head of the queue.

Hopefully the conductor shouts "End Titles, please," but seeing the tea wagon at the door, resigns and cries even more optimistically, "O.K., make it ten minutes." We make it a quarter of an hour, and half a session is through.

CHAPTER VI

FILM MUSIC FORUM

—◆—

*Composers, Music Directors, Producers, Musicologists
and Film Critics air their views.*

In 1935, film music journalist and composer, Kurt London,
put the position before the public clearly and concisely. He
said :—

"The music which accompanies the film is still struggling
for its place in the sun ; the film people themselves almost
invariably treat it very casually and are not quite clear in their
own minds about its importance ; musicians take it up more
for the sake of fees than for art's sake, and he is a rare exception
among them who shows any sympathy for its novel forms ;
the public finally does not trouble overmuch about music
because it almost always fails to understand the cause and
effect of film-musical ideas. . . ."

To-day we look back over the past ten years to see whether this
statement still holds true or whether we have overcome the problems
and difficulties. Peter Noble, actor and theatrical journalist,
author of the "British Film Yearbook," thinks we have.

"Much of the music specially written for British films
during the war," he says, "has been first rate. . . . In addition
to the musical scores composed by ' pure ' film composers
like Mischa Spoliansky, Allan Gray, Hans May and John
Greenwood, a number of other eminent composers have entered
the field of documentary and feature films, with extraordinarily
fine results. Who can forget the brilliant music for *Things To
Come* by Arthur Bliss just a few years ago ? And the rolling
grandeur of Vaughan Williams' score for *49th Parallel* was
equalled only by the power of William Alwyn's music for
Desert Victory and *The Way Ahead*. The growing interest in
films is reflected in the number of outstanding composers who
have been engaged in writing film music in recent years.
Among them may be noted William Walton, whose music
for *Henry V* contributed much to that film's excellence, Clifton
Parker, a young composer whose distinguished scores for such

films as *Western Approaches* augur well for his future work, Richard Addinsell (of ' Warsaw Concerto ' fame), Benjamin Britten, the late Walter Leigh, Geoffrey Toye, Constant Lambert, Ernest Irving and the late Hubert Bath. More than ever is it to be seen that the finest artists in the country are going to be allied in the creation of films of intelligence and quality."

Hubert Clifford, himself a film music composer and a critic, is inclined to agree. He is more cautious, but sees great possibilities of film music replacing the opera as an outlet from dramatic scoring :—

" ' If Puccini were alive to-day, he'd be writing for the films.' A friend of mine recently expressed this provocative opinion, one consideration of which propounds the interesting questions of the economic possibility of opera surviving, and of the measure of fulfilment which the composition of film music affords to a composer whose leanings are towards the dramatic. The former question will probably be decided quite automatically. The financial strength of the film industry offers handsome rewards for the professional composer ; the opera house does not. Opera was a living art in the countries most affected by the war, and it seems probable that its survival at all in these countries can only be on the basis of the well tried repertoire. If this be so, the opera house cannot avoid taking on the artistic value and functions of a museum.

" The question of whether writing for the films provides a satisfactory alternative to the composition of opera is one which can only be decided by the individual composer. Judging by the enthusiastic way in which such composers as Vaughan Williams, Bliss and Walton have taken to the films, and judging by the results, it looks as if, given the right film, composers have a new vehicle for whatever dramatic urges and talents they possess."

This may be largely true, but one composer, Benjamin Britten, has turned down a number of film music commissions in order to compose opera, for which he has become very famous. He says he finds the writing of opera is still of primary importance and has shown that the art is very far from dead. The writer of " Peter Grimes " does, however, admit that :—

" there are great possibilities in music for the films, but it must be taken seriously by the director and composer, and used as an integral part of the whole thing—not just as a sound effect, or to fill up gaps during the talking. The nearest approach to this I've seen has been in the Disney cartoons and a few French films."

Paul Rotha, author, director and producer in the documentary film world, has something to say here :—

" Music always has and, I believe, always will form a valuable part of film creation. It performs certain duties in the exciting of human emotions which cannot be replaced by the use of either speech or sound. To use Walter Leigh's phrase ' It is an artificial organisation of sound for purely emotional purposes, a representation of physical movement in terms of sound and rhythm.' But one thing is obvious, that music required to-day for incorporation into the sound band, along with natural sound and speech, is absolutely different from either orthodox concert music, or from the kind of music which was written as an accompaniment to silent films and later to synchronised scores. The old idea that music must fulfil the function of an undercurrent to the picture, just quiet enough to prevent distraction from the screen, being faded down when the commentator speaks, and faded up again when he has finished, this is as antiquated as the type of film for which it is still used.

" Modern music for sound film must be an integral part of the sound script, must on occasions be allowed to dominate the picture, must on others perform merely an atmospheric function and frequently it must be intermixed with natural sound and speech."

Which leads us to consider the exact functions of film music, and here first we call on one of the outstanding British contemporary composers to give us his impression of the exact purpose of film music. Arthur Bliss explains it this way :—

" When you see a well-dressed man, you are not conscious of his clothes ; you are just pleasantly aware that here is somebody well turned out. The total impression is satisfying, though you can't exactly say why. Film music should have this effect on the cinemagoer ; he should not be conscious of it as something distinct from the film itself. The twin principles of vision and sound should merge and achieve a unity—as they do in ballet, or in the music-drama of Wagner ; but, of course, the business of writing for the screen requires a very special technique. The composer has to be a kind of musical epigrammist, compressing the sense of an idea into the shortest possible time and conveying it with the greatest economy and effectiveness."

Darius Milhaud, French composer, who has been to this country to score for documentary, says :—

" Film music must never be obtrusive. It should be a necessary function of the film, simple and sparing. Therefore, I always use a small orchestra for film work. Too many instruments sound thick and confused when reproduced in the cinema."

Rollo H. Myers, musical journalist and author, is not so enthusiastic :—

" In film music, the composer is a mere cog in the machinery, contributing just as much and no more than he is told to the general effect. He is literally on ' piece-work,' and must be prepared to cut out or tack on so many bars here or there at a moment's notice, working, as it were, with a slide rule and composing so many notes to the yard. On the technical side, notwithstanding, great progress has been made in the photography of sound and on the artistic side a good deal of excellent work has already been accomplished in this sphere. It is probable then that if the cinema industry continues to develop in the future as it has in the past, it will attract more and more serious composers who will see in it one of the few remaining fields in which to exercise their art."

Constant Lambert, composer and conductor, has more faith in the new medium :—

" Film music," he says, " should not be despised because it is inevitably more ephemeral and less important than symphonic and operatic music. We do not despise the first-rate poster artist or the first-rate journalist, and the fact that the sound film has already attracted, in this country alone, composers as eminent as Walton, Bliss, Benjamin, Leigh and Britten is in itself ample justification of the seriousness and thoroughness with which the composer should approach his task. In addition to its intrinsic interest as a new craft, writing for films will have the salutary effect of keeping composers in touch with a large audience and its human reactions. It stands to reason that film music must above all be expressive, and the demands made by the film for colourful and expressive music may well be the decisive factor in turning composers away from the drab and fruitless avenues offered by the post-war ideals of ' abstraction ' and ' neo-classicism.' "

Arnold Bax, Master of the King's Music, and prominent contemporary composer, however, does not think much of this film business. He has always had a livelihood assured and has not had to depend on his music to earn him a living. He has tried the films once (*Malta G.C.*) and the music was a very successful score and concert suite, but Arnold Bax is, nevertheless, quite emphatic :—

"I do not think the medium is at present at all satisfactory as far as the composer is concerned, as his music is largely inaudible, toned down to make way for—in many cases—quite unnecessary talk. This is, in my opinion, quite needless as it is possible to pay attention to two things at the same time if they appeal to different parts of the intelligence."

Arthur Bliss suffers no delusions on the subject either. He says :—

"I'm afraid I have to be brutally frank and say that the chief incentive to write for the screen is £ s. d., because a composer is likely to make far more money in a little time by this sort of work than he is from the casual and not-too-frequent performances of his works in the concert hall or over the radio. But even while working against all the mechanical restrictions on inspiration imposed by this form of composition, it may still be possible for a musician to preserve his artistic integrity. But he must bear several things in mind ; one is that the atmosphere of the film studio may encourage complacency, because film people have a way of exaggerating and bestowing praise that is not always justified by hard artistic standards. Secondly, it must be remembered that the dramatic quality of a piece of film music is enhanced by the correspondingly dramatic content of the picture itself. The person watching the film is already in an emotionally responsive condition and will tend to invest the music with wonderful qualities that it doesn't really possess. My argument is that in the last resort film music should be judged solely as music—that is to say, by the ears alone, and the question of its value depends on whether it can stand up to this test."

And without a doubt, Bliss has proved his point. All the film scores that he has done so far have become first-class concert hall suites and met with the cordial approval of the music critics. As well as *Things To Come*, there is *Conquest Of The Air*, the French march from a documentary, and most recently, *Men Of Two Worlds*.

John Croydon is a film producer with strong ideas on music :—

"Most really good British composers are difficult to get for film work," he says. "Even when they are able to spare the time to score a good British picture, they write their music with one eye on concert hall receipts which may later accrue from the score, and as a result, the unity of the film suffers."

He admits, however, that it is highly desirable to have as many big name composers as possible scoring for pictures in order that British films may be given a true artistic background, incorporating the full range of musical creation for which our modern contemporary musicians are justly famous.

I think Arthur Bliss raises a good point, for after all, most of the men writing for the films must think at times " Is it really worth the trouble? " Richard Addinsell voices the opinion of many when he says :—

"I enjoy working for films very much, but occasionally after a specially hard job one can't help wondering if anyone listens or notices certain passages in a score that have been the cause of particular trouble or excitement in the making. Muir Mathieson and I have often discussed this point, for unlike the theatre where you can watch and gauge an audience reaction, the cinema, as far as the music is concerned, remains for ever an unknown quantity."

This, unless you work on the basis of writing music that can later become a concert suite, is very true and not much fun for the composer. Arthur Unwin, musical journalist, is inclined to agree, though he offers a " safety in numbers " solution that is rather unconvincing :—

"How often is the ordinary filmgoer conscious of the music he is hearing? The more successful the composer is in welding his work to the picture, the less likely is it to be noticed, for it becomes simply a contribution to the general teamwork, generally overshadowed by the glamour of the acting. Nevertheless, the fact that so many serious composers have been commissioned to write for the screen indicates the importance film producers attach to music's share in this hybrid art and this recognition should at least give some satisfaction to music lovers."

Sam Heppner, also a musical journalist, has something more positive to say, calling for an entirely new approach to the subject.

" The future of film music ? Who can say ? At present it is clearly subordinate to the film itself, except in certain rare and unexpected cases, but if any music of lasting value is to be written for the screen, a completely new production technique must be employed, releasing the composer from the mechanical limitations under which he now suffers and bringing his background music to the fore."

However, there is a large group of specialist film music composers who really believe in their music as it is practised to-day, and they have the backing of the majority of modern movie musicians. One of them, William Alwyn, puts the case :—

" I am passionately fond of films, and I think all good film composers are. You must believe in pictures, have faith in your artistic medium, and you can produce good scores. I like going to the pictures and I like doing music for the pictures. It is an absorbing job, it is good fun and if you believe in what you are doing, it will be good music. I like to feel part of the team that is working to provide screen entertainment for such a vast audience."

Documentary expert, Ernst Meyer, will gladly second that :—

" It is a fascinating business. Here you can really get into contact with reality, maintain your contact with the people. With a good director, you can get right into the atmosphere of real creative work. For example, I had to write music for a film about the sea and the fishing fleets. The director sent me into the fishing towns, I went to sea with the trawlers, I got the atmosphere and reality of the picture being made. Then I wrote the music from life, from what I had seen and heard. No matter if the music only served to put across the story of the film, in itself passing almost unnoticed. It was the music of reality and gave me a chance to break away from the isolated vacuum into which modern serious music is tending to go as a result of an ever-widening gap between the composer and his audience."

But here is someone who is not so keen. Miss Elizabeth Cross, filmgoer, just does not like film music :—

" We hate the music, or most of it. Not only is it painfully loud, but equally painfully obvious. Even when someone fresh is allowed to write the ' incidental ' music to a so-called serious film, they are so cowed that they do it in their sleep and merely cough up the good old phrases that indicate ' came the dawn ' or ' a gallant ship sailed on to her doom,' etc., etc., ad infinitum. It's very cosy and reminiscent of the days when we admired our village pianist at the pictures with her lovely indexed book which gave you the right music for death-beds, first kisses, galloping horses, and what have you, all at the flick of the thumb. But surely, after all these years, we can grow up just a bit . . . or do most audiences really like having the traditional tunes for each emotion ? Maybe they do, but lots of us don't. Incidentally, thinking of incidental music, isn't it still most terribly overdone ? Can't people be contented to look at a really grand pictorial shot without being distracted by moaning violins ? And isn't it maddening to everyone to have suitable soft music braying out just when the hero and heroine are murmuring sweet nothings ? After all, some people would like to hear what the pair of them are saying. No, on the whole we think a lot of the music is plain lousy."

Joan Cook, also a filmgoer, takes that to heart. She asks simply :—

" Don't you think all this music is absolutely unnecessary and that just natural sound would be very much better ? It's all so unnatural."

Muir Mathieson, musical director of over 200 films and the country's leading authority on the subject, gives the answer:—

" Music is and always must be a vital part of film art. . . . Music can help to humanise the subject and widen its appeal. Music can make a film less intellectual and more emotional. It can influence the reaction of the audience to any given sequence. . . . It can develop rhythmic suggestions from words. It can carry ideas through dissolves and fade-outs. It can prepare the eye through the ear. It can merge unnoticeably from realistic sound into pure music. It can shock. It can startle. It can sympathise. It can sweeten. But for the love of mike, never let it be mediocre."

For those of you who are still in doubt, the best method would be for me to take you into a studio and show you a drama on the screen with and without its music. It quickly becomes apparent how much of the effect is often obtained by music, music which as it is, passes unnoticed in the cinema, yet carries a kick behind it that makes all the difference to the dramatic effect. Kurt London says of music in the ordinary " straight " film that :—

> " it has to connect dialogue sections without friction ; it has to establish associations of ideas and carry on developments of thought ; and, over and above all this, it has to intensify the incidence of climax and prepare for further dramatic action."

Maurice Jaubert, famous French composer, who scored for British documentary at one time, will tell you that " we do not go to the cinema to hear music. We require it to deepen and prolong in us the screen's visual impressions. Its task is not to explain these impressions, but to add to them an overtone specially different—or else film music must be content to remain perpetually redundant. Its task is not to be expressive by adding its sentiments to those of the characters or of the director, but to be decorative by uniting its own rhythmical pattern with the visual pattern woven for us on the screen."

And now to conclude " Film Music Forum " here are three surveys of British film music by people who each have special angles of approach to the subject. First, we have the views of an independent critic writing in Hollywood about British films ; secondly, a British film composer gives a clear account of his reactions to the work of composing for the films ; and, finally, a film music director sums up his attitude to the matter. May I introduce Margery Morrison[1] writing from an office on the famous Hollywood Boulevard.

HOLLYWOOD LOOKS AT BRITISH FILM MUSIC

" My impressions of recent British releases in America ? Well, for better perspective I mention first two early top-

[1]Margery Morrison is one of the most prominent American film music critics. She is associate editor of the only magazine in the world devoted solely to screen music—" Film Music Notes," published monthly in Hollywood. She writes here of British films that have recently received an American release ; if your favourite British movie is missing from her review it is probably because it had not been screened in the States at the time we went to press. There follows a series of extracts from film reviews published by " Film Music Notes " for the guidance of American film music enthusiasts, music schools, colleges, etc.

notchers ; Noel Coward's *In Which We Serve* (1943) and Norman Walker's *The Great Mr. Handel* (1944). From my point of view you have had nothing to approach the first of these to catch the real tempo of British life. The fundamental love of sea and ships : the singing of the men, hearty and unashamed : deeply human characterizations : the burial service at sea : the original treatment of flashbacks giving an epitome of national life. *The Great Mr. Handel* is unexcelled in its reconstruction of a period : the re-creation of a masterpiece (' The Messiah ') with all the soul-agony involved, showing the ' divine fury ' of creative work to a duller public. The massive majesty of the music is successfully created.

"In the same category with these I place *The Seventh Veil*, in which you have the best recording to date. Here we have the evolution of an artist. We are made to share her experiences, her inhibitions from childhood—and so share the psychiatric problem suggested by the title. The music is spontaneously cued in, it never halts the action nor the story value and the change to the bravura type is gradual. Eileen Joyce plays it magnificently, with virtuosity, and it is creditably and convincingly dubbed by lovely Ann Todd.

"Among the war pictures *Colonel Blimp, Mr. Emmanuel, The Silver Fleet* and *The Way Ahead* come to mind. The first gives us wonderful glimpses of London and Berlin at various periods, with dated and well chosen music. Though the recording in general is not up to our standards, the arrangement and distribution of music throughout the film are very fine. The score contains excerpts from ' Mignon,' ' Zampa,' Offenbach, the Fate motif from ' Lohengrin,' a parody on the ' March of the Wooden Soldiers ' (so popular in the days of the inimitable Balieff and his ' Chauve Souris ') and, especially well used, the ' Fingal's Cave ' overture of Mendelssohn and the British Grenadiers at the end.

"Unlike *Colonel Blimp, Mr. Emmanuel* takes us to Berlin in the early days of the war and helps us to understand the problems of his people : a fine lesson in tolerance.

"*The Silver Fleet*, with the valuable co-operation of the British Navy and that of the Royal Netherlands, shows us how the impossible was accomplished by the deep-seated patriotism of the Dutch and belief in their national hero, Piet Hein. We are shown how a submarine was built in a conquered country and how the Germans were delivered into English hands. The score by Allan Gray is the best integrated and recorded one to follow on from *In Which We Serve,* and the choral singing has inspirational quality and lift ; the children sing naturally and with conviction, noteworthy for achieving such beautiful floating quality.

" *The Way Ahead* was a superb presentation of human reactions to modern warfare as exemplified by a group of average British citizens, recruited from all walks of life, who form the army (some with reluctance) and after a period of severe training go into battle and prove that they are, indeed, made of noble stuff. Fundamentally national in quality, yet universal in its appeal, this picture is high in ethical values. Music is used very little except at the outset. There it begins in the main title with a drum roll and a military theme, frank, brave and dashing, which fades into minor as the story begins. From that point on it is heard only occasionally except to strengthen the mood and then is almost entirely military save for the ' concert ' which is faithfully funny and the very fine sequence where all the men sing in hearty, unashamed British fashion. There is a sincerity in values and characterizations which are deeply human and not in the Hollywood manner. Sound effects, warnings, muffled explosions, licking flames, and the crash of tanks are most convincing. Direction, also, is outstanding. All honour to Britain for making and giving us this poignant and real document.

" What a delightful picture—*Vacation From Marriage* (British title : *Perfect Strangers*). We quote from ' Time Magazine ' : ' Mr. Korda gives to the story that air of authenticity and apparent artlessness which has become a sort of hall-mark of the best British pictures.' Here is a wonderful balance of construction ; the story and the documentary become one and there is a grand sense of humour. The main title of the score is appropriately humdrum and conservative. As the tale progresses there is a corresponding change in mood and tempo, with intriguing rhythms. That is a remarkable shot from the crow's nest. I felt as though I were there with Donat.

" Addinsell's distinguished score for the Noel Coward *Blithe Spirit* might well be integrated into a single orchestral number. Deft, sophisticated, extra-dimensional like the picture itself—there is a whimsical, sardonic vein all too seldom found in music.

" Much less expert is the cheerful *You Can't Do Without Love* (British title : *One Exciting Night*). There is an unusual publicity angle and timely background, your Tiller Girls gave us our first example of precision dancing—from them evolved our ' Rockettes.' Our correspondent for ' Film Music Notes ' wrote : ' There is bound to be a difference of opinion as regards this British made musical with its unmistakably English flavour. For while an effort has been made to suit the music to the plot and, in this case, to the star, in general it is so far outside of our standards that it is difficult to judge it fairly. Some will like its undertone quality, its over-simplification and lack of almost everything in the way of eye appeal. The rather homely and badly costumed heroine, on whom almost the entire burden of the music rests, they will find refreshing. Her voice is pleasing but utterly without shading, giving somewhat the effect of a cornet-a-piston. Production values are like a flat drawing and sympathetic and sincere though the leading lady may be, others of us will long for just a dash of that Hollywood glamour which heretofore we have been prone to criticize, and for some of the Hollywood staging and costumes which make our conception of even wartime budget pictures, acceptable to eye and ear. For those of us who feel this way, everything in the picture sounds dry and dull, the singing mediocre in quality and the recording poor and lacking in overtones. The lyrics have little sparkle and contribute nothing, the pace is too slow, and the arrangement of the small orchestra is such as to make it seem thin and inadequate. No music credits are given, perhaps wisely so."

[NOTE.—This masterly summing-up of a typical British second-feature musical is well worth considering when reading the section above regarding British musicals in general.—J.F.H.].

" *A Yank In London* (British title: *I Live In Grosvenor Square*)—beautifully produced and with a well-knit story this war drama has good social value and is still timely, offering as it does a sane presentation of national differences and points of contrast as well as striking contrasts. Direction shows sensitive understanding of the characters and narrative and the cast is a fine one. Photography is good and the English scenery actual and ingratiating. Mr. Collins proves a good choice to do the score. Being British, with years of American experience, it is a happy mixture of both. His

17th century music is charmingly fitting as background for the life in the old family estate and is just as traditional as the life of the English upper classes. The score is amply seasoned with American swing and jitterbug and Irene Manning offers the saccharine song ' Home,' which being over-sentimental, adds nothing to the music of a score which is shorter than for the usual American film of that type, but for that reason probably more effective and by the most part, very good.

" The British Ministry of Information has given us two wonderful documentaries—*The United States* (British title : *U.S.A., The Land And The People*) and *Journey Together*. First, *The United States* : Though made in Britain this straightforward documentary presents a truer picture of the real United States than many of our own films, for if the film is a criterion the British producers have a better knowledge of the vastness and wonders of our country than do some of us. It should certainly do much to promote a better understanding of the U.S.A., not only in their military forces, but throughout the Empire. Many of our own films must give foreigners a strange idea of us— what with the stressing of gangsters, outlaws, café society, night clubs and drinking. This one showing our cities, commerce and industry and, in addition, the home life of an average small town boy, brings things into their proper perspective and our thanks are due to the producers for their laudable effort. The accompanying score has an unusual accumulation of fine sequences and is of distinct value. It contributes to the emotional content—in the factories it is mechanical, in the home soft and tender, leading up to grand climaxes in the western scenes. Too bad no credits are given.

" The Gordon Jacob score for *Journey Together* is outstanding. Fundamental, sturdy rhythm is joined with a soaring quality in keeping with the picture itself, and humour which is not dependent on the bassoon. There is a feeling of youth, of unlimited horizons. The sound effects are skilfully dubbed. To our ears the orchestra sounds a bit thin ; there is a lack of strings. It may not have our incisiveness, but it is most delightful as music and fits the situations admirably.

INSTRUMENTS OF THE ORCHESTRA. Dr. Malcolm Sargent conducts the London Symphony Orchestra while Muir Mathieson surveys the scene during the performance of Benjamin Britten's Variations and Fugue on a Theme of Purcell.

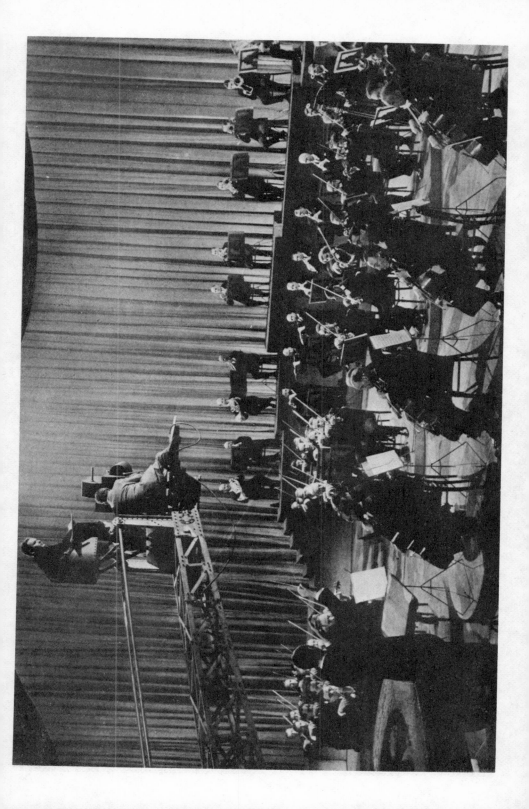

It is a friendly gesture to include Edward G. Robinson in the cast. The photography is spectacular and unusual.

" Looking back over the years, we find other interesting titbits amongst British productions. There was *The Yellow Canary* with music by the London Symphony Orchestra, giving a rich and harmonious foundation to an engrossing spy melodrama ; the recordings of ' Blue Danube ' in *Jeannie*, or the outstanding score to *Tunisian Victory*, jointly handled by American Dmitri Tiomkin and Britisher William Alwyn.

" In general, we find the British pictures give less recognition to pace than we do, but this is more than compensated by the direct approach to human values, and a sophisticated humor that does not ignore nor over-emphasize the facts of life. Your recording, except for *The Seventh Veil*, has not had our frequency potential."

MARGERY MORRISON, Hollywood, May, 1946.

" Films represent, perhaps, the most important of all outlets for the music of the future."

CONSTANCE PURDY

" Somewhat to my surprise, I am constantly finding that the field of film music is in the doldrums with the intelligentsia. ' We are not interested in popular music,' they say. Or else ' quite in the Hollywood vein,' faintly damning the product. We confess that the public, by and large, prefers Freddy Martin's version of ' To-night We Love ' to the Tchaikowsky B Flat Minor Concerto ; the Victory Theme to Beethoven's Fifth Symphony.

" But people are listening with keen and open minds to a new type of score. They realise that a change is coming over movie and musical psychology. Younger students and composers are obtaining a new set of values to which the ever-increasing and intelligent fan mail bears witness. The older compilations and arrangements from the classics are being definitely demoded.

MEN OF TWO WORLDS. At the music recording session of this film are (left to right) Arthur Bliss, director Thorold Dickinson, Desmond Dew, the Denham sound recordist, Eileen Joyce, (seated) Walter Legge of the H.M.V. Studios, Muir Mathieson and the negro artist Robert Adams.

The average synchronized score now being composed illustrates the story, gives proper atmosphere and setting, points the situations and often has a dramatic continuity of its own."

MARGERY MORRISON

" Musicians should realise the prime necessity of informing themselves about the engineering and mechanical problems, the general procedure of the cinema. The technical and the artistic must co-operate."

MARGERY MORRISON

" The motion pictures should seek for a new type of music which in its simplicity and directness, its lack of formalism and of emotional exaggerations, would be truly human. The heart of mankind is one ; the blood-plasm of any man may save the life of any other man. The ' music of man ' yet to come should sing to this one heart and stir this one blood in all human beings."

DANE RUDHYAR

" The fundamental difference between symphonic program music and descriptive cinema music lies in the fact that the first, though following a programmatic purpose, creates freely its own form. It is not bound by detailed description or a dramatic outline, whereas the descriptive cinema music illustrates lavishly the happenings of a given scene. This deprives it of a logical musical development—in short deprives it of its own musical ' raison d'etre.' "

MIKLOS ROZSA

" Not only musical America, but the whole world, is interested in more and better music in films. The future is brighter than ever before because our seeing and listening audience is music conscious."

NATHANIEL SHILKRET

HENRY V

An American Analysis of the Score

◄◆►

by *STANLIE McCONNELL*

William Walton's score, remarkable for its beauty, appropriateness and the musicianship we know as " English," actually begins when the roulades of a flute accompanies a breeze-tossed handbill. The paper unfolds and we read that *Henry V* is to be performed at the Globe Theatre. As the camera gives a panoramic view of the Thames of Shakespeare's day, the sound of voices singing an old plain chant reaches our ears. Gradually this song is embellished by orchestral counterpoint as our tour progresses and encircles the Globe Theatre. This part of the score comes to a satisfying musical conclusion as the flag of the theatre is raised. We hear the orchestra tuning up and inside we get a glimpse of them as they start the overture. It is not intended that we should have a chance really to study these instruments, for Mr. Walton wisely decided not to confine himself to the limitations of the Elizabethan orchestra. However, if you are quick you will see a chest of viols, a recorder and the straight trumpet of that period. The musicians sit in a balcony as in Shakespeare's day, and not in front of the stage according to the present custom. Then, many of the ultra-fashionables sat or reclined upon the stage itself, for which privilege they paid extra. This is shown while the overture, a sprightly piece reminiscent of an old English contra-dance, is played. The musicians finish. There is applause.

You will note that the play is introduced wordlessly—camera work, pantomimic action, sound effects and music being used to establish the place and the mood. In such a technique, music becomes a vital factor and an indispensable part of the action.

A trumpeter announces the beginning of the play. Chorus appears. This so-called " chorus," of course, is not a group of singers but a single character who explains the play somewhat in the manner of the ancient Greek choruses. Where the Hellenic chorus chanted, the Elizabethan speaks his lines in Shakespeare's eloquent verse.

As chorus reaches the line " On your imaginary forces work," music of a modal quality is heard faintly in the background to assist us with this request. Each time he reappears throughout the play similar music is heard. Similar, but not identical. Frank Howes, writing of Walton, tells us that one of his notable characteristics is " the fluidity of his themes, which are rarely heard in identical spellings at their various reappearances." In his score for *Henry V* one of the two pieces he repeats exactly is the overture, done obviously for realistic purposes. It comes back briefly after Chorus has finished, taking us to Scene I.

At the end of this scene with the Archbishop of Canterbury and the comical Bishop of Ely, there is some very interesting music for the back stage activities. It leads into a fanfare of trumpets for the opening of Scene II. There is no music in the following sequences of the play until a flourish of trumpets announces the approaching entrance of the French ambassadors. This plan is followed throughout the production. Background music never clouds the rendition of important Shakespearean lines. It is used infrequently to stir up imaginative power, but for the most part the music of this film is used as a distinct factor in the dramatic action.

French horns usher in Mountjoy, the Herald. This instrument is used quite consistently throughout for the French, while the trumpet speaks for the English. Twice in the play, *Henry V*, at the entrance of Mountjoy, the script calls for the sounding of the " tucket." Authorities say that this is quite possibly a historic touch and class it as most interesting among these announcing signals used in Shakespeare. You will easily recognize the pattern of the tucket used in this film to announce Mountjoy.

The overture is repeated briefly at the end of the act. Again we have music for Chorus' prologue. The orchestra helps with the sound effects for the sudden storm and then changes to a humorous style as a page announces the locale of the next scene, " The Boar's Head." The following comic scene between Pistol and his friend is cleverly underscored.

One of the most moving parts of the score is the theme treated in passacaglia form which accompanies the death of Falstaff. Beginning in the bassoon it moves upward with simple classical dignity, adding great pathos to this memorable scene. It is first suggested when Pistol is told that Sir John is very ill. It is fully developed two scenes later after our film has left the confines of the Elizabethan theatre and gone into the fanciful realms of our imaginations.

At Southampton, the Archbishop is blessing the journey with a service on shipboard. Everything has become idealized. As Chorus fades into the mist we realize the entire style of the music is changing. We hear that romantic invention of melody which has been developing in Walton of late years—a lyrical romanticism of which Hubert J. Foss writes, " There is in him some Keatsian beauty, some sense of old unhappy far-off things and battles long ago." The exquisite French court appears. Its languorous beauty is emphasized through the ear, as the music associated with the scenes played in this castle develops.

Background music supports the siege of Harfleur. French horns announce the yielding of the town and a single drum accompanies the marching men as they enter to take it over.

Harry turns his gaze to the distant castle. The French theme returns. We see the lovely Katharine and her duenna entering the garden. The exquisitely played scene of the English lesson needs no music. It comes back again as they leave the garden and the horn call of the departing knights blends with its soft harmonies as they watch them ride into the distance. A delicate melody appears in the flute and accompanies our exquisite heroine as she descends the stairs to join the others.

The sound track for the scene of the night before the battle is notable for its dramatic silences. There is a background of stillness as the French noblemen show their disunity and over-confidence. The horn announces the passing of the hours. They gaze at the twinkling lights of the opposing camp as a trumpet tells eloquently of its nearness.

There is faint music only as Chorus speaks and we are taken to the other side to see " a little touch of Harry in the night." Again the impressiveness of the silence for the inspired scene that links this bygone battle with our recent ones. As dawn approaches we hear with Harry the sound of Masses being sung. Trumpets call him from his fervent prayer. The camps come to life.

The music takes over as the French are seen confidently attiring themselves in their cumbersome armour. Back in the English camp only the words of King Henry's inspiring St. Crispian's Day speech are heard. You may be surprised to hear from the French side a familiar horn call we associate with English hunting. Its use at this time is an incongruous reminder of the interchange of cultures. Then, that first wonderful shot of the row of red drums ! Mountjoy's tucket is heard as he rides to the English camp and says . . . "Once more I come to know of thee, King Harry." A drum rolls distantly during Harry's answer. Again the tucket as the black horse rides back.

The French mounted in their armour, drink a battle toast— the red drums roll—flourishes in the brass—the battle music has begun. Approaching gradually, the French gather greater and greater momentum. The synchronization of the music with their gallop is unbelievably perfect. The clanking of the armour and the increasing thud of the horses hoofs are cleverly intermingled with the music. King Henry's sword is raised, ready to give the signal to his archers. At the peak the director suppresses the sound effects and the music is allowed its full force. Suddenly the climax is reached and only the zing of the English arrows is heard. It is a never-to-be-forgotten sound.

The music dies out as Henry discovers the English camp has been set afire and the boys slain. " I was not angry since I came to France, until this instant," he says, as he gallops off to engage the Constable of France in the encounter that decides the day.

There is no tucket as Mountjoy comes this time to the English camp.

Mountjoy. The day is yours.

King Henry. Prais'd be God and not our strength for it ! What is this castle that stands hard by ?

Mountjoy. They call it Agincourt.

King Henry. Then call we this the field of Agincourt.

Here one of the oldest traditional songs, The Agincourt Song, from that historic day in 1415, is sung in part. Although it is not fully given at this time, its significance is great both dramatically and educationally.

There is silence as Henry hears the list of the English dead. " Do we all holy rites," he says, " Let there be sung Non Nobis and Te Deum." These lines are historically authentic. Instead of accepting adulation, the King commanded that thanks be given to God. The best known versions of the " Non Nobis " and the " Te Deum " are used. We hear the first part of the Non Nobis in its traditional canonic form, followed by the Te Deum in organal style, as the men wind their way to the castle.

Then follows a curious interlude in which we hear an exquisite Christmas carol sung by children. It is a welcome relief after the heaviness and sorrow of battle. There is also humorous music for the scene played by Pistol and the Welsh captain.

Spring comes. Inside the castle, Henry is meeting with the French Court to bring about a final peace. The choir boys are singing a delicate chanson that would be delightful to use in classes preparing to see this film. It ends as King Henry says " Peace to this Meeting, wherefor we are met ! " The Duke of Burgundy laments the ruin of their war-torn countryside as the French theme returns in a scene superbly blending the arts of poetry, scenic beauty and music. The choir repeats its delicate refrains as the court bows out and leaves Harry and Katharine together.

The charming love scene follows, in which Harry's reference to " broken music " is interesting to music students. Music was said to be " broken " when a consort of viols was imperfect through the absence of one of its players and an instrument of another kind, for example, a flute, was substituted. Thus Henry is saying Kate's English is like " broken music " in the sweetness of her voice.

" We are makers of manners, Kate." The chorus comes back as they are dressed in their betrothal robes. Full chorus and bells are added as they approach their thrones. We see only King Henry as they turn. He has changed. He is the play-actor King we saw at the beginning ! We hear the overture and applause and we know we are back in London on the stage of the Globe even before we are startled to see a youth in a curly wig impersonating the beautiful Katharine.

There is a boy's choir here, too, but they are led by Bishop of Ely. They sing a madrigal as the flag of the theatre is lowered. The handbill and the roulades of the flute return. The bill unrolls and we read the names of the distinguished people who were responsible for this magnificent production. As the names appear, the music is similar in style to that which accompanied our original tour to the theatre but this time the voices are singing the famed " Agincourt Song." The music reaches great grandeur as the credits are complete and we are given the final view of Old London that brings this truly aesthetic experience to an end.

Last among the credits, impressively spaced, we read :

Music by
William Walton
Conducted by
Muir Mathieson
Played by
The London Symphony Orchestra

175

This, at the first preview in London, brought an enthusiatic round of applause from the sophisticated press. It is sure to bring similar praise from all music lovers and students of cinematic art in this country. Such results are obtained only when a country's best composers write the music for their films. *Henry V* rouses again our appreciation of the indomitable spirit of our English ally, whose artists made this rare thing of beauty, while the sound of war still resounded in their land.

FILM MUSIC

by R. VAUGHAN WILLIAMS

" Some years ago I happened to say to Arthur Benjamin that I should like to have a shot at writing for the films. He seemed surprised and shocked that I should wish to attempt anything which required so much skill and gained so little artistic reward. However, he mentioned my curious wish to Muir Mathieson, whom, at that time, I hardly knew, though we have since become firm friends. The result was that one Saturday evening I had a telephone call asking me to write some film music. When I asked how long I could have, the answer was ' till Wednesday.'

" This is one of the bad sides of film writing—the time limit. Not, indeed, that it hurts anyone to try to write quickly ; the feeling of urgency is often a stimulus. When the hand is lazy the mind often gets lazy as well, but the composer wants to have the opportunity, when all is approaching completion, to remember emotion in tranquility, to sit down quietly and make sure that he has achieved the *mot juste* at every point. That is where the time-limit inhibits the final perfection of inspiration.

" On the other hand, film composing is a splendid discipline, and I recommend a course of it to all composition teachers whose pupils are apt to be dawdling in their ideas, or whose every bar is sacred and must not be cut or altered.

" When the film composer comes down to brass tacks he finds himself confronted with a rigid time-sheet. The producer says, ' I want forty seconds of music here ! ' This means forty, not thirty-nine or forty-one. The picture rolls on relentlessly, like fate. If the music is too short it will stop dead just before the culminating kiss ; if it is too long it will still be registering intense emotion while the screen is already showing the comic man putting on his mother-in-law's breeches.

" A film producer would make short work of Mahler's interminable codas or Dvorak's five endings to each movement.

" I believe that film music is capable of becoming, and to a certain extent already is, a fine art, but it is applied art, and a specialised art at that ; it must fit the action and dialogue ; often

177

it becomes simply a background. Its form must depend on the form of the drama, so the composer must be prepared to write music which is capable of almost unlimited extension or compression; it must be able to 'fade-out' and 'fade-in' again without loss of continuity. A composer must be prepared to face losing his head or his tail or even his inside without demur, and must be prepared to make a workmanlike job of it; in fact, he must shape his ends in spite of the producer's rough hewings.

" It may be questioned, ' Is any art possible in these conditions ? ' I say, emphatically, ' Yes, if we go the right way to work.' It is extraordinary how, under the pressure of necessity, a dozen or so bars in the middle of a movement are discovered to be redundant, how a fortissimo climax really ought to be a pianissimo fade-out.

" There are two ways of viewing film music : one, in which every action, word, gesture or incident is punctuated in sound. This requires great skill and orchestral knowledge and a vivid specialised imagination, but often leads to a mere scrappy succession of sounds of no musical value in itself. On this the question arises : Should film music have any value outside its particular function ? By value I do not mean necessarily that it must sound equally well played as a concert piece, but I do believe that no artistic result can come from this complex entity, the film, unless each element, acting, photography, script and music are each in themselves and by themselves intrinsically good.

" The other method of writing film music, which personally I favour, partly because I am quite incapable of doing the former, is to ignore the details and to intensify the spirit of the whole situation by a continuous stream of music. This stream can be modified (often at rehearsal !) by points of colour superimposed on the flow. For example, your music is illustrating Columbus's voyage and you have a sombre tune symbolising the weariness of the voyage, the depression of the crew and the doubts of Columbus. But the producer says, ' I want a little bit of sunshine music for that flash on the waves.' Now, don't say, 'Oh well, the music does not provide for that, I must take it home and write something quite new.' If you are wise, you will send the orchestra away for five minutes (which will delight them). You look at the score to find out what instruments are unemployed—say the harp and two muted trumpets. If possible, you will call Muir Mathieson in to assist you. You write in your flash at the appropriate second, you re-call the orchestra and the producer, who marvels at your skill in writing what appears to him to be an entirely new piece of music in so short a time.

" On the other hand, you must not be horrified, if you find that a passage which you intended to portray the villain's mad revenge has been used by the musical director to illustrate the cats being driven out of the dairy. The truth is, that within limits, any music can be made to fit any situation. An ingenious and sympathetic musical director can skilfully manœuvre a musical phrase so that it exactly synchronises with a situation which was never in the composer's mind.

" I am only a novice at this art of film music, and some of my more practised colleagues assure me that when I have had all their experience my youthful exuberence will disappear, and I shall look· upon film composing not as an art, but as a business. At present I still feel a morning blush in my art, and it has not yet paled into the light of common day. I still believe that the film contains potentialities for the combination of all the arts such as Wagner never dreamt of.

" I would, therefore, urge those distinguished musicians who have entered into the world of the cinema—Bax, Bliss, Walton, Benjamin and others, to realise their responsibility in helping to take the film out of the realm of hack-work and make it a subject worthy of a real composer.

" If, however, the composer is to take his side of the bargain seriously, the other partners in the transaction must come out to meet him. The arts must combine from the very inception of the idea. There is a story of a millionaire who built a house and showed it to a friend when it was near completion. The friend commented on the bare and barrack-like look of the building. ' But you see,' said the millionaire, ' we haven't added the architecture yet.' This seems to be the idea of music held by too many film producers. When the photography is finished, when the dialogue and the barking dogs and the whistling trains and the screeching taxis have been pasted on to the sound-track (I expect this is an entirely unscientific way of expressing it), then, thinks the producer, ' Let us have a little music to add a final frill.' So the music only comes in when all'the photography is done and the actors dispersed to their homes or to their next job. Perhaps the composer has (unwisely from the practical point of view) already

179

read the script and devised music for certain situations as he has imagined them before seeing the pictures, but what can he do about it ? The photograph is already there, the time is rigidly fixed, and if the composer's musical ideas are too long or too short they must be cut or repeated, or, worse still, hurried or slowed down, because the photograph once taken, there can be no re-timing.

" What is the remedy for all this ? Surely the author, producer, photographer and composer should work together *from the beginning*. Film producers pay lip service to this idea ; they tell you that they want the ideal combination of the arts, but when all is finished one finds that much of the music has been cut out or faded-down to a vague murmur, or distorted so that its own father would not know it, and this without so much as ' by your leave ' to the unhappy musician.

" I repeat, then, the various elements should work together from the start. I can imagine the author showing a rough draft to the composer ; the composer would suggest places where, in his opinion, music was necessary, and the author would, of course, do the same to the composer. The composer could even sketch some of the music, and if it was mutually approved of, the scenes could be timed so as to give the music free play. Let us suppose, for example, that the film contains a scene in which the hero is escaping from his enemies and arrives at a shepherd's hut in the mountains. The composer finds he wants a long theme to ' establish ' the mountain scenery, but the producer says ' That will never do ; it would hold up the action.' And so they fight it out. Perhaps the producer wins and the composer has to alter or modify his music, or the producer is so pleased with the composer's tune that he risks the extra length. My point is, that all this should be done *before* the photographs are taken.

" This would not prevent further modifications in the final stages.

" An outsider would probably consider this procedure obvious, but, so far as my limited experience goes, it has never occurred as a possibility to the author, or the producer, and certainly not to the composer.

" Again, when music is to accompany dialogue or action, surely the actors should hear the music before they start rehearsing, and at rehearsal act to the music, both from the point of view of timing and of emotional reaction.

" I need hardly say that the same give and take would be necessary here ; that is, that the composer must be ready occasionally to modify his music to fit the action and dialogue.

" It is objected that this is unpractical ; one could not have a symphony orchestra day after day in the studio accompanying a long-drawn-out rehearsal for each scene. The expense, it is said, would be impossible. When I hear of the hundreds of thousands of pounds which are spent on a film production, it seems to be rather queer to cavil at the few extra hundreds which this would involve—but let that pass. If an orchestra is impossible, how about the pianoforte ? The trouble would be to eliminate the pianoforte sounds and substitute an orchestral equivalent which would absolutely synchronise. I am told that no method has yet been devised that can do this. I know nothing about the mechanics of film making ; the skill of the whole thing fills me with awe, so I cannot believe that the engineers, if they really wished, could not devise a method—where there's a will there's a way. At present, where film music is concerned, there is not the will.

" A third method would be to rehearse with the music played, I presume, on the pianoforte, and then, having registered the exact timing and the exact emotional reaction of the actors to the music, to act it all over again in exactly the same way without the music. I cannot help feeling that the result would be intolerably mechanical.

" Of these three methods, the pianoforte accompaniment (afterwards to be eliminated) seems to be the best solution of the problem. Does it really pass the wit of those marvellous engineers of the film to devise some method by which it can be achieved ?

" I believe that this and many other problems could be solved by those who have had much experience, if the composer insisted. As long as music is content to be the maid-of-all-work, until the musicians rise to their responsibilities, we shall achieve nothing.

" Perhaps one day a great film will be built up on the basis of music. The music will be written first and the film devised to accompany it, or the film will be written to music already composed. Walt Disney has pointed the way in his *Fantasia*. But must it always be a cartoon film ? Could not the same idea be applied to the photographic film ? Can music only suggest the fantastic and grotesque creations of an artist's pencil? May it not also shed its light on real people?

" I have to confess to a desire to see a film built up on Bach's ' St. Matthew Passion.' Of course, it must be done by the right people ; but then, does not that apply to every work of art, and when I say the ' right people ' I naturally mean the people that I should choose for it. ' Orthodoxy is my doxy, heterodoxy is other people's doxy.'

" What a wonderful *via crucis* could be devised from the opening chorus, the daughter of Sion summoning all women to weep with her ; then the sudden call ' See Him, the bridegroom,' and the culmination in the choral ' O Lamb of God Most Holy.'

" Then could not the opening narrative be illustrated by a realisation of Da Vinci's ' Cenacolo,' and at the *choral* we should switch over, as only a film can, to St. Thomas at Leipzig and the huge congregation singing ' O Blessed Jesus how hast Thou offended.' But I could go on for ever with these vague imaginings, and this is only one example of how music can initiate the drama.

" Does what I have written sound like the uninstructed grouse of an ignorant tyro? I hope not, indeed. I venture to believe that my very inexperience may have enabled me to see the wood where the expert can only see the trees.

" I have often talked over these difficulties with authors, producers and musical directors, and they have been inclined in theory to agree with me. I acknowledge with gratitude that when I have worked with them they have, within their scheme, stretched every possible point to give my ignorantly composed music its chance ; but they have not yet been able to break down the essentially wrong system by which the various arts are segregated and only reassembled at the last moment, instead of coming together from the beginning. It is only when this is achieved that the film will come into its own as one of the finest of the fine arts."

ASPECTS OF FILM MUSIC

by MUIR MATHIESON

" I believe that film music is capable of becoming, and to a certain extent already is, a fine art, but it is applied art, and a specialized art at that." Dr. R. Vaughan Williams said this in an article he wrote for the R.C.M. Magazine It would seem that " Tempo " agrees with Vaughan Williams, proof of which is its decision to publish regular critical articles on contemporary film music in future issues.

For my part, I am delighted. It must be nearly ten years since I expressed the belief that film music was destined to become something more than a mere colourful background to a film. I felt that music written for the screen could not only become an integral part of the film—an integral part even in the development of the film—but would soon be valued as an entity in itself. To-day there is much evidence to show that this is so. It is beginning to be obvious that some of the music from the film scores of the last few years will take its place with the best of theatre music—for example, the " Peer Gynt " and the " Midsummer Night's Dream " suites. It is in regard to the critical appreciation of the public and its relation to composers through the medium of the film that I want to write ; there are some factors, possibly not appreciated by everyone, which have affected the progress we are making to-day.

Many of the best British composers are now writing regularly for the film. It is not surprising, when you look at the list of distinguished names, that some of their film music is beginning to find its way into the contemporary repertoire. It is fitting, therefore, that this music should be criticized in an enlightened fashion when it is first heard ; but criticized always with an eye to the context, as well as to its purely musical value.

To understand the problems of film music, it is necessary to remember that until recently it was not considered seriously, neither was it consciously appreciated by the average film-goer. But there has been a change. I believe that the new public has been educated, firstly in an appreciation of the film as a whole, and secondly, in an understanding of the details. Instead of noticing only the weakness in badly written or clumsily handled music, the film-goer is rapidly learning to understand and enjoy some of the finer music which has been written for him. The man in the street can not only discern good acting from bad (see box office receipts !) but is capable of discussing and criticizing, as well as enjoying, the varying merits of a film. I have often been amazed at the amount of constructive criticism one hears on buses and trains in connection with such technical aspects of film-making as cutting, editing and direction. Music is probably the latest of the technical ingredients to have captured this attention. This may be due to the new awareness and appreciation of music, as seen in all the concert halls around the country ; it may have been helped by the romantic success of the " Warsaw Concerto " : it has certainly been stimulated by the quality of the work that composers have put into films during the last few years. Whatever the cause, I can vouch for it that people are as quick to notice the distinguished in music on the screen as they are to deplore the commonplace.

What better encouragement could a composer ask for than an intelligent appreciation of his music by the public. From letters I receive it is obvious that the cinema audience knows its composers well. Could there be a better reason to write for the films ? I believe this is being understood by composers, hence the ever-increasing output of specially written, worthwhile music. This change in the public attitude appears to be general throughout the country. Whereas in earlier days people were apathetic and almost wholly unaware of the musical or aural aspect of the film, they now *demand* the best. And how do we know this ? The film, after all, is a commercial enterprise, based on the idea of supplying a commodity that the public wants. With regard to the musical score, surely the composers' names on the credit titles of the successful money-making films are a reliable indication of the public's discrimination.

One should remember that the film-goer comes from classes more widely divergent than in any other form of entertainment. Most people go to the cinema, and they have one thing in common (again I refer you to box office receipts). They all insist on the

THE MAGIC BOW. Director Bernard Knowles watches Stewart Granger practising violin for his screen part of Paganini under the watchful eye of David MacCullum, well-known orchestra leader.

184

best stars, directors, producers and cameramen, the best stories. And now, because universal taste has been raised by the composers themselves, they begin to demand good music.

Several of the leading composers in this country have each done a great deal to develop public taste, using the film as a medium. I believe the composer finds a spur in the dramatic quality of the film he is working on : there is for him something to be gained from the style and quality of the production, and, as this improves, he in turn is able to give his best, simply because the dramatic influence of the picture may have been a direct encouragement to his imagination. Incidentally, if composers—already established or not—can derive a certain income from writing for the films, it will enable them to have time and opportunity to relax in order to concentrate on their concert works. In return, the time they spend in this way comes back to the film in a tangible form.

Some composers do find the film—its real dramatic worth— a positive stimulus to invention, and a help towards the attainment of facility in writing. Dr. Vaughan Williams says that film-composing is a splendid discipline, and I agree with that. But I have also found in the case of most composers, that the very encouragement to be prolific, while writing for the films, is an incentive to shake themselves free from any of the weaker stuff of which even the best composers have to rid themselves at some time or other. All this can be corrected, and then there is room for the better musical thoughts to find their way through. For the composer who writes with great facility, the opportunities for hearing his music simplify the problems of correction and second thoughts.

The film is a young art. Surely young men should be allowed to write for it. It may be good for the film, and good for *them*. It is a tradition that the young composer has to struggle for recognition, even after he has found himself. Here is an opportunity for him to do both more speedily. There is, I hope, encouragement and stimulus. There are, moreover, a few technical advantages which could help some composers.

I would not for a moment suggest that writing for films should be the one aim of any composer, but it is well to remember that his music can be heard, first by himself, and then by an audience

BRITISH COMPOSERS.
Arthur Bliss, R. Vaughan Williams, (top) ; William Walton, Hubert Bath (below).

(in this case possibly an audience of millions) a very short time after he has written it. That, surely, is a thing which has seldom happened, even in the days when Haydn and Mozart had their music commissioned ; it is almost as though there were a return to the old system of " commissioned " music, but on a very grand scale. There is one drawback, however. Though fertility and invention may be encouraged, there is not always sufficient time for adequate reflection on what has been written. This is being speedily rectified !

It would, I think, be fair to say that the standard of music in British films is at the present time as high, if not higher, than in any other country. This applies more especially to the serious type of film. Let me hasten to explain that I refer more to the quality of the music than to the technical handling of it. I would say that the technique of the Americans is more advanced, or at least infinitely " slicker " than ours. Their management of music on the sound-track is brilliant, and their composers seem to have trained themselves to write with a precise care and appreciation of the dramatic significance of each turn in a story. Perhaps because he has been at it longer, the American composer has turned himself more thoroughly into a music dramatist than the British. On the other hand, I think the average score written here has more intrinsic musical value. If British composers can achieve a balance between the technical dexterity of the Americans and their own standard of writing, then we shall have made another big step forward in the development of a real film music.

I felt a temptation, when contemplating this article, to draw parallels between operatic and film music ; but that must wait a year or two because, at the present time, the composer is to a certain extent limited by the equipment at his disposal, and there are various technical difficulties of a purely mechanical nature. There is no doubt that those difficulties will disappear as soon as the war is over, and recording and re-recording equipment and experiments can be renewed.

Experiment is essential. Orson Welles, who is probably one of the most active present-day experimenters, was a radio producer before he went into films. His experiments with radio seem to have given him a healthy regard for the significance of sound in film ; the sound track in his film *Citizen Kane* was a revelation in many ways.

In this country the "documentary" film makers have always been the adventurers. One of the latest and most interesting experiments was a sound track, planned and constructed before the film was photographed. The natural sounds, the music, and the speech were blended together to make a coherent whole, not a mere aural accompaniment to the visuals on the screen. It was exciting to meet with a certain degree of success. The scope for experiment is unlimited, and as far as I can see it always will be. We have learnt that it is wisest not to require music to do things which natural sound can interpret more faithfully, and we have learnt that very great care must be taken in deciding where music must go and what it must do : too many films have been ruined by the indiscriminate use of music.

We have learnt, too, that sound-tracks often suffer from over-loading due to an attempt to make them carry too many elements—for example, music, speech and natural sound simultaneously.

We are beginning to learn that the transition from music to speech is of the greatest importance to the flow of the sound track ; this is a point that has not always been as carefully considered as it should be.

We are finding that the quality of dialogue and its level must be considered in relation to the orchestration and musical balance. If the dynamic level and tone-colour can be kept constant between dialogue and music, ugly clashes and uncomfortably discordant effects can be avoided. Registers which compete directly with the human voice often appear. It is these problems that call for the most precise writing and technical control from the composer, when he is working to synchronise sound and action to one-third of a second.

We are still learning ; and as I began with a quotation from Dr. Vaughan Williams, here is another from the same article which will help to make my point : "At present I still feel a morning blush in my art, and it has not yet paled into the light of common day. I still believe that the film contains potentialities for the combination of all the arts such as Wagner never dreamt of."

BIOGRAPHICAL INDEX

Who's Who of film music composers, music directors, sound recordists, sound track stars and film music writers.

Note.—A film title quoted against the name of a composer means that he has made some contribution to the music of that film. It does not necessarily mean that he has written the entire score, though in many instances this will be the case. Where the same film appears under two different composers, the music track was a joint undertaking.

No credits are given here for orchestrating or arranging, though in some cases the results may have been considerably influenced by this means. The term " musical arranger " for the purposes of the index refers to the work of assembling previously composed music into background accompaniment for films, for example, the use of gramophone records in compiling a music track.

Certain studios have not shown the full composition credits in many of their earlier pictures ; where possible an attempt has been made to go beyond the sparse information given on the credit titles of such films.

The year shown against films listed here normally refers to the trade or press show date, but in certain cases may indicate the year in which the music was composed.

ABADY, TEMPLE. Composer. *Railways* (Crown, 1946), *Hausa Village* (Taurus, 1946), *The Three A's* (Crown, 1947) and *Boy Builders* (Crown, 1947).

ADDINSELL, RICHARD. Composer. Born in London, 1904. He was educated privately and at Hertford College, Oxford, where he studied law. His real interest, however, was music for the theatre, and at the age of 21 he began to devote the whole of his time to the study and practice of composition in this field. During a short period of studentship at the Royal College of Music he set a number of light lyrics, and contributed substantially to one of Andre Charlot's revues. His first complete musical setting for a stage play was his score to Clemence Dane's " Adam's Opera," produced at the Old Vic at the end of 1928. His collaborative association with the famous playwright has been rejoined from time to time over the past 17 years ; their names have frequently appeared together on theatre playbills, in broadcast introductory announcements, and on the film credit titles. In 1929 Addinsell left England for three years of study and travel on the Continent. He visited all the principal theatres and musical centres, but spent most of his time in Berlin and Vienna. In 1932 he returned to England to take up a commission to write the music of Le Gallienne production of " Alice in Wonderland," and he visited New York in connection with this production in 1933. Then followed six months in Hollywood under a contract to write film background music for R.K.O. Later the same year he returned to America for the production of " Come of Age," a " play in music and in words." Besides writing the score, Addinsell had collaborated with Clemence Dane in the general treatment of this highly experimental piece, and he produced it jointly with her at the Maxine Elliot Theatre in January, 1934. His next two scores for Clemence Dane plays were for her version of Rostand's " L'Aiglon " (Le Gallienne production, New York, 1935) and " The Happy Hypocrite " produced as " a play with music " at His Majesty's Theatre in 1936. Addinsell's subsequent work for the theatre was the incidental music for " The Taming of the Shrew," in which Edith Evans appeared at the New Theatre in 1937, and a new adaptation by Clemence Dane of " Alice in Wonderland " introduced at the Scala Theatre for the Christmas season, 1943, and revived at the Palace Theatre for the Christmas season, 1944. Addinsell has frequently written direct for the radio, including (in 1941) the music for a series of six radio plays by Clemence Dane, broadcast under the general title of " The Saviours." A number of his light songs have been written for and in collaboration with Joyce Grenfell, notably " I'm Going to See you To-day," " Turn Back the Clock " and " Oh, Mr. Du Maurier," which was one of the successes in Noel Coward's revue " Sigh No More." It was in 1936 that Addinsell entered films in collaboration with Muir Mathieson with the score to the Alexander Korda London film *The Amateur Gentleman*, featuring Douglas Fairbanks, Jnr. This was followed by a series of feature film scores for many London film productions, all recorded by Muir Mathieson, including *Dark Journey, Farewell Again, South Riding* and *Fire Over England* in 1937, and *Vessel Of Wrath* in 1938. In 1939 he produced a very fine score to the M.-G.-M. British production *Goodbye, Mr. Chips*, and went on to compose for the first feature made after the commencement of war in Alexander Korda's studios at Denham *The Lion Has Wings*. Then followed a series of documentary and Army films for which Addinsell supplied the music, interspersed with further feature film scores : *Contraband* (London, 1940), *Gaslight* (1940), *Men Of The Lightship* (M.O.I., 1940), *Britain At Bay* (M.O.I., 1940) and *Ulster* (M.O.I., 1940) in 1941, *This England* (British National), *Camouflage* (Army Unit), *Special Despatch* (Army Unit), *W.R.N.S.* (M.O.I.), *The Big Blockade* (Ealing), *Love On The Dole* (British National), *The Green Belt* (Strand films for the British Council), *This Is Colour* (I.C.I.) and the most famous of all the Addinsell scores, perhaps the most remarkable piece of film background music ever written, the score to *Dangerous Moonlight* featuring the " Warsaw Concerto." In 1942 he scored *The Siege Of Tobruk* (Army Unit), *A Day Will Dawn, We Sail At*

Midnight (Crown Unit) and *A.T.S.* (Army Unit), followed by *Troopship* (Army Unit) and *The New Lot* (Army Unit). Then for a time he was engaged in work for the radio and the stage, but in 1945, he returned to the screen with a first-class score (which is available on a gramophone record) for the Noel Coward film *Blithe Spirit*. In 1946 appeared the music for the film *Diary For Timothy*, made by the Crown Film Unit. Addinsell resides in London just a short distance from the B.B.C., and at present has further film scores in production. His unique contributions to the screen, notably the music to *Goodbye, Mr. Chips*, *Gaslight*, *Blithe Spirit*, and of course, the " Warsaw Concerto," make him one of Britain's outstanding personalities of the film music world.

ALWYN, WILLIAM. Composer. Born in Northampton, 1905. William Alwyn studied music at the Royal Academy of Music, and had a distinguished career prior to his entry into films in 1936. His compositions include a piano concerto, a violin concerto, string quartets, songs and piano music, many being notable works of unusual quality, such as his " Divertimento " for unaccompanied flute, which has been described as " the attainment by such unlikely means of eminently musical results." From 1937-40, he held the Colland Fellowship in Music of the Worshipful Company of Musicians, while in 1940 he was elected an Honorary Freeman of the Musician's Company. But it is in the sphere of the cinema that Alwyn is such a familiar figure, having appeared on the credit titles of many of the country's most outstanding documentary pictures as well as a number of prominent feature productions. His first film score was for the Strand film *The Future's In The Air* (1936), followed by a great series of factual films which include : *New Worlds For Old* (Paul Rotha, 1937), *Air Outpost* (Strand, 1937), *Monkey Into Man* (Strand Zoological Films, 1938), *Zoo Babies* (Strand Zoological, 1938), *The Zoo And You* (Strand Zoological, 1938), *Birth Of The Year* (Strand, 1938), *Roads Across Britain* (Realist, 1939), *Wings Over Empire* (Stuart Legg, 1939), *These Children Are Safe* (Strand, 1939), *S.O.S.* (Eldridge and Curtis for M.O.I., 1940), *W.V.S.* (Verity, 1941), *Steel Goes To Sea* (Merton Park, 1941), *Spring On The Farm* (Greenpark, 1942), *Wales* (Strand, 1942), *The Countrywomen* (Seven League, 1942), *Life Begins Again* (Paul Rotha, 1942), *Winter On The Farm* (Greenpark, 1942), *The Harvest Shall Come* (Realist, 1942), *Western Isles* (Merton Park, 1942), *Fires Were Started* (Crown Unit, 1942), *Crown Of The Year* (Greenpark, 1942), *Citizens Of Tomorrow* (Realist, 1942), *Border Weave* (Turner-M.-G.-M., 1943), *World Of Plenty* (Paul Rotha, 1943), *There's A Future In It* (Strand, 1943), *Desert Victory* (Army and R.A.F. Film Units, 1943), *Tunisian Victory* (Army and R.A.F. Units, 1944), *Summer On The Farm* (Greenpark, 1943), *Our Country* (Strand, 1944), *Welcome To Britain* (M.O.I. for American Army), *Soldier-Sailor* (Realist, 1944), *French Town* (Realist, 1944), *The Gen* (R.A.F. Newsreel), *To-day and To-morrow* (World Wide, 1945), *The Proud City* (Greenpark, 1945), *The True Glory* (British and American Service Film Units, 1945), *Total War In Britain* (Paul Rotha, 1945), *Worker And Warfront* (magazine series) (Paul Rotha), *Land Of Promise* (Paul Rotha, 1946). William Alwyn entered the field of feature films in 1941 and has scored the following pictures : *Penn Of Pennsylvania* (British National, 1941), *They Flew Alone* (R.K.O. Radio-British, 1942), *Squadron Leader X* (R.K.O. Radio-British, 1942), *Escape To Danger* (R.K.O. Radio-British, 1943), *The Way Ahead* (Two Cities, 1944), *On Approval* (Independent, 1944), *Medal For The General* (British National, 1944), *The Rake's Progress* (Individual, 1945), *I See A Dark Stranger* (Individual, 1946), *Odd Man Out* (Two Cities, 1947), *Green For Danger* (Individual, 1947), *Take My Life* (Cineguild, 1947) and *The City Speaks* (Paul Rotha, 1947).

AURIC, GEORGES. Composer. Born in Lodève, Hérault, 1899. He studied at the Paris Conservatoire, and under the composer D'Indy at the Schola Cantorum. His first compositions appeared when he was 15 years old ; since when he has written much piano music, songs, orchestral works and ballets. He is a member of the music group known as " Les Six," which includes Honegger and Milhaud, both film music writers. As a musical journalist, Auric was the pre-war critic of " Les Nouvelles Litteraires " for all its musical sections, and is now critic for " Les Lettres Francaises," " La Liberation " and "Paris Presse." In 1945, he came to England and was introduced to the British Press by Benjamin Britten on arrival in London for consultations with G. B. Shaw and Gabriel Pascal. Among his French film scores are included : *Le Sang D'un Poète* (An " avant garde " film directed by Jean Cocteau, 1932), *A Nous La Liberté* (Rene Clair), *La Mort Du Sphinx* (1937), *L'Affaire Lafarge* (Triannon Films, 1938), *Alibi* (1938), *Heart Of Paris* (Triannon Films, 1939), *Entrée Des Artistes* (1939) and *L'Eternel Retour* (made during the German occupation of France, 1944). His British films include *Dead Of Night* (Ealing, 1945), which was his first score for an English picture, and the Gabriel Pascal production of 1944-45 *Caesar And Cleopatra*, also *Hue And Cry* (Ealing, 1946). His recent French scores include *La Belle Et La Belle* (Jean Cocteau, 1946), and the Cannes Film Festival Prize-winning Score of 1946 *La Symphonie Pastorale*, quoted as the best musical background of any film of the year.

BART, UNA. Composer. Assistant to Ernest Irving in the music department of Ealing Studios. She contributed music to the film *Champagne Charlie*.

BATH, HUBERT. Composer. Born in Barnstaple, 1883. Died in London, 1945. He studied at the Royal College of Music under Beringer (piano) and Corder (composition). His compositions include comic operas, popular cantatas and orchestral works, also many songs and recitations with musical background. His most ambitious work is a symphonic poem " The Visions of Hannele (1913, revised 1920) based on the incidental music he wrote for a production of Gerhard Hauptmann's "Hannele." Other works include "Symphonic Poem" (played at the Albert Hall), " Devonia," and a choral work performed at the Leeds Festival. He has written a very large amount of music for the stage, and was for a time musical adviser to the London County Council, directing the organisation of its park bands. Hubert Bath was one of the pioneers of British film music, a man who did tremendous work in raising the standards of film background music from the very beginning. It was he who wrote music for the first sound films made in this country including *Kitty* in 1929 (half sound, half silent), and *Blackmail*, the first British all-talking picture, directed by Alfred Hitchcock for Gaumont-British. Next, he scored *Under The Greenwood Tree* for British International Pictures, followed by a background score and arrangements of Strauss waltzes for the Gaumont-British musical film *Waltzes From Vienna* (1934). This again was directed by Alfred Hitchcock and produced by Tom Arnold. In 1933, Bath joined the permanent staff of Louis Levy's music department at the studios in Lime Grove, Shepherd's Bush, working with them continuously except for a break between 1937 and 1943. Among the pictures he scored for them are included : *Wings Over Everest* (filmed by G.-B. News cameraman S. R. Bonnett on a flight over Mount Everest), *Chu Chin Chow* (orchestrations and background score), *Tudor Rose*, *Rhodes Of Africa* (from which comes the march " Empire Builders "), *The Passing Of The Third Floor Back* (Conrad Veidt), *His Lordship* (George Arliss), *Bulldog Jack* (sequences only), *The Thirty-Nine Steps* and *Doctor Syn* in collaboration with Jack Beaver, *The Great Barrier*, *Evensong* (Evelyn Laye ; background score only), *A Yank At Oxford*, *Dear Octopus*, *Millions Like Us*, *The Adventures Of Tartu*, *A Place Of One's Own*, *Love Story* (from which comes " The Cornish Rhapsody."), *They Were Sisters*, *The Air Plan* (R.A.F. Unit), *Operational Height* (R.A.F. Unit) and other Gainsborough films. His last complete score was for the highly successful *They Were Sisters* ; he began the rough sketches for *The Wicked Lady* and at that time when his " Cornish Rhapsody " was at the height of its fame both in the film and as a gramophone record, Hubert Bath died after a life devoted to the cause of film music. He was a great believer in the " unobtrusive score," music that gives greater emotional depth to a film and passes unnoticed into the pattern of the entertainment without emerging as a separate entity. His work has been very ably taken on by his son, also a film musician.

BATH, JOHN. Composer and Music Director. Born in West Kensington, London, 1916. The son of the composer Hubert Bath. He was educated at the Westminster Cathedral Choir School, and has been recorded by H.M.V. as a soloist in the cathedral choir. His musical education came mainly from his father, and he grew up in an atmosphere of music and film scores. He served in the Army during the war for the War Office film section, editing, composing and conducting music for Army training films. Before this he was in the H.M.V. record advertising department, with Walter Legge at Gaumont-British studios as film librarian, with Associated British at Elstree as a film cutter, with the B.B.C. in the recorded programme department, and with Keith Prowse as manager of their educational department. He has composed over 150 pieces, including a ballet founded on Chaucer's " Merchant's Tale," due for production at the Whitehall Theatre. He is at present at work on his " Sussex Suite," and hopes to be soon producing films about Sussex with a new film company which is to be formed for that purpose. To-day, he is film editor and music director at Merton Park Studios. His films are mainly scores for Army kinematograph pictures and include *According To Our Records* (A.K.S., 1944), *You Too Can Get Malaria* (Verity, 1944), *Technique Of Instruction* (A.K.S., 1944 ; includes a cartoon section), *Eastern Background* (D.A.K., 1944), *The Story Of D.D.T.* (A.K.S., 1944), *Borne On Two Wings* (A.K.S., 1945 ; cartoon in colour), *A Letter From Home* (a series of A.K.S. newsletters, 1945), *Read All About It* (A.K.S., 1945), *A Day In The Line* (A.K.S., 1945), *The Hospital Team* (Verity, 1945), *Food Manufacture* (World Wide Films, 1945), *Tackling The Problem* (A.K.S., 1945), *This Is China* (Merton Park, 1946), *Jean's Plan* (Merton Park for the Odeon Children's Clubs), *Flying With Prudence* (Merton Park for the Air Ministry, 1946), and one feature film *The Voice Within* (Grand National, 1946). Additional documentaries and short films include *Pool Of Contentment* (Central Office of Information, 1946), *The Glen Is Ours* (Verity, 1946), *New Hobbies* (Shell, 1946), *Heat Treatment* (Verity, 1946), *Can We Be Rich?* (Cecil Musk, 1946), *This Modern Age : Number One* ; *Scotland Yard* (Arthur Rank, 1946), *A Place In The Sun* (Julian Wintle, 1946), *Shell Magazine, Number Nine* (Shell Unit, 1946) and *Circus Boy* (G.B. Children's Club, 1947).

BAX, ARNOLD. Composer. Born in London, 1883. He entered the Royal Academy of Music at the age of 17 for a five-year course, studying piano with Tobias Matthay, and composition with Frederick Corder. Before completing his apprenticeship, he already displayed considerable skill in composition, and showed an amazing faculty for sight-reading. He has devoted a lifetime to composition, and, never having been obliged to earn a livelihood, he has held no official musical appointment. He was knighted in 1937, and in 1942 became Master of the King's Music. Although a fine pianist, he has never appeared before the public in that capacity, nor has he done any conducting of his own works, but has spent his time in producing a very large output of composition, including seven symphonies. Bax is a romantic composer with exceptional powers of creative imagination. His inventiveness reveals itself in highly poetic music, often very subtle, and hence requiring an alert ear to obtain full enjoyment, a factor which has tended to prevent his music from attaining full public recognition. In 1942, he wrote his only film score to the picture *Malta G.C.*, made by the Crown and R.A.F. Film Units. Although Bax did not find that the film medium suited his highly individualistic approach to music, the score was subsequently converted into a concert suite and has received many public performances during the last three years, enjoying a wide popularity.

BAYCO, FREDERICK. Composer. *Three Cadets* (Greenpark, 1945).

BEAVER, JACK. Composer and Music Director. Born in Clapham, London, 1900. He studied at the Royal College of Music under F. Corder in composition and Waller and Matthay for pianoforte. He was associated with music for the silent cinema, and during the last ten years has done a great deal of work for the B.B.C. and the theatre ; he was responsible for scoring practically all the radio adaptations of films from 1936 to 1941 in collaboration with Douglas Moodie, and in 1946 became musical director to the Peter Eton radio programme " Picture Parade." His first work for talkies was in 1932 when he scored *Baroud* (R.K.O.-British). Next, he worked with Louis Levy and the music department at Shepherd's Bush, collaborating on such films as *Channel Crossing, Lady In Danger, Dr. Syn* and *The Thirty-Nine Steps* with Hubert Bath, *Everything Is Thunder, Foreign Affairs* and other Tom Walls films. From 1934 onwards, Beaver became resident composer to the famous Gaumont-British instructional series *Secrets Of Life* and *Secrets Of Nature,* and in 1939, in addition to writing the music, he took over the work of conducting the recording sessions. He was music director for a time to Premier Stafford Corp., for whom he wrote and directed music for *Ball At The Savoy, The Wife Of General Ling* and *Wings Over Africa.* He wrote and directed music for Warner Bros. at Teddington for *The Prime Minister* (1940), *Atlantic Ferry* (1941), *This Was Paris* (1941), *Flying Fortress* (1942), *The Peterville Diamond* (1942), *The Night Invader* (1942), *The Dark Tower* (1942) ; in addition, Beaver musically directed *The Chinese Bungalow* (1939), *The Case Of The Frightened Lady* (1940), *Candlelight In Algeria* for British Aviation Pictures in 1945, and most recently *Gaiety George* at Denham in 1946. For the picture *The Case Of The Frightened Lady,* he wrote what may be considered the first tabloid piano concerto, a style of writing which later produced such music as the " Warsaw Concerto " and the " Cornish Rhapsody."

BENJAMIN, ARTHUR. Composer. Born in Sydney, New South Wales, 1893. He studied at the Royal College of Music, returning to Australia as professor of the pianoforte at the Conservatory in Sydney. He again came to England, and became a member of the R.C.M. staff, but in 1937 he left to settle in Vancouver. After a series of radio talks and concerts in addition to music teaching, conducting and composing, he has now become an outstanding figure in Canadian musical life. He is a frequent visitor to the United States, broadcasting and arranging many performances of modern British music in America. His own works include operas, piano and chamber music, and numerous orchestral pieces that have received widespread performances. While in England, Benjamin wrote music for a number of important feature and documentary films, including : *The Man Who Knew Too Much* (Gaumont-British, 1934), *Wharves And Strays* (London Films, 1935), *The Clairvoyant* (Gaumont-British, 1935), *The Scarlet Pimpernel* (London Films, 1935), *The Turn Of The Tide* (Gaumont-British, 1935), *Lobsters* (Bury Prods., 1936), *Wings Of The Morning* (the first British Technicolor feature film, 1937), *The Return Of The Pimpernel* and *Under The Red Robe.* In 1947 he wrote the music for *The Crowthers of Bankdam* (Holbein Films), including the aria " The Fire of Your Love," sung in the picture by Maria Var.

BENNELL, RAYMOND. Composer. Scored some early documentaries, including *Sea Change* (New Era-Alex Shaw, 1935), *Cover To Cover* (Strand, 1936), also collaborated with William Alwyn on *The Future's In The Air* (Strand, 1936).

BERKELEY, LENNOX. Composer. Born in Boar's Hill, near Oxford, 1903. He is partly of French descent, though his general education was completed at Oxford. However, for his musical training he went to Paris, where he studied from 1926-32 with Nadia Boulanger ; to-day, his music sympathies are largely Parisian, or at any rate, Continental. He has written an oratorio " Jonah," performed at the Leeds Festival in 1937, a ballet " The Judgment of Paris," performed at Sadler's Wells in 1938, as well as orchestral, piano and chamber music. He entered films in 1944, scoring *Hotel Reserve* (R.K.O. Radio-British), and later that year *Out Of Chaos*, the film story of the war artists made by Two Cities. Some of the music from *Hotel Reserve* has been recorded and played by the B.B.C. Although his work for the commercial cinema dates from 1944, he scored a short picture *The Sword Of The Spirit* for the Catholic Film Society in 1942.

BERKELEY, MOLLY. Composer. *Out To Play* (Short Film Productions, 1936).

BERNERS, LORD. Composer. Born in Arley Park, Shropshire, 1883. Family name : Gerald Hugh Tyrwhitt-Wilson. He was educated at Eton College, but spent much of his youth on the Continent studying languages for the diplomatic service. He began his career as an attaché to the British Embassy at Constantinople, but had by that time made serious musical studies at Dresden and in London. He was mainly self-taught, although during eight years at the Embassy in Rome, he sought the advice of Cassella and, as opportunity offered, had some lessons from Stravinsky. His original compositions appeared under the name of Gerald Trywhitt, but in 1918, he succeeded to the barony of Berners. He wrote a ballet for Diaghilef " The Triumph of Neptune," and has composed a good deal of modern music, much of it prompted by a sense of irony ; he is considered a foremost musical humorist. He is also a painter, having exhibited his works in London in recent years, and is an author of some note, publishing in 1934, the first part of an autobiography " First Childhood." His first film score was in 1944 for the Ealing film *Halfway House*, and in 1945, he contributed two songs to *Champagne Charlie*. A recent score of his is for the Ealing film of 1947 *Nicholas Nickleby*.

BIDGOOD, HARRY. Composer and Music Director. Dance band leader and popular music expert, Harry Bidgood has been associated with a number of British musical films, including the George Formby pictures *Bell-Bottom George, He Snoops To Conquer, I Didn't Do It, Let George Do It* and *George In Civvy Street*. He was music director to the Vera Lynn film *One Exciting Night*, and for the Butchers musical *I'll Turn To You* (in which he conducted the London Symphony Orchestra).

BLAIN, KENNETH. Composer. *The Ghost Train* (song : " The Seaside Band "). Gaumont-British, 1941.

BLISS, ARTHUR. Composer. Born in London, 1891. Bliss was educated at Rugby and at Pembroke College, later going to Cambridge, where he obtained his B.A. and his Mus.Bac. in 1913. While at Cambridge, he studied under Charles Wood, continuing his musical education at the Royal College of Music in 1914 with Stanford, Vaughan Williams and Gustav Holst. During World War I, he served with the Royal Fusiliers and the Grenadier Guards, taking a commission. He was wounded on the Somme, gassed at Cambrai, and was mentioned in despatches. On leaving the army, he continued with his music, writing such works at " Madame Noy " (a song for soprano and six instruments), " Ballad of the Four Seasons " and the " Colour Symphony." In 1923 Bliss went to America, where he settled in California for a time, but in 1925 he returned to this country again. His film music career began in 1935 with one of the most significant scores in the whole of film music annals, *Things To Come*. This was written in collaboration with H. G. Wells, and was recorded by Muir Mathieson and the London Symphony Orchestra. It was an immediate success and was performed at the Promenade Concerts as a concert suite in the same year as the film appeared. Next, Bliss wrote the music for the London Films production *Conquest Of The Air*, and the music was heard as an orchestral suite at the Proms. in 1938. However, the film was held up a great deal during production, and although planned as early as 1937, it was not until the war years that it made its much revised appearance and then only on a limited basis. The suite, which plays for twelve minutes, is, however, excellent music and has received a number of performances. For a long time after this, he was occupied with other forms of composition, including works such as the Piano Concerto, first performed at the New York World's Fair in 1939. In 1943 the Soviet newsreel production *Defeat Of The Germans Near Moscow* carried opening fanfares by Bliss. Then in 1945 he composed a stirring march for a French film *Presence Au Combat*, a factual picture of the French fighting services. Finally, in 1946, he composed one of his greatest scores, the epic music to the picturisation of African social problems, *Men Of Two Worlds* (Two Cities). Arthur Bliss has written very few film scores, but all the music that he has contributed to the cinema has been of the highest order, and in each case has become a concert work of considerable importance, for he believes that film music, to be good, should be capable of standing on its own, to be judged as music suitable for concert hall performance. Thus his scores are always impressive, often elaborate, and always good solid music.

BLOOD, DENNIS. Composer. A composer for documentary films. His scores include *The True Story Of Lili Marlene* (Crown Film Unit, 1944), and *Crofters* (Greenpark, 1944), also *Farmer's Boy* (Greenpark, 1945) and music for the R.A.F. newsreel *The Gen.* In 1947, *Power in the Land* (World Wide).

BLORE, JOHN. Composer. *Welcome, Mr. Washington* (British National, 1944) and *The Butler's Dilemma* (British National, 1944).

BOUGHTON, RUTLAND. Composer. Famous composer of "Immortal Hour." He contributed music to the film *Lorna Doone.*

BOULT, ADRIAN. Conductor. The famous concert hall conductor made a screen appearance conducting the London Philharmonic Orchestra in *Battle For Music* (Strand Films, 1944).

BRAV, LUDWIG. Composer and Musical Arranger. He has arranged and scored music for a number of documentary films and also fitted gramophone music to a number of silent pictures. His films include *Jerusalem, Petra, Wanderers Of The Desert* and *Temples Of India* (all Technicolor travel films from the *World Window* series), *War Front* (Strand, 1941) and *The House We Live In* (Crown Film Unit).

BRAHAM, PHILIP. Composer and Music Director. Early talkie music director at Wembley Studios; he died in about 1934. Among the films he handled musically are *City Of Song* (Wembley, 1930), *Wedding Rehearsal* (1932) and *The First Mrs. Fraser* (Wembley, 1932).

BRAITHWAITE, WARWICK. Conductor. This well-known concert hall conductor makes a screen appearance in *Battle For Music* (Strand Films, 1944), conducting the London Philharmonic Orchestra.

BRIDGEWATER, LESLIE. Composer and Music Director. He has been responsible for the music in a number of documentary pictures, including *Progress, Looking Through, Down To Earth* and *The Village That Found Itself*, all made by Merton Park Studios in recent years. He is also well-known as a conductor and leader of his own orchestra.

BRILL, CHARLES. Composer. His most well-known film is *Pastor Hall* (Charter Films, 1940). He has also written music for documentary, including *Battle Of The Books* (Paul Rotha, 1941); his orchestra is familiar to radio listeners, while the recording of the Benjamin Britten music from *Village Harvest* is by the Charles Brill Orchestra.

BRITTEN, BENJAMIN. Composer. Born in Lowestoft, 1913. He was educated at Gresham's School at Holt in Norfolk, and afterwards at the Royal College of Music from 1930-33, studying composition under John Ireland and piano under Arthur Benjamin (both of whom have also written music for films). Up to the age of 12 he was a pupil of Frank Bridge. He first came into prominence with an elaborate set of unaccompanied choral variations called " A Boy Was Born," followed by music for the International Society for Contemporary Music, and works for the radio and stage. In 1938 he provided music for the production of " The Ascent of F.6," and in 1945, the music to " This Way To The Tomb," produced at the Mercury Theatre. His opera " Peter Grimes " made history in the story of British contemporary music, and met with a very favourable reception in all parts of the world. He entered films in 1936, and has scored many documentaries, including such famous G.P.O. Film Unit pictures as *Coal Face* (1936), *Night Mail* (1936), *Line To Tschierva Hut* (1937), *The Calendar Of The Year* (1937) and *The Savings Of Bill Blewitt*. Other documentary scores include *The Tocher* (a silhouette film made to popularise the Post Office Savings Bank, and produced in 1938 by Lotte Reiniger for the G.P.O. Film Unit), *Advance Democracy* (a Realist Film Unit production made for the Royal Arsenal Co-operative Society in 1939), *Around The Village Green* (Travel Association Film Unit, 1937), *The Way To The Sea* (Strand Films, 1937), and *Sixpenny Telegram* (G.P.O. Film Unit, 1938). In 1937 Britten scored his only feature film, *Love From A Stranger* (directed by Rowland V. Lee). In 1946 he wrote a special score, based on a theme by Purcell, for use in a Crown Film Unit production *Instruments of the Orchestra*. The film was directed by Muir Mathieson with music conducted by Malcolm Sargent. The " Irish Reel " from the film *Village Harvest*, scored by Britten, is available on a Decca gramophone record.

BRODSZKY, NICHOLAS. Composer. Born in Odessa, Russia, 1905. After an early musical education in Russia, he left that country and came to Europe where he continued his musical studies in Rome, Vienna and Budapest. He has scored over 60 films, and wrote his first film music in Vienna in 1930 for a picture featuring Richard Tauber and Gitta Alpar. This was followed by a long series of Continental films, before coming to England where, in 1936, he was engaged by C. B. Cochran to write music for the Coronation revue "Home and Beauty." His first film score in England was for *French Without Tears* (1938). Since then he has scored the following pictures : *Freedom Radio* (1940), *Spy For A Day*, *Quiet Wedding* (1940), *Unpublished Story*, *Tomorrow We Live*, *The Demi-Paradise* (Two Cities, 1944), *The Way To The Stars* (Two Cities, 1945), *English Without Tears* (Two Cities, 1944), *Carnival* (Two Cities, 1946) and *Beware Of Pity* (Two Cities, 1946). Music from *The Way To The Stars* and *Carnival* has been published, while a gramophone record is available of *The Way To The Stars*. Brodszky is one of the most prominent of our film musicians who employ the Hollywood system of having a large number of collaborators and orchestrators engaged on each score, whereby the composer may concentrate on the production of the straightforward melodies, which are then passed on for orchestration and working-out. The excellence of this system may be judged by the fine *Way To The Stars* music. Among the composers and arrangers who have collaborated with Brodszky are Clive Richardson, Charles Williams, Roy Douglas and Sidney Torch. A recent score of his is the delightful music to *While The Sun Shines*, the film based on the Terence Rattigan play, also the scores for *A Man About The House* (Edward Black Productions, 1947) and *The Turners Of Prospect Road* (Grand National, 1947).

BUCHANAN, MABEL. Composer. *Give Me The Stars* (song : " Throughout the Years "). British National Films, 1944.

BURGESS, GEORGE. Sound Supervisor. Born in London, 1897. He was educated at Dulwich College from 1909 up to 1914 when he joined up, first in the East Surrey Regiment, later transferring to the Royal Flying Corps and eventually leaving the Royal Air Force (as it had then become) in 1919. There followed five busy years at London University and at Barts Hospital. In 1925, Burgess joined the Radio Communication Company, in 1926 he was with Mullards, and in 1928 he entered films, first with B.T.P. and Pathé Natan in Paris. He returned to England in 1929 and continued to gain film experience at the studios at Wembley. 1934 saw him at the Associated Talking Picture Studio at Ealing, but in 1935 he again went overseas to Italy, working for Cines in Rome. Back to England in 1936, George Burgess did a year with Riverside Studio, a year at Gainsborough, and in 1938, he worked for the British Acoustic Sound people. From 1938 until 1940, he was with the Studios Sonart in Brussels, but after the invasion of Belgium and France, he returned to England to become sound supervisor at the Riverside Film Studios at Hammersmith, a position he has held right up to the present. During the course of such a varied career, Burgess has gained a great deal of experience in the recording of music for the screen, and is at present designing a new music recording studio which is to be built at Riverside. His very extensive list of films include the following pictures : *City Of Song* (the first film to feature the singer, Jan Kiepura), *Wedding Rehearsal* (the first London Film Production made by Alexander Korda), *The First Mrs. Fraser, Two White Arms, Money For Speed, Divine Spark* (*Casta Diva*, a special film commissioned by Mussolini for the centenary of the composer Bellini, produced in Italy in four languages—Italian, German, French and English), *Can You Hear Me, Mother ?* (Sandy Powell), *Her Last Affair* (Googie Withers), *O.K. For Sound* (the first Crazy Gang film), *Everybody Dance* (Cicely Courtneidge), *Windbag The Sailor* (Will Hay), *Front Line Kids* (Leslie Fuller), *He Found A Star* (Vic Oliver), *Somewhere In Camp, Somewhere In Civvies* and *Somewhere On Leave* (Frank Randle), *I'll Walk Beside You* and *For You Alone* (Leslie Brook, the London Symphony Orchestra), *I Love To Sing* (Vera Lynn), *Happidrome* (Harry Korris), *Gert And Daisy Clean Up, Under New Management, Variety Jubilee, Th Seventh Veil* (Ann Todd, James Mason), *The Years Between* (Sydney Box, 1946), *A Girl In A Million* (Sydney Box, 1946), *Daybreak* (Sydney Box, 1947) and *A Convict Has Escaped* (Alliance, 1947).

BUSBY, BOB. Composer. Born at Maidenhead, 1901. He commenced pianoforte lessons at the age of 7, and from 10 onwards at the Trinity College of Music. He began study in counterpoint and harmony at the age of 11 ; among the instruments he learnt to play were the cornet, clarinet and 'cello. His concert experience dates from his ninth year, beginning with cornet solos in various bands, followed by clarinet work in military bands, and by the beginning of World War I, he was playing the 'cello in a London cinema orchestra. He commenced writing for films as early as 1922 on the Continent (for Ufa in Berlin), followed by a long spell of composition and arranging for orchestras in Austria, Hungary, France, Spain and Holland. In 1932, he commenced writing music for British films, and in 1942, joined the music department at Gainsborough Studios. Recent films to which he has contributed include : *King Arthur Was A Gentleman* (1942), *Give Us The Moon* (1944), *Bees In Paradise* (1944), *I'll Be Your Sweetheart* (1944), *Waterloo Road* (1944).

BYRD, BRETTON. Composer and Music Director. Born in Ramsgate, Kent, 1904. His real name is James Thomas Byrd. He was educated at St. George's School in Ramsgate, where he received his first music instruction consisting of elementary piano lessons, and some experience as a solo boy soprano in the church choir attached to the school. During World War I he sang regularly at charity concerts, while from 1918-20 he gained valuable experience playing the piano for dances and at local picture houses. At the age of 16 he became dependant on his earnings as a professional musician, starting with a concert party season as pianist at Sandy Hollow Pavilion in Pokesdown, Bournemouth, with a show known as " Wraggle Taggles." Then followed over 400 one-and-two-night stands in Scotland with J. M. Hamilton, a contemporary of Harry Lauder and W. F. Frame. The five-octave piano was carried round with the show in a large basket, and had to be loaded and unloaded by the pianist with the assistance of the cast. This was followed by a spell on the piano of an old-time " flea-pit " in Coatbridge, where the picture was often stopped and some of the audience lectured by the manager on their behaviour, or thrown out by the attendants, after which the picture proceeded as if nothing had happened. Then he conducted and wrote music for travelling revues and pantomimes, played in dance bands, conducted for a musical comedy called "The Beauty Prize," and also for Hetty King, Harry Jolson (brother of Al Jolson) and other variety acts. In 1930, he was introduced to Louis Levy, and joined the music staff at the Gainsborough Studios. His first job in films was to sing in a vocal trio (an arrangement which he made himself), after which he did certain orchestrations and compositions for the film *Love On Wheels*, a Jack Hulbert musical picture. Since then he has worked on about a hundred films in various capacities and for different companies. Apart from musical composition, he has evolved systems of shooting musical sequences, and has specialised in the post-synchronisation of accompaniments for song and dance scenes, the making of guide tracks, musical sound cutting (he is an expert film cutter as well as a musician and has a mechanical frame of mind that is very useful for this type of musical work), and he has devised a method of positively checking the balance of a recording orchestra. This is done by using a special composition which, when played by an orchestra of the size for which the music is written, allows an accurate balancing of recording level to be obtained quickly for any given recording session. In addition, he has written a number of shooting scripts for musical production numbers. His strong mechanical mind he attributes to his music studies ; apart from a few lessons in early life he is largely self-taught musically. Recently he has invented a new type of tandem bicycle which incorporates many improvements, including an easy system of conversion from a " bicycle built for two " to an ordinary single type bike. This combination of musician-engineer is surely unique amongst a class of men who are usually regarded as being highly unpractical and pre-occupied in matters of the mind and the soul. His extensive list of films for which he provided incidental music, orchestrations, songs, musical direction, or in any way contributed to the musical aspect, include the following titles : *George And Margaret* (Marie Löhr, Judy Kelly), *Two For Danger* (Barry K. Barnes), *That's The Ticket* (Syd Fields), *The Briggs Family* (Edward Chapman, Jane Baxter), *The Midas Touch* (Michael Redgrave, Frank Cellier), *Hoots Mon* (Max Miller), *His Brother's Keeper* (Tamara Desni), *Confidential Lady* (Jane Baxter, Ben Lyon), *Murder Will Out* (Jane Baxter, John Lodge), *Those Were The Days* (Max Miller), *A Gentleman's Gentleman* (Eric Blore), *The Nursemaid Who Disappeared* (Edward Chapman), *They Drive At Night* (Emlyn Williams), *The Return Of Carol Deane* (Bebe Daniels), all made by Warner Bros., *A Window In London* (Michael Redgrave, Sally Gray, Paul Lucas), *So This Is London* (Gordon Harker, Alistair Sim), *Inspector Hornleigh* (Robertson Hare, Alfred Drayton), *Keep Smiling* (Gracie Fields), *We're Going To Be Rich* (Gracie Fields), and these films now listed, all made at the Gaumont-British Studios : *Gangway* (Jessie Matthews), *Head Over Heels* (Jessie Matthews), *Take My Tip* (Jack Hulbert, Cicely Courtneidge), *It's Love Again* (Jessie Matthews), *Jack Of All Trades* (Jack Hulbert), *First A Girl* (Jessie Matthews), *Car Of Dreams* (John Mills), *Oh ! Daddy* (Frances Day, Leslie Henson), *Roadhouse* (Violet Loraine), *A Song For You* (Jan Kiepura), *A Cup Of Kindness* (Tom Walls, Robertson Hare), *Evergreen* (Jessie Matthews), *Jack Ahoy* (Jack Hulbert), the four Will Hay films *Good Morning Boys*, *Windbag The Sailor*, *Where There's A Will* and *Boys Will Be Boys*, *Everybody Dance* (Cicely Courtneidge), *Seven Sinners*, *Me And Marlborough* (Cicely Courtneidge), *Evensong* (Evelyn Laye), *Jew Süss* (Conrad Veidt), *The Good Companions* (Jessie Matthews), *Sleeping Car* (Ivor Novello), *Britannia*

Of Billingsgate (Violet Loraine), *Falling For You* (Jack Hulbert, Cicely Courtneidge), *Love On Wheels* (Jack Hulbert), *Follow Your Star* (Belgrave Films, Arthur Tracy), *The Goose Steps Out* (Ealing Studios, Will Hay), *Happidrome* (M.-G.-M. British), *Turned Out Nice Again* (George Formby), *Caravan* (Stewart Granger), *I'll Be Your Sweetheart* (Margaret Lockwood), *Time Flies* (Tommy Handley), *The Saint's Vacation*; recently he collaborated closely with Yehudi Menuhin during his recording work for the film *The Magic Bow* (Stewart Granger).

CARR, MICHAEL. Song Writer. A composer of popular songs such as " South of the Border " and " Old Faithful." He has contributed a number of songs to various films such as *Follow Your Star, Flight From Folly* (Warner Bros., 1944).

CHAGRIN, FRANCIS. Composer. Born in Rumania. He lived and worked in Paris from 1932-36, when he came to England. Then for a time he was in Paris again scoring for French films, but in 1938, he settled in this country permanently. His first associations with the French cinema were in 1934 and his first British film was in 1937. Chagrin has written a good deal of French music and songs for the B.B.C.; during the war he handled the musical side of the B.B.C. service for the French Resistance movement. His Paris films (scored between 1934 and 1936) include *Ce Colle* (with Fernandel), *La Lutte Pour Le Vie*, *Le Grande Croisiere* and *David Et Goliath*. In England he has been closely associated with the documentary film and the propaganda trailers of the M.O.I. These include : *Animal Legends* (1938), *Five Faces* (Strand, 1937), *Behind The Maginot Line* (March of Time, Paris and London, 1938), *Britain's Youth* (Strand, 1939), *Behind The Guns* (Merton Park, 1940), *Telefootlers* (Verity, 1941), *A-Tish-oo* (Verity, 1941), *Canteen On Wheels* (Verity, 1941), two films for the Dutch Government in 1944, two cartoon trailers for the M.O.I., 1944, and some industrial and advertising films, including *Castings* (Merton Park, 1944), also *Near Home* (Basic Films, 1945) and *Homes For The People* (Basic Films, 1945). He has also scored two British feature films, *Silent Battle* (John Loder, 1939) and *Law And Disorder* (Barry K. Barnes, 1940). Recent short films include : *Picture Paper* (Verity, 1946), *The Bridge* (Data Films, 1946), and a large number of publicity and advertising trailers.

CLIFFE, FRED E. Composer and Song Writer. He has written songs for a number of George Formby films, including *Come On George* and *Let George Do It*, both made at Ealing Studios.

CLIFFORD, HUBERT. Composer. Born Bairnsdale, Victoria, Australia, in 1904. He became a composition scholar at the Conservatoire of Music in Melbourne, and a pupil of Firby Hart. Later he came to London, where he studied at the Royal College of Music under Vaughan Williams. From 1941-44 he was the B.B.C. Empire music supervisor, followed by a post as music advisor to the B.B.C. Eastern Service. In 1944 he became Professor of Composition of the Royal Academy of Music. Dr. Clifford is an authority on music in schools ; his compositions include a " Serenade," first performed by the B.B.C. on Empire Day, 1944, and a suite " Five English Nursery Tunes," first performed by the B.B.C. Orchestra in Bristol in 1941. He is a comparative newcomer to films, his first score being for *Power On The Land* (Verity, 1943), then a series of documentary films including *The Second Freedom* (Verity, 1943), *Road To Moscow* (M.O.I., 1944), *Battle Of Britain* (M.O.I.), *Left Of The Line* (Army Film Unit) and *Steel* (Technique) in 1944, *Shakespeare's Country* (Verity), *General Election* (for the British Council), *Letter From Britain* (Merton Park) and *Their Invisible Inheritance* (Merton Park) in 1945. He has also written a series of film music articles and reviews in the Boosey & Hawkes magazine "Tempo," and late in 1946 he was appointed Music Director to Alexander Korda's London Film Productions, going in 1947 to Hollywood to study American film music and sound-recording methods on behalf of the Korda group.

COATES, ERIC. Composer. Well-known British composer. Wrote " The Eighth Army March " used in the film *Nine Men* (Ealing, 1943).

COLLINS, ANTHONY. Composer and Music Director. Born in Hastings, 1903. After an extensive musical education, he commenced his career as an orchestral player with the Covent Garden and the London Symphony Orchestras. He entered films as a composer and conductor in 1937 for the film *Victoria The Great*, the first of a long series of collaborations with Herbert Wilcox Films. In 1938 he scored *Sixty Glorious Years*, followed by *The Rat, Nurse Edith Cavell* and *A Royal Divorce*. In the spring of 1939 Collins went to the States and settled in Hollywood, where he wrote the music for many famous films, including *Irene, No, No, Nanette, Sunny, Forever And A Day, Swiss Family Robinson, Tom Brown's Schooldays* and *Destroyer*. Apart from his work for these R.K.O. Radio pictures, he had two years composing and conducting for the Orson Welles radio programme for the Lockheed Aviation Company of California, while he founded and conducted the Mozart Orchestra of Los Angeles. While in America he had a unique opportunity of studying and comparing film music methods in Hollywood to those of Britain, and he has very definite views on the subject. In the spring of 1945 he returned to a very different London from the one he left in 1939, to score the film *I Live In Grosvenor Square* (Herbert Wilcox : Anna Neagle), and *Piccadilly Incident*, also for Wilcox in 1946. During his return to England, he has been a guest conductor to a number of our national orchestras, including the B.B.C. Orchestra, and a specially formed Mozart Orchestra of London. On completing the *Piccadilly Incident* score, Collins returned to America for a series of concerts with the Orchestra of the Columbia Broadcasting System, finally going back to Hollywood to continue his work for R.K.O. Radio Pictures. In 1947 he scored *The Courtneys Of Curzon Street* (Wilcox-Imperadio, 1947).

COLLINS, WALTER. Composer. *The Good Companions* and *Britannia Of Billingsgate* (Gaumont). Part score only.

COOKE, GREVILLE. Composer. *For All Eternity* (Strand, 1935).

COOPER, J. E. N. Composer. *Spring On The Farm* (1934).

COWARD, NOEL. Composer, Playwright, Actor, Producer. Born in Teddington, 1899. This famous figure of stage and screen was educated in Croydon, and first appeared on the stage in 1910. Since then he has been associated with a great series of successes like " Bitter Sweet," " Cavalcade," " Private Lives," etc. He composed the music themes for his films *Cavalcade* (1933), *In Which We Serve* (1942) and *This Happy Breed* (1944).

CRAWFORD, JAMES. For ten years, has been assistant to Ernest Irving in the music department of Ealing Studios.

CRISP, A. Musical Arranger. *Echo Of Applause* (1946).

CROWHURST, CYRIL. Music Recordist. Chief Sound Recordist and Sound Engineer at Denham Studios. He was responsible for the design of the large music-scoring stage opened at Denham in 1946, and known as the " Stage One Music Theatre."

CROWTHER, FRANK. Musical Arranger. Recorded music for short films, including *Southward Ho !* (C. E. Hodges Prods., 1937).

DARNTON, CHRISTIAN. Composer. Born in Leeds, 1905. He early evinced a passion for music, and commenced piano lessons at the age of four. His first compositions were written when he was nine years old. At 15 he began to take lessons in composition, and studied under Harry Farjeon and Professor Charles Wood at Cambridge. In 1927 a concert of his chamber music was given

G*

at Grotrian Hall, London. During 1928-29, Darnton lived in Berlin, where he studied with Max Butting. Returning to England he took an appointment as music master at Stowe School, and subsequently was assistant editor of " The Music Lover." His works include chamber music, concertos and many orchestral works. His " Stalingrad Overture " was performed at the Royal Albert Hall and later broadcast, while his symphonies have also been given concert and broadcast performances. He is also well-known as the author of the Penguin book " You and Music," published both in this country and in America. His first experience in film music was the composition of title music for the R.A.F. newsreel *The Gen* in 1944. Then came the music for *Route To Moscow* (M.O.I., 1944) in which three composers contributed, including Hubert Clifford and Darnton. In 1945 he scored the following films : *A Harbour Goes To France* (Crown Unit), *Birth Day* (Data Films), *Marine Salvage* (Data Films), *You Can't Kill A City* (Canadian Army Film Unit), *River Tyne* (Merlin Films), *Channel Islands* (Crown Unit), *Muscle Menders* (Canadian Army Film Unit), *The Antwerp Story* (Canadian Army Film Unit) ; also *Green Fields Beyond* (Canadian Army Film Unit, 1946).

DAVIE, CEDRIC THORPE. Composer. Master of Music at St. Andrews University, he won a prize in the " Daily Express " Music Contest of 1946 with a Symphony. He scored the documentary *Scotland Speaks*, and in 1947 wrote the music for *The Brothers* (Sydney Box).

DAVIES, HUBERT. Composer and Arranger. *The Hidden Land* (Visonor Educational Films, 1937).

DE JONG, FLORENCE. Pianist. Provided the piano music to *Echo Of Applause* (1946), a history of the silent cinema.

DEL MAR, NORMAN. Composer. He has written music for Service short films, including the R.A.F. newsreel *The Gen*. The Battle Sketch " Landing Party " from one of these newsreels has been recorded by the B.B.C. Northern Orchestra for broadcast purposes.

DEMUTH, NORMAN. Composer. Born in South Croydon, Surrey, 1898. He was educated at St. George's, Windsor, at Repton, and then at the Royal College of Music, but in the larger forms of composition he was mainly self-taught. He became professor of composition at the Royal Academy of Music in 1929, and is an honorary associate of the R.C.M. He was secretary and co-founder of the R.C.M. New Music Society. His music includes six symphonies, a ballet " Planetomania," concertos, and much orchestral and instrumental work. In 1943 he composed the official regimental march of the Pioneer Corps. Demuth entered films during the war, arranging music for various short films (War Office, etc.). His only feature film score to date was for the Ealing film of 1945 *Pink String And Sealing Wax*.

DENNIS, JOHN. Music Recordist. Chief production mixer at Pinewood Studios, John Dennis recorded the Arthur Bliss score for *Men Of Two Worlds* (Two Cities, 1946).

DEW, DESMOND. Music Recordist. Born in Warmley, Gloucestershire, 1912. He was educated at Allhallows School, Honiton, Devon, and then went on to a two-years' course in mechanical engineering at Manchester University. This was followed by a course in electro-acoustics at the London Polytechnic, after which Dew served a two-year apprenticeship with a firm of wire manufacturers in Warrington, Lancs. It was in 1935 that he entered films as a microphone operator with Alexander Korda at Worton Hall, and a year later, he graduated to the dubbing and music recording department as an assistant mixer. Later the studios at Denham were built by Alexander Korda, and by 1942, Desmond Dew had become chief mixer there. In 1945 he became head of the dubbing and music recording departments at both Denham and Pinewood Studios. He now handles nearly all the music recording from these two studios of the Rank organisation, and in 1946, he undertook a mission to Hollywood to investigate the sound recording methods and equipment of their studios. In addition, Dew has travelled to many parts of the world in the course of his film career, including France, India, China and Japan, as well as America. The list of films for which he has recorded the music is very large, and includes the following films : *Henry V*, *Brief Encounter*, *I Know Where I'm Going*, *Colonel Blimp*, *On Approval*, *The Silver Fleet*, *The Gentle Sex*, *First Of The Few*, *The Way Ahead*, *This Happy Breed*, *Blithe Spirit*, *The Way To The Stars*, *Perfect Strangers*, *In Which We Serve*, *Caesar And Cleopatra*, *Men Of Two Worlds*, *Gaiety George*, *Carnival*, *I See A Dark Stranger*, *Tawny Pipit*, *Thunder Rock*, *Hotel Reserve*, *Pimpernel Smith*, *English Without Tears*, *Get Cracking*, *The Demi-Paradise*, *Great Day*, *A Canterbury Tale*, *The Lamp Still Burns*, *Journey Together*, *They Knew Mr. Knight*, *Convoy Story*, *The Flemish Farm*, *Epitaph For A Spy*, *A Matter Of Life And Death*, *Great Expectations*.

DE WOLFE. Wardour Street Music Library. Established in 1909, it is claimed as the world's largest library of " ready-canned " film music. The music is used mainly for commercial, advertising and specialised short films.

DOUGLAS, ROY. Composer. Born at Tunbridge Wells, 1907. A musician of widely varied experience both as a composer and as an executant, Roy Douglas has had a very varied career as an orchestral player for every type of keyboard instrument, including the piano, celesta, harpsichord, Novachord, and most types of organ from the humble Mustel to those of Queen's Hall and the Albert Hall, much of this work having been with the London Symphony Orchestra. His compositions include several chamber music works for rather unusual combinations of instruments. In addition, he has done a great deal of arranging and orchestrating for the radio, for the recording theatre and for the stage. For ballet, Douglas has produced several transcriptions and orchestrations, and as an orchestral player, has played the solo piano parts for a number of modern ballets at their first English appearance, including works by Poulenc, Auric and Konstantinov, also " Petrouchka." He entered films in 1932 as a backroom boy, orchestrating and transcribing scores of all types in collaboration with the various composers, and it was not until 1942 that we find him scoring films on his own. Since then he has been responsible for the music of a number of documentaries and feature films, including *All For Norway* (Strand, 1942), *Seeds And Science* (Strand, 1943), *Voyage To Freedom* (Strand, 1943), *Candlelight In Algeria* (British Aviation Pictures, 1943), *The Bells Go Down* (Ealing, 1943), *Night And Day* (Verity, 1944) and *Central Front Burma* (Gryphon-Verity, 1945).

DRAKE, TED. Music Recordist. *School for Secrets*, *Great Expectations*, *Green For Danger*, *Carnival* (part only) and *Hungry Hill*, all in 1946 at Denham. Before joining the studios at Denham, he was with the Variety Department of the B.B.C.

EASDALE, BRIAN. Composer. Born in Manchester, 1909. He was educated at the Royal College of Music, where he gained the Foli Scholarship for composition. In 1931 he gave a concert of his own works with Herbert Murrill at Wigmore Hall, London, and at Florence a concert of music by English composers in 1934. He has composed music for the theatre, including Eugene O'Neill's play " Mourning Becomes Electra " (1937), and has written a piano concerto, some orchestral music and two operas. His film music has been for documentary, including work for the G.P.O. and Crown Unit. In 1937, *Big Money* (G.P.O. Unit) and *Kew Gardens* (Short Film Prods.) ; *Men In Danger* (G.P.O. Unit, 1939), and *Ferry Pilot* (Crown Unit, 1942), also *Job In A Million* (G.P.O. Unit, 1937), *Health In Industry* (G.P.O. Unit, 1938) and *Spring Offensive*.

ELLIS, VIVIAN. Composer and Song Writer. He has contributed songs to a number of films such as *Jack's The Boy* (Jack Hulbert), *Men Are Not Gods* (London Films, 1936) and *Piccadilly Incident* (Herbert Wilcox, 1946).

EVANS, DAVID MOULE. Composer. Born in 1905, and studied composition under Herbert Howells at the Royal College of Music, where he gained the Mendelssohn scholarship. After leaving the College, he devoted most of his time to teaching, and it was not until 1941 that he was able to devote himself wholly to composition. His works include an overture " The Spirit of London " (which has had a number of broadcast performances as well as public concert hall interpretations) and a number of other orchestral works as well as a trio for flute, oboe and piano, and a " Divertimento." He has composed for a number of documentary films, including music for the R.A.F. newsreel *The Gen, London,* 1942 (Greenpark Films, 1942), *Make Fruitful The Land* (Greenpark Films, 1944), *National Health* (Technique).

FAGAN, GIDEON. Composer and Music Director. Born in South Africa, he came to England in 1922 to the Royal College of Music, and from 1927 onwards was writing music for the theatre. He has appeared as guest conductor of the B.B.C. Orchestra in London, and at the outbreak of World War II, he became conductor of the B.B.C. Orchestra in Manchester, where he worked for three years. When James Fitzpatrick came to England to produce films in Britain for Metro-Goldwyn-Meyer in 1936, Fagan became music director to the unit. The first production was *David Livingstone* ; the tone poem " Ilala," written in 1941, is founded on themes which the composer originally wrote for this picture. Next came *Auld Lang Syne, Last Rose Of Summer* and *The Captain's Table*, all in 1936, for which Fagan either composed or arranged the music. There followed three interesting films in a series known as *The Music Masters*. They consisted of half-hour pictures on Chopin, Lizst and Rossini ; Fagan arranged the music in each case. Finally, comes two films in the series for which James Fitzpatrick is most famous, namely, *Traveltalks* ; they were *Quaint Quebec* (music arranged from Canadian folk tunes) and *Highlights Of Capetown* (for which Fagan composed the music). Since then he has frequently been associated with Ernest Irving on various scores for Ealing Studio productions as assistant music director.

FEHER, FREIDRICH. Composer and Music Director. *The Robber Symphony* (1936).

FERBER, ALBERT. Composer and Concert Pianist. *The Hangman Waits* (Five Stars Production, 1947).

FOLEY, ADRIAN. Composer and Song Writer. *The Butler's Dilemma* (Song : " Romance ") (British National Films, 1944).

FORESYTHE, REGINALD. Composer. He has written music for two R.A.F. Film Unit productions.

FOSS, HUBERT. Composer. Born in Croydon, 1899. His musical education consisted mainly of private study. He is well-known in musical circles, his main connection with films being through William Walton and Ralph Vaughan Williams. He has so far scored only one film, an Army training short *The Sergeant Was A Corporal* (World Wide).

FOULDS, J. H. Composer. Born in Manchester, 1880, died in Calcutta, 1939. At 14, he was a member of a theatre orchestra, then for ten years he was in the Hallé Orchestra. Later, under Richter's direction, he conducted stage music and made regular Continental visits for opera experience, composing all the time a great deal of music for the stage. During World War I, he organised weekly concerts for the Forces, and in 1918, became musical director for the London

Central Y.M.C.A., giving Saturday orchestral concerts and lectures. In 1921, he was conductor of the University of London Musical Society. He composed music for films at one time, including *So This Is Lancashire* and *Northern Summer*, both for Strand Films in 1935.

FRANKEL, BENJAMIN. Composer and Music Director. Born in London, 1906. He studied composition and pianoforte at the Guildhall School of Music under R. Orlando Morgan. Then he went on to the Trinity College of Music to study the violin with Mark Greenfield, followed later by private study in Cologne and Berlin (with Victor ‚Benham). He has had a long period of association with film music in this country and has specialised in the lighter type of scoring, being one of our leading experts in the jazz and comedy score. His list of films includes : *Radio Parade Of* 1935 (British International Pictures, 1934), *Public Nuisance No.* 1 (Cecil Films, 1936), *Love In Exile* (Capitol Films, 1936), *The Singing Cop* (Warner Bros., 1937), *No Monkey Business* (G.F.D., 1937), *Music Hath Charms* (British International Pictures, 1937), *He Found A Star* (John Corfield, 1943), *They Met In The Dark* (Marcel Hellman, 1944), *Flight From Folly* (Warner Bros., 1944), *The Great Circle* (Shell Film Unit, 1944), *Bon Voyage* (Phœnix Films-M.O.I., 1944), *The Fire Of London* (Phœnix Films-M.O.I., 1945), *The New Teacher* (Crown Film Unit, 1945), *Macbeth* and *Julius Caesar* (British Council, 1945), *The Seventh Veil* (Sydney Box, 1945), *The Broad Fourteens* (Crown Film Unit, 1945), *The Years Between* (Sydney Box, 1946), *A Girl In A Million* (Sydney Box, 1946), *Dear Murderer* (Betty Box, 1947).

FULTON, NORMAN. Composer. He has written music for documentary productions, including the R.A.F. Newsreel *The Gen* and the industrial film *Optics* (1945).

GALLIARD, MARIUS FRANCOIS. Composer. French composer. He scored one G.P.O. Unit production called *Forty-Million People*. In 1947 he scored *The Convict Has Escaped* (Riverside).

GAY, NOEL. Composer and Song Writer. Born in Wakefield, Yorkshire, 1898. He has received an extensive musical education as the following impressive list of letters indicate : " R.M. Armitage, M.A., Mus.Bac. (Cantab), F.R.C.O., A.R.C.M." After considerable experience as an organist at the Chapel Royal, St. Anne's, Soho, and Christ's College, Cambridge, Noel Gay eventually found fame as a writer of music and song for the stage and the screen. Among the stage successes for which he wrote are " Charlot's Show of 1926," " Clowns in Clover," "Hold My Hand," " Me and My Gal " " Light Up " and many others. His first contribution to films was in 1930—*Tondeleyo* (" White Cargo.") Then in 1932, *Soldiers Of The Queen* (Gaumont) and *Sleepless Nights* (British International Pictures, 1934) ; thence up to the last few years with songs and music for the Arthur Askey film *I Thank You* (Gaumont), the film of the stage show " Me and My Girl," which was retitled *The Lambeth Walk*, Tommy Handley's film *Time Flies*, and two Ealing Studio films *Let's Be Famous* (1939) and *Champagne Charlie* in 1945. He also wrote songs for *Sailors Three* (Ealing) and *Let The People Sing* (British National).

GERALDO. Dance Band Leader and Musical Director. *Laugh It Off* (British National, 1940).

GIBBS, C. ARMSTRONG. Composer. *Lorna Doone*.

GIFFORD, HARRY. Composer and Song Writer. He has written songs for George Formby films, including *Come On George* and *Let George Do It* (both Ealing films).

GOEHR, WALTER. Composer. Walter Goehr came to England from Austria in 1933 as musical director for H.M.V. and Columbia after a good deal of film work on the Continent, including a number of Julien Duvivier's early French films. He has composed a great quantity of chamber, piano and orchestral music, and is well-known as a concert hall conductor. He is known to radio listeners as " George Walter,". and as the conductor of his own orchestra " The Orchestre Raymonde." Some of his film scores are also credited under the name of George Walter. His music for radio includes the feature programmes " The Harbour Called Mulberry," " Radar " and " Marching On." Film music includes incidental music for the Gaumont-British News, the scores to *The Ghost Train* (Gainsborough, 1941), *For Freedom* (Gaumont-British, 1940) and most recently *Great Expectations* (Denham and Pinewood, 1946). He has conducted a number of film recording sessions, including *A Canterbury Tale* (Archers, 1944), *The Volunteer* (Archers, 1944), *I Know Where I'm Going* (Archers, 1945) ; the music for these films was written by Allan Gray.

GOLDSBOROUGH, ARNOLD. Conductor. Well-known concert hall conductor. He conducted the choir and orchestra for the dubbed version of the Russian film *Volga-Volga* (Mosfilm, Moscow, 1940 ; dubbed in England, 1945), and appeared in the part of an Italian conductor in the Sydney Box film of 1945 *The Seventh Veil.*

GOOSSENS, EUGENE. Composer. Born in London, 1893. He is a member of a famous musical family that includes Leon Goossens, first oboist of the Queen's Hall Orchestra at the age of 17, and Sidonie and Marie Goossens, both well-known harpists. He studied at Bruges Conservatoire, Liverpool College of Music, and the Royal College of Music in London. He first made his name as a concert violinist ; later he was associated with the Carl Rosa Opera, The National Opera Company, Sir Thomas Beecham and the Russian Ballet. He left England in 1934 and became conductor of the Symphony Orchestra of Rochester, N.Y., toured the States as a guest conductor, and lately has been conductor of the Cincinnati Orchestra, having settled permanently in America. He was associated with the early British sound cinema, collaborating on a number of film scores, including *The Constant Nymph* (1932, Victoria Hopper).

GOUGH, JOHN. Composer. Born in Tasmania, 1903. He came to London and studied under R. Vaughan Williams at the Royal College of Music. He has written music for short films, including the R.A.F. newsreel *The Gen.*

GRAY, ALLAN. Composer. Born in Poland. He studied music on the Continent, and later was musical director for some time to Max Reinhardt. Since coming to England, he has been responsible for the music in several Shakespearian productions, and many radio and stage successes. He has written for films in many Continental countries as well as in England ; his pictures include : *The Challenge, Marriage Of Corbal, Emil And The Detectives, No Reply From F.P.1, The Countess Of Monte Cristo, School For Husbands, Secrets Of Stamboul, First Offence, Latin Quarter* (British National, 1945), *Christmas Week-End* (Columbia-British, 1946) ; he is music writer to the Archers Film Unit, scoring most of the films made by director Michael Powell in recent years, including *The Volunteer* (Archers, 1943), *The Life And Death Of Colonel Blimp* (Archers, 1943), *A Canterbury Tale* (Archers, 1944), *The Silver Fleet* (Archers, 1943), *I Know Where I'm Going* (Archers, 1945), *A Matter Of Life and Death* (Archers, 1946) and *This Man is Mine* (Columbia, 1946).

GREEN, PHIL. Composer. *The Magic Bow* (" Romance," based on a theme by Paganini, first performed at the Royal Albert Hall in May, 1946). Gainsborough, 1946.

GREENWOOD, JOHN. Composer. Born in London, 1889. He was musically educated at the Royal College of Music, where he held a scholarship in composition. He studied under Stanford, and on leaving the College, he wrote extensively, frequently conducting his own works with such orchestras as the B.B.C. Symphony, London Symphony and the National. His works include two symphonies, symphonic poems, chamber music, songs, a ballet, etc. He has also written a great deal of film music, and a list of his pictures includes the following titles : *To What Red Hell, Stranglehold, The Sleeping Cardinal, At The Villa Rose, Alibi, A Tale Of Two Cities, Prison Without Bars, Twenty-One Days* (1939), *The Drum* (London Films, 1937), *Elephant Boy* (London Films, 1937), *Man Of Aran* (Robert Flaherty, Gaumont, 1933), *East Meets West* (1936), *The Constant Nymph* (with Eugene Goossens ; Gaumont, 1933), *Contraband* (1940 ; in collaboration with Richard Addinsell), *A.1 At Lloyd's* (Strand, 1940), *Pimpernel Smith* (British National, 1941), *Wavell's* 30,000 (Crown, 1942), *The Lamp Still Burns* (Leslie Howard, 1942), *The Gentle Sex* (Leslie Howard, 1943), *Painted Boats* (Ealing, 1945), *Nine Men* (Ealing, 1943), *San Demetrio* (Ealing, 1944), *They Knew Mr. Knight* (G.H.W. Prods., 1944), *Men Of Rochdale* (Verity, 1945), *Switchover* (Verity, 1945), *Hungry Hill* (Denham, 1946), *Frieda* (Ealing, 1947).

GREVILLE, URSULA. Composer. *The Key To Scotland* (Strand, 1935).

GRUN, BERNARD. Composer. *All That I Have* (Peak Films, 1947).

HAMBOURG, MARK. Concert Pianist. World-famous concert pianist. Appeared in the British National film *The Common Touch*, playing the first movement of the Piano Concerto No. 1 by Tchaikowsky. He also recorded for the film *Let The People Sing*.

HESS, MYRA. Concert Pianist. Myra Hess studied pianoforte under Tobias Matthay at the Royal College of Music, and afterwards gained a world-wide reputation as a concert pianist, taking part in tours in England, Holland, France, Germany, Austria, Hungary, Canada, America, and so on. She was closely connected with the organisation of the famous series of lunch-time concerts in the National Gallery in London. In 1936 she was awarded the C.B.E., and in 1941, became a Dame of the British Empire (D.B.E.). She appeared in the documentary films *Listen To Britain* (1942) and *Diary For Timothy* (1946), both made by the Crown Film Unit and featuring her in the hall of the National Gallery. From material shot for *Diary For Timothy*, a special short film entitled *Myra Hess* was issued in 1946.

HODGSON, W. Music Director. *This Is England* (G.B.I., 1935), *Nursery Island* (G.B.I., 1936), *Strength And Beauty* series (six films made by G.B.I., 1937), *As We Live* (G.B.I., 1937), *Where Love Is, God Is* (G.B.I. religious film, 1937), *They Made The Land* (G.B.I., 1938), *Flashbacks* (history of the film : C. B. Cochran, 1938), *Defeat Of The Germans Near Moscow* (Soviet Film Agency, 1943).

HOLLINGSWORTH, JOHN. Music Director. Born in London, 1916. He was educated at Bradfield College and at the Guildhall School of Music in London. He directed his first concerts with the London Symphony Orchestra at the age of 23. With the coming of World War II, he joined the R.A.F. in 1940, where he became associate conductor to the newly-formed Royal Air Force Symphony Orchestra in conjunction with Squadron-Leader R. P. O'Donnell. With this organisation he toured extensively, both in this country and in America, during which he was able to study closely the methods of recording film music as used in Hollywood as a result of a visit by the R.A.F. Orchestra to that city. In 1945, he flew with the Orchestra to Potsdam for three concerts given before the delegations of the Three Power Conference, which included Winston Churchill, President Truman and Marshal Stalin. Since demobilisation, he has directed concerts with all the leading music groups in the country, including the B.B.C. His first work for films was in 1942 when he conducted the R.A.F. Orchestra in the recording of the Leighton Lucas score for *Target For To-night* (Crown Film Unit : recorded

207

at Warner Bros. Studio in Teddington). Then in 1944, he conducted the music for *Cornish Valley* (Greenpark ; music by Leonard Isaacs) and *Crofters* (Greenpark ; music by Dennis Blood), in 1945 *Burma Victory* (Army Film Unit ; music by Alan Rawsthorne), *Tackling A Problem* (Army Film Unit ; music by John Bath), *Ship Busters* (R.A.F. Unit ; music by Leighton Lucas), *Farmer's Boy* (Greenpark ; music by Dennis Blood) and *Three Cadets* (Greenpark ; music by Frederick Bayco). In 1946, *The Voice Within* (Grand National ; music by John Bath), *Children On Trial* (Crown Unit ; music by Clifton Parker), *The Way From Germany* (Crown Unit ; music by Elizabeth Lutyens), *A Soldier Returns*. His introduction to the feature film music world was made by Muir Mathieson, to whom he became assistant musical director in 1945 ; he collaborated with Mathieson on the music for *Brief Encounter* (music by Rachmaninoff) and *Jungle Mariner* (music by Elizabeth Lutyens). More recent scores he has conducted include *Hausa Village* (music by Temple Abady, 1946), *The Glen Is Ours* (music by John Bath), *Aircraft Carrier* (Paul Rotha ; music by Kenneth Pakeman), *Pool Of Contentment* (C.O.I. ; music by John Bath), all in 1946, *Boy Builders* (Crown, 1947 ; music by Temple Abady), *Pacific Hitch-Hike* (Paul Rotha ; music by Kenneth Pakeman, 1946), *North-East Corner* (Greenpark ; music by Kenneth Pakeman, 1947), *The Three A's* (Crown ; music by Temple Abady, 1947). He also carried out the extensive musical research for the Sydney Box production *Life Of Melba* (1947), and conducted the music for *The Silver Darlings* (A.B.P.C., 1947).

HOLST, GUSTAV. Composer. Born 1874. Died 1934. The famous composer of the " St. Paul's Suite " and " The Planets " wrote the music for *The Bells*, produced at Wembley in about 1931 by Associated Sound Film Industries. George Burgess (who recorded the score) says that Gustav Holst showed a remarkable and speedy insight into the requirements of music for the screen in this one score that he did for pictures shortly before he fell ill and died.

HONEGGER, ARTHUR. Composer. Born in Le Havre, France, 1892, of Swiss parents. He studied music in the Conservatories of Zurich and Paris, and came into prominence as a member of " Les Six," the modernist French group of composers that included two other film music men, Auric and Milhaud. Honegger is known for his often violently modernistic and unusual works, such as " Pacific 231," a locomotive tone poem based on music written for a film, and " Rugby," a tone poem on that most rigorous of ball games. His work for the cinema in France has been extensive and includes such Gallic classics as *Les Misérables*, *Rapt*, *Cessez Le Feu*, *L'Idée*, *Crime Et Châtiment*, *Mademoiselle Docteur*, *Harvest*, *L'Equipage* and the well-known Charles Boyer-Danielle Darrieux romance *Mayerling*. In 1938 he wrote an excellent score to the British film *Pygmalion*, produced by Gabriel Pascal and directed by Anthony Asquith from the play by G. B. Shaw.

HUGHES, KEN. Music Arranger. Born in Liverpool, 1922. In 1938, he became a sound technician at Gaumont-British, and in 1940 was on the " features and drama " staff of the B.B.C., where he arranged background music for the first 500 performances of " Front Line Family," the famous overseas programme that later became " The Robinson Family." In 1942, he became music advisor to Spectator Films, a director with Verity in 1943, and a writer-director with World Wide in 1944. He is a specialist in the construction of musical backgrounds made up of ready existing music such as gramophone records and music library material. Films he has fitted tracks to include : *London Scrapbook*, *Free French Navy*, *Little Ships Of Britain*, *The Freedom Of Aberfeldy* and *Clyde Built* in 1942 ; *Catholics In Britain* and *Soho* in 1943 ; *Tyneside Story* in 1944 ; *Housing in Scotland* and *Our Enemy Japan* in 1945 ; *Strategy In The South West Pacific* in 1946. Nine of these productions were for the Ministry of Information.

HUGHES, SPIKE. Composer. *Fiddlers Three* (Ealing, 1944).

HELY-HUTCHINSON, VICTOR. Composer. Born in Capetown, South Africa, 1901. He developed early, and at 9, a volume of his compositions was published under the title "A Child's Thoughts." He was educated at Eton, Oxford and the Royal College of Music, became for a time a member of the staff of the B.B.C., and in 1934, became Professor of Music in the University of Birmingham. He is a Doctor of Music (Oxon.). He has written effective compositions, orchestral and other, usually in a cheerful vein. He is the present music director of the B.B.C. His film work has so far been for documentary : *Battle Of Supplies* (Strand, 1942), *New Zealand* (Crown, 1945), *Camouflage Airview* (Verity, 1945), *Teeth Of Steel* (Technique), *The Gen* (R.A.F. newsreel), *When We Build Again* (Strand, 1944), *The Call Of The Sea, South Africa* (Crown, 1944).

HYDEN, WALFORD. Composer. A specialist in Spanish music. He scored *Caravan* (Gainsborough, 1945). Born at Hanley, Staffordshire in 1892, he has contributed music to a number of films, including one based on his famous radio programme " Café Collette," and a large-scale industrial film on rayon.

IRELAND, JOHN. Composer. Born at Bowdon, Cheshire, 1879. His youth was spent in a literary atmosphere, for his parents were both well-known authors, and Carlyle, Leigh Hunt and other men of letters had been family friends. At the age of 14 he went to the Royal College of Music, studying composition under Stanford. He first became known as a composer of chamber music ; he has written for the piano, composed many songs and orchestral works, also the well-known piano concerto. He is a slow and methodical composer, and his output has been fairly small, but has shown great sincerity. For many years he has been asked to write for films, but it is only recently that he has entered the studios for Ernest Irving at Ealing to score the Harry Watt picture *The Overlanders*, made in Australia, and musically interpreted by John Ireland in 1946.

IRVING, ERNEST. Composer and Music Director. Born at Godalming, Surrey, 1878. Ernest Irving is a pioneer of British film music and British theatre music, having devoted a long and active life to composition and conducting of every type of music. After a sound musical education, Irving became associated with the stage. He has been music director of nearly all the West End theatres at one time or another, and has great memories of the days of the Edwardian stage and of the London of forty years ago. He has written music for sixteen plays, including "Hamlet" (modern version), "Twelfth Night," "The Circle of Chalk," "The Two Bouquets" and "Elephant in Arcady." He has musically directed "The Dubarry," "The Immortal Hour," "The Land of Smiles," "The Chocolate Soldier," and "Lilac Time," all in London productions. He has had seasons as a guest conductor at the Odeon and Mogador Palace Theatres in Paris, and at the Comedy in Madrid. He is a member of the Honorary Committee of Management of the Royal Philharmonic Society. He lives at present in a house adjoining Ealing Studios. His extensive knowledge of the great classical composers—Mozart, Handel, Bach, Haydn —is very much in evidence in his choice of music in many of his films, such as the use of Handel's "Water Music" in *Find, Fix And Strike*, or the picture of that composer's life *The Great Mr. Handel*. Irving has been associated with Ealing film studios for well over ten years, and has musically directed all their films during that period. These include : *Nine To Six* (1933), *Autumn Crocus* (1934), *Java Head* (1935), *Death Drives Through* (1936), *The High Breakfast* (Cartoon film, 1937), all the Gracie Fields films made at Ealing Studios, *Return To Yesterday* (1938), *Young Man's Fancy* (1938), all the George Formby films made at Ealing, including *It's In The Air, Come On, George, Let George Do It*, etc., *The Proud Valley* (1939), *The Ware Case* (1938), *There Ain't No Justice* (1938), *The Gaunt Stranger* (1938), *Four Just Men* (1938), *The Foreman Went To France* (1942), *The Great Mr. Handel* (1943), *The Black Sheep Of Whitehall* (1941), *Find, Fix And Strike* (1942), *Went The Day Well?* (1942), *Next Of Kin* (1942), *Convoy*

(1940), *Saloon Bar* (1940), *Nine Men* (1943), *The Bells Go Down* (1943), *Greek Testament* (1943), *Halfway House* (1944), *My Learned Friend* (1943), *Laburnum Grove* (1934), *For Those In Peril* (1944), *San Demetrio, London* (1944), *The Big Blockade* (1942), *Ships With Wings* (1941), *Champagne Charlie* (1944), *They Came To A City* (1945), *Return Of The Vikings* (1945), *Painted Boats* (1945), *Pink String And Sealing Wax* (1945), *Dead Of Night* (1945), *The Captive Heart* (1946), *The Overlanders* (1946), *Hue And Cry* (1946), *The Good Samaritan* (puppet film, 1945), *Nicholas Nickleby* (1946), *The Loves of Joanna Godden* (1947), *Frieda* (1947).

ISAACS, LEONARD. Composer. He has composed the music to a number of short films, including the R.A.F. newsreel series *The Gen* and *Cornish Valley* (Greenpark, 1944).

JACOB, GORDON. Composer. Born in Norwood, London, 1895. He studied at the Royal College under Charles Stanford, Adrian Boult, Vaughan Williams and others, having begun his education on general lines at Dulwich College in 1908. He served during World War I and was a prisoner from 1917-18. Orchestral and chamber music, part songs, and two ballets are included among his compositions, in addition to many orchestral arrangements for the Sadler's Wells Ballet. He is considered an authority on orchestration, and has written a text book " Orchestral Technique " as well as a little guide book to music lovers called " How to Read a Score." He is a Professor of Composition at the R.C.M., and examiner in music in the Universities of London and Wales. Jacob has contributed more than twenty musical arrangements to the B.B.C. show " Itma." He entered films in 1943 with the score to *Before The Raid* (Crown Unit), followed by *Close Quarters* (Crown Unit, 1943), *For Those In Peril* (Ealing, 1944), *Maintenance Command* (R.A.F. Film Unit, 1944), *The Big Pack* (R.A.F. Film Unit, 1944), *On The Face Of It* (Verity Films, 1944), *Journey Together* (R.A.F. Film Unit, 1945), *The Way We Live* (Two Cities, 1946).

JACOBSON, HARRY. Composer and Song Writer. *Fiddlers Three* (Ealing, 1944).

JAUBERT, MAURICE. Composer. Maurice Jaubert scored some of France's most famous films : Rene Clair's *Quatorze Juillet*, two early documentaries *La Vie D'un Fleuve* and *Easter Island, Tarakanova, Quai Des Brumes* (1938), *Bizarre, Bizarre* (1939), *La Fin Du Jour* (1939), *Le Jour Se Leve* (1939), *Pays Du Scalp, Zero De Conduite, Le Dernier Milliardaire* and many others. In 1937, he scored *We Live In Two Worlds* for Cavalcanti, the French director, who came from Paris to join the Post Office Film Unit, and is now a feature film director at Ealing Studios.

JENNINGS, AL. Music Director. *West Indies Calling* (Paul Rotha, 1943).

JOYCE, EILEEN. Pianist. Well-known concert pianist. She has done considerable work for the films, beginning with an appearance in the Strand picture of the story of the London Philharmonic Orchestra *Battle For Music* (1944), followed by a recording for the sound track of the Piano Concerto No. 2 by Rachmaninoff, which was featured in the Noel Coward production of 1945 *Brief Encounter*. It was Eileen Joyce who played the music of Mozart, Beethoven, Grieg and Rachmaninoff for the track of *The Seventh Veil*, in which Ann Todd appeared in the screen portrayal of the psychological study of a concert pianist. In 1946, she recorded the Arthur Bliss music to *Men Of Two Worlds*, which includes a remarkable film piano concerto. Finally, in *A Girl In A Million*, she makes a screen appearance, playing César Franck's Symphonic Variations (Sydney Box, 1946).

KENTNER, LOUIS. Concert Pianist. Sound track recordings for *Dangerous Moonlight* (Denham, 1942).

KING, FRANK. Music Director. *Sweethearts Forever* (Empire Films, 1945).

KING, HAROLD. Music Recordist. Born in Nottingham, 1907. He entered films with British Lion in 1928 during the last days of the silent films, but at the beginning of talkies, he was for a short while associated with British International Pictures. However, in 1930, he went back to British Lion Films, where he was in charge of the sound department up to 1940. Next came two pictures for Grand National, and in the middle of 1940, King became recording director for British National Films, where he now does all the music recording. Harold King is one of the country's leading music recordists, and has been responsible for the music track of a very large number of films. His own method is that of using only the minimum of microphones and arranging his orchestra so as to give correct balance. He says : " To record a piece of music successfully, the first and most important factor is to know the piece of music. To do this, one listens direct to the band rehearsing and studies the score." In addition, Harold King suggests that " to study the composer is very helpful," as in this way you " get to know his style." Among his recent film music recordings are the following British National pictures : *In The Rear Of The Enemy, Let The People Sing, Salute John Citizen, Those Kids From Town, Love On The Dole, The Common Touch* (featuring the recording of Mark Hambourg playing the Tchaikowsky Piano Concerto No. 1), *Twilight Hour, Strawberry Roan, The World Owes Me A Living, The Agitator, Murder In Reverse, The Trojan Brothers, Waltz Time, The Lisbon Story* and many other films.

LAMBERT, CONSTANT. Composer and Conductor. Born in London, 1905. He was trained at the Royal College of Music, since when he has been closely associated with ballet in particular, and also with the world of musical journalism and composition. In 1925 and 1927 he was commissioned to write ballets for Diaghilef, while to-day, he is musical director for· the Sadler's Wells organisation in London, recently conducting for the ballet seasons at Covent Garden. His vivid and original " Rio Grande " for Chorus, Pianoforte and Orchestra (1929), with its strong jazz influence, is his best known earlier composition. He has published a book entitled " Music Ho ! A Study of Music in Decline " (1934), and he wrote the foreword for Kurt London's book " Film Music," published in 1936. However, he has so far only scored one film *Merchant Seamen*, made by the G.P.O. (later Crown) Film Unit in 1940. It was recorded on the film sound track by the Sadler's Wells Orchestra, conducted by the composer. In 1943, the music from the film was presented during a large-scale pageant at the Royal Albert Hall in shortened form as a suite in three movements : " Fanfare," " Safe Convoy " and " March : Merchant Seamen." It became popular, and in October, 1943, the full version of the suite was given its first performance by the London Philharmonic Orchestra in Bristol, consisting of five movements : " Fanfare," " Convoy in Fog," " The Attack," " Safe Convoy " and " March : Merchant Seamen." In this form it has received many public performances in all parts of the country. The work is dedicated to the orchestras of the Royal Marines. Lambert appeared in *Battle For Music* (1944) conducting the London Philharmonic Orchestra.

LAW, EDGAR. Music Recordist. Entered films in 1929 on the staff of Western Electric, working on various sound installations in this country and in France. He was on music and dubbing at Denham from 1936-1937, and recorded music for *Wings of the Morning, Southern Roses, Elephant Boy, Fire Over England, Farewell Again, Under The Red Robe, Moonlight Sonata, Knight Without Armour* and *Rembrandt*. Law was with Paramount News from 1937 to 1944, when he became chief recordist to Merton Park Studios, recording music for such documentaries as *Flying With Prudence, Steel, Men of Rochdale, Mosquito, Crofting, Fenlands* and *Jean's Plan*. In 1946 he was appointed in charge of dubbing and scoring at Sound City studios.

LEEVERS, NORMAN. Music Recordist. As head of a company that specialises in providing music " ready canned " for use in short films, Norman Leevers has recorded a great deal of music designed for use with films, and in some cases, has played a large part in fitting the music track to the picture. During the last ten years, the company has recorded sound tracks for nearly 3,000 films, practically all of which have included music recording. Norman Leevers has recorded library music for Boosey & Hawkes, the Royal Netherlands Government, the Polish Government, Ace Distributors, Halas-Batchelor Cartoons, Anson Dyer Cartoons and Inspiration Pictures. In the course of this work he has supervised music recording at his own studio in Wardour Street, and at a large number of well-known halls, including the Cambridge Theatre, the Scala Theatre, Kingsway Hall and Unity Theatre, using his own specially designed mobile unit.

LEIGH, WALTER. Composer. Born in Wimbledon, 1905. Died in the Middle East, 1942. Walter Leigh studied at Cambridge and later in Berlin with Hindemith, also a screen music writer. His music includes piano works, songs, jazz, a sonata for violin and piano (International Music Festival, 1932), and a comic opera " The Jolly Roger," performed in Birmingham and London in 1933. He entered films with the G.P.O. Film Unit, and was responsible for a number of their scores. One of his earliest jobs, *Song Of Ceylon*, is a classic amongst film music annals, and pointed the way to much of the initial experiment in music and the documentary film. Other scores of his are 6.30 *Collection* (G.P.O. Unit, 1934), *Dawn Of Iran* (Strand, 1937), *Face Of Scotland* (Realist, 1938), *Work-A-Day* (advert. film), *The Fourth Estate* (Paul Rotha, 1940) and *Squadron* 992 (Crown Unit, 1940). Walter Leigh was killed in action with the Tank Corps in the Libyan campaign during the summer of 1942.

LESLIE-SMITH, KENNETH. Composer and Song Writer. *The Rugged Island* (Jenny Brown, 1934).

LEVY, LOUIS. Composer and Musical Director. Born in London, 1893. Louis Levy is a pioneer of the early silent film days, and has devoted almost his whole life to film music. He started his career in 1910, arranging and performing music for silent pictures, and in 1916, he became musical director at the New Gallery Cinema in London. In 1921, he went to the Shepherd's Bush Pavilion as music chief, and it is said that Louis Levy was the first man ever to develop the theme song in pictures, back in the silent days. Later, America adopted the idea, and a great flood of theme song films were a feature of the first three or four years of Hollywood talking pictures. At the beginning of talkies, he joined the Gaumont-British Studios at Shepherd's Bush, where he is still to-day the head of the music department for all Gainsborough productions. In his capacity as music director, he has been responsible for all the films made there, and runs a kind of music " casting bureau " whereby composers are brought in to score the type of pictures that suit their particular style. Amongst the composers that have been associated with Levy are Hubert Bath, Hans May, Bretton Byrd, Leighton Lucas, Jack Beaver, Bob Busby, Cedric Mallabey, Walford Hyden and many others. The films for which Levy has been music director include : *Sleeping Car* (1933), *Waltzes From Vienna* (1934), *Car Of Dreams* (1935), *The Thirty-Nine Steps* (1935), *Road House* (1934), *Tudor Rose* (1936), *The Tunnel* (1935), *King Of The Damned* (1936), *Seven Sinners* (1936), *First Offence* (1936), *It's Love Again* (1936), all the Jack Hulbert, Jessie Matthews, Will Hay and Alfred Hitchcock films made by Gainsborough, *Nine Days A Queen* (1936), *Doomed Cargo* (1936), *Secret Agent* (1936), *Head Over Heels In Love, Evergreen, Hey, Hey, U.S.A.* (1937), *King Solomon's Mines* (1937), *Good Morning, Boys* (1937), *Oh, Mr. Porter* (1937), *Convict* 99 (1938), *The Citadel* (1938), *Follow Your Star* (1938), *Alf's Button Afloat* (1938), *Pot Luck* (1938), *The Lady Vanishes* (1938), *Old Bones Of The River* (1938), *Pygmalion* (1938), *The Frozen Limits* (1939), *Ask A Policeman* (1939),

To The Victor (1938), *Sailing Along* (1938), *Spare A Copper* (1940), *An Englishman's Home* (1940), *For Freedom* (1940), *I Thank You* (1941), *Kipps* (1941), *The Ghost Train* (1941), *Cottage To Let* (1941), *Hi, Gang!* (1941), *We Shall Rise Again* (1941), *King Arthur Was A Gentleman* (1942), *Uncensored* (1942), *The Young Mr. Pitt* (1942), *The Adventures Of Tartu* (1943), *Millions Like Us* (1943), *Dear Octopus* (1943), *The Man In Grey* (1943), *We Dive At Dawn* (1943), *Miss London, Limited* (1943), *It's That Man Again* (1943), *Fanny By Gaslight* (1944), *Bees In Paradise* (1944), *Time Flies* (1944), *Give Us The Moon* (1944), *2,000 Women* (1944), *Love Story* (1944), *Madonna Of The Seven Moons* (1944) ; the following are films shown in 1945 : *Waterloo Road, A Place Of One's Own, They Were Sisters, The Wicked Lady* ; in 1946 : *Caravan, Bedelia, The Root Of All Evil*. He was associate producer to *I'll Be Your Sweetheart* (1945).

LONDON, KURT. Kurt London is a musician, technician and writer. He studied philosophy, music and literature in Berlin, Heidelberg, Wurzburg and Freiburg. In the early twenties, he entered the world of film criticism and film music in Germany, becoming chief editor of " Der Film " in 1929, and in 1932 with the aid of Siemens, he established a microphone Institute for sound film, radio and gramophone. He also composed music for German films. In 1933 he left for Paris, coming to London in 1935, where his book " Film Music " was published in 1936 by Faber & Faber. Born in 1899, he has studied film music in all parts of Europe, and his book has become the standard textbook on the subject of film music in many parts of the world ; numerous quotations from it appear in this present work. Kurt London is at present living in Washington, U.S.A. Eloquent comment on the extent of his perception and grasp of film music problems is given by the fact that although his volume is now ten years old, and the film industry is one of the most rapidly progressive of all the fields of entertainment, the vast majority of Kurt London's writings remain as true to-day as when they were first written in Paris in 1935.

LUCAS, LEIGHTON. Composer. Born in London, 1903. Largely self-taught from a musical point of view, Leighton Lucas has spent a life-time of composing, conducting and ballet dancing. He was with Daighilef's Russian Ballet as a solo dancer when still a boy, and has been closely connected with ballet ever since ; at present he is working on music for a new ballet production. He has conducted the B.B.C. Orchestra, was for a time conductor and choreographer to the Birmingham Reportory Opera Company, and for some years was conductor of the Arts Theatre Ballet. During the war, he served with the R.A.F., and has recently formed his own orchestra. He has written a good deal of incidental music for the radio, including music for the radio version of " Just William." He entered films soon after the beginning of sound, his first full score being for the film *Hyde Park Corner* (Grosvenor Films, 1934). For over three years he was associated with Louis Levy at the Gaumont-British Studios, working on *The Ghoul, Waltz Time* (with Evelyn Laye), *Britannia of Billingsgate, The Cardinal* (with Mathieson Lang), and on a number of Jessie Matthews and Jack Hulbert films made by Gaumont. Later, he went on to other forms of composition, and did little film work up to 1942, apart from a few documentaries such as *The Key To Scotland* (Strand, 1935). On joining the R.A.F., he wrote the score to the Crown Film story of the R.A.F. *Target For To-night*. Other wartime documentaries include *A Date With A Tank* (Army Unit, 1945), *Pacific Thrust* (Greenpark Films, 1944), *Ship Busters* (R.A.F. Film Unit, 1945), while his most recent score is for *We Of The West Riding* (Greenpark Films, 1946).

LUTYENS, ELIZABETH. Composer. *Jungle Mariner* (Crown Film Unit, 1944) and *The Way From Germany* (Crown Film Unit, 1946).

MACKEY, PERCIVAL. Composer and Music Director. Born in London, 1894. Percival Mackey began his career as a dentist, but at a very early age his deep interest in music took charge and he set out on tour with a one-man act as accompanying pianist. The act included ventriloquist interludes, conjuring, comedy material—and an item that was a great novelty in those days, the showing of a film, for which Mackey, aged 14, provided the music. This early show was a dangerous affair, the projector being run on top of a pile of old boxes right in the middle of the audience, and two large gas cylinders stuck behind to provide the incandescent illumination. And the pianist got 2/6 a week, plus keep ! At the age of 18, he went to Ireland, where he toured with the Royal Irish Animated Picture Company with a three-piece band, accompanying a touring film show. Following this, he did four years in the army during World War I, and was wounded in France. For a time he was engaged in organising army concert parties. Up to the coming of the sound film, he worked in many cinema orchestras, eventually forming his own dance band and making a large number of gramophone records. For a time he was an orchestrator with Jack Hylton's band. His first talkie score was for the Gracie Fields film made in 1931 called *This Week Of Grace*, for which Harry Parr-Davies composed the song hits. In the same year he scored *These Charming People* for Paramount-British, followed by music for the first film made by Alexander Korda in this country, *Service For Ladies*, with Leslie Howard. Since then he has musically directed, orchestrated and composed for a very large number of films ; among them are included the following titles : *Girls Please* (British and Dominions, 1931), *Stamboul* (Paramount-British, 1931), *This Is The Life* (British Lion, 1934), *Death At Broadcasting House* (Phœnix Films, 1934), *While Parents Sleep* (British and Dominions, 1935), *Cheer Up* (Gaiety Films, 1935), *S.O.S.* (1935), *Honeymoon For Three* (Gaiety Films, 1935), *Charing Cross Road* (British Lion, 1935), *Talk Of The Devil, Silent Passenger* (Phœnix Films, 1936), *Accused* (Criterion Films, 1936), *Chick* (Leslie Howard : British and Dominions, 1936), *Crime Over London* (Douglas Fairbanks, Jun. : Criterion Films, 1936), *Skylarks, Lightning Conductor* (Gordon Harker), *Make Up* (Standard International Films, 1937), *Jump For Glory* (Douglas Fairbanks, Jun. : Criterion Films, 1937), *Minstrel Boy* (Butchers, 1937), *Sam Small Leaves Town* (Stanley Holloway : Grand National Films, 1937), *Lily of Laguna* (Butchers Films, 1937), *Old Mother Riley In Paris* (Butchers Films, 1938), *This Man Is News* (Pinewood Studios, 1938), *A Spot Of Bother* (Clapham and Dwyer, 1938), *Almost A Gentleman* (Butchers Films, 1938), *Mountains Of Mourne* (Butchers Films, 1938), *Anything To Declare* (Butchers Films, 1938), *Night Journey* (1938), *Missing People* (1939), *Music Hall Parade* (Butchers Films, 1939), *You Will Remember* (Jack Raymond Productions, 1940), *Sailors Don't Care* (Butchers Films, 1940), *Somewhere In England* (Butchers Films, 1940), *Danny Boy* (Butchers Films, 1941), *Facing The Music* (Butchers Films, 1941), *Gert And Daisy's Week-end* (Butchers Films, 1941), *Jailbirds* (Butchers Films, 1940), *Garrison Follies* (Butchers Films, 1940), *Pack Up Your Troubles* (Butchers Films, 1940), *Front Line Kids* (Butchers Films, 1941), *Sheep Dog Of The Hills* (Butchers Films, 1941), *Bob's Your Uncle* (Butchers Films, 1941), *Hard Steel* (G.H.W. Productions, 1941), *The Mind Of Mr. Reeder* (Jack Raymond Productions, 1939), *Somewhere In Camp* (Butchers Films, 1942), *Somewhere On Leave* (Butchers Films, 1942), *The Missing Million* (Jack Raymond Productions, 1942), *The Rose Of Tralee* (Butchers Films, 1942), *Gert And Daisy Clean Up* (Butchers Films, 1942), *Old Mother Riley Overseas* (British National, 1943), *Variety Jubilee* (Butchers Films, 1942), *Demobbed* (Butchers Films, 1943), *Somewhere In Civvies* (Butchers Films, 1943), *In The Bag* (Butchers Films, 1943), *Up With The Lark* (Renown Films, 1943), *Headlines* (John Corfield Productions, 1943), *Kiss The Bride Goodbye* (Butchers Films, 1944), *I'll Walk Beside You* (Butchers Films, 1944), *Meet Sexton Blake* (British National, 1944), *Night Of Magic* (Premier Films, 1944), *The Echo Murders* (British National, 1945), *Don Chicago* (British National, 1945), *Old Mother Riley At Home* (British National, 1945), *What Do We Do Now ?* (Grand National, 1946), *Loyal Heart* (British National, 1946), *Under New Management* (Butchers Films, 1946), *Home Sweet Home* (Butchers Films, 1945).

MALLABEY, CEDRIC. Composer. *The Man In Grey* (Gainsborough, 1943), *Fanny By Gaslight* (Gainsborough, 1944).

MARLY, ANNA. Composer and Song Writer. *Dead Of Night* (song : " Hulla-looba," Ealing, 1945).

MATHIESON, JOHN. Music Director. Brother of Muir Mathieson, John Mathieson has recently returned from service in India with the army. He is now an assistant to Ernest Irving at Ealing Studios.

MATHIESON, MUIR. Music Director. Born in Stirling, Scotland, 1911. Muir Mathieson first began to conduct with the Stirling Boys' Orchestra when 13 years old and did his first B.B.C. broadcast at this time. Then he got the Leverhulme and Boult Scholarships and studied at the Royal College of Music. After leaving the College, he began to work as assistant musical director for Alexander Korda at the age of 20. At 21 he went to Canada with the ballet and conducted there. One night, during a performance of " Hiawatha " at the Royal Albert Hall, Dr. Malcolm Sargent, who was conducting, was taken ill after the second act. " I had to take over and conduct for the remainder of the performance," says Muir ; " I was very young then and was lucky enough to continue conducting for the rest of the season." He has conducted many programmes for the B.B.C., for a number of operettas in London, for the ballet and the opera, and for numerous concert performances with most of our national orchestras. His films are : *The Private Life Of Don Juan, The Ghost Goes West, Conquest Of The Air, The Scarlet Pimpernel, The Thief Of Baghdad, Wings Of The Morning, The Spy In Black, Q Planes, Fire Over England, Elephant Boy, Things To Come, Sanders Of The River, Wharves And Strays, The Gannets, Vessel Of Wrath, Old Bill And Son, St. Martin's Lane, On The Night Of The Fire, The Four Feathers, A Royal Divorce, Sixty Glorious Years, The Rat, Victoria The Great, Prison Without Bars, Over The Moon, The Challenge, The First And The Last, The Divorce Of Lady X, Under The Red Robe, Action For Slander, Storm In A Teacup, Farewell Again, South Riding, Dark Journey, The Return Of The Pimpernel, The Drum, Paradise For Two, Four Dark Hours, The Squeaker, Knight Without Armour, Men Are Not Gods, Rembrandt, Forget Me Not, The Man Who Could Work Miracles, Moscow Nights, Catherine The Great, The Turn Of The Tide, They Flew Alone, Dangerous Moonlight, Major Barbara, Gaslight, 49th Parallel, Wavell's 30,000, Love On The Dole, Men Of The Lightship, The Lion Has Wings, Contraband, A Day Will Dawn, First Of The Few, Green Girdle, War Front, Pimpernel Smith, Escape To Danger, Squadron Leader X, The Flemish Farm, We Sail At Midnight, The Gentle Sex, Close Quarters, Fires Were Started, The Demi-Paradise, The Yellow Canary, Power In The Highlands, In Which We Serve, Henry V, Hotel Reserve, Tawny Pipit, Britain At Bay, Before The Raid, Christmas Under Fire, Coastal Command, Factory Front, Ferry Pilot, Heart Of Britain, Letter From Ulster, Listen To Britain, Britain Can Take It, Malta G.C., Merchant Seamen, North Sea, The Silent Village, Target For To-night, Big City, New Britain, Spring Offensive, Squadron 992, Scotland Speaks, Ulster, This Is Colour, The Siege Of Tobruk, Teeth Of Steel, The People's Land, Wales, The W.R.N.S., The Big Pack, This Happy Breed, R.A.F. Regiment, Desert Victory, Second Freedom, Steel, The Gen* (R.A.F. newsreel), *The Call Of The Sea, Camouflage, Troopship, We Serve, Highland Doctor, The True Story Of Lili Marlene, Western Approaches, The Lamp Still Burns, Freedom Radio, Quiet Wedding, This England, Penn Of Pennsylvania, On Approval, The Way Ahead, Caesar And Cleopatra, Blithe Spirit, Perfect Strangers, Our Country, Stricken Peninsula, The Rake's Progress, Journey Together, The Seventh Veil, Brief Encounter, Great Day, Acacia Avenue, The True Glory, Tunisian Victory, To-day And To-morrow, The Years Between, A Girl In A Million, Men Of Two Worlds, Burma Victory, School For Secrets, Hungry Hill, Odd Man Out, Daybreak, The Upturned Glass, The Brothers, Instruments Of The Orchestra.* Muir Mathieson has made two personal appearances on the screen as a conductor when he was seen with the London Symphony Orchestra in *The Seventh Veil* and *A Girl In A Million.* He directed the film *Instruments Of The Orchestra*, featuring the London Symphony Orchestra conducted by Dr. Malcolm Sargent.

MAY, HANS. Composer and Music Director. Born in Vienna, 1891. His musical education was carried out at the Academy of Music in Vienna, where he studied under Auton Door in pianoforte, and Richard Hauberger for composition. At the age of 10, he gave his first public piano recitals, and by the age of 18, he had qualified as a conductor. Touring as a conductor of the operatic world, he travelled extensively from Berlin to Cairo and Istanbul. He was one of the earliest of film music pioneers, being associated with the " Kinothek," a catalogued library of music used for the musical accompaniment to silent films, which was originated by Giuseppe Becce in 1919. Becce was an Italian musician, who set up this first attempt at organised film music in Berlin, and it was in this connection that Hans May arranged the music for over a thousand silent films, in addition to composing hundreds of special pieces for early pre-talkie film scores. Amongst these, the most important were those written for the German presentation of the Russian silent " classic " *Panzerkreuzer Potemkin* and for the silent version of *Midsummer Night's Dream.* His work for films continued after the change-over to sound, and in 1930 he scored *Flame Of Love* (featuring Anna May Wong), followed by *Bridegroom Widow* in 1931, both for British International Pictures. These were his first British scores and since then Hans May has provided music for well over a hundred Continental and English films ; among them are included the following titles : *The Lilac Domino, My Song Goes Round The World, A Star Fell Out Of Heaven, Viennese Waltz, Give Her A Ring, Radio Parade, How's Chances, Student's Romance, Everything In Life, Southern Roses, Ein Leid Geht Um Die Welt, Mademoiselle Docteur* (English version), *I Killed The Count* (1939), *La Paradis Perdu* (1939), *We Will Rise Again* (1942), *The Stars Look Down* (1939), *Thunder Rock* (Boulting Brothers, 1942), *It's That Man Again* (Gainsborough, 1942), *Candlelight In Algeria* (British Aviation Pictures, 1944), *2,000 Women* (Gainsborough, 1944), *Waltz Time* (British National, 1945), *The Trojan Brothers* (British National, 1945), *Murder In Reverse* (British National, 1945), *The Wicked Lady* (Gainsborough, 1945), *Twilight Hour* (British National, 1944), *The World Owes Me A Living* (British National, 1945), *Latin Quarter* (British National, 1945), *Madonna Of The Seven Moons* (Gainsborough, 1944), *Uncensored* (Gainsborough, 1943), *Backroom Boy* (Gainsborough, 1942), *Mayerling* (Charles Boyer : French film), *The £100 Window* (Warners, 1944), *The Lisbon Story* (British National, 1946), *Salute The Soldier* (1945), *Flying Dutchmen* (1945) and *R.A.F. Over Europe* (1944), *Bedelia* (Gainsborough, 1946), *The Laughing Lady* (British National, 1946), *Springsong* (British National, 1946), *Woman To Woman* (British National, 1947).

MELACHRINO, GEORGE. Composer. Dance band leader and composer, he recently scored and musically directed the British National film *Appointment With Crime* (1946).

MENON, NARAYANA. Instrumentalist. Expert on Indian music. He has worked with the music side of the B.B.C. Indian Service. In 1945, he provided the score for the Merton Park film *19-Metre Band*, an experiment in background and feature music involving a synthesis of East and West in music never before attempted.

MENUHIN, YEHUDI. Concert Violinist. Born in New York, 1916. He began to learn on a miniature violin at the age of 3, and made his first public appearance at a Young People's concert organised by the San Francisco Symphony at the age of 7. Two years later he appeared with full orchestra in a performance of Lalo's " Symphonie Espagnole," and in 1927, at the age of 10, he played the

Beethoven Violin Concerto with the New York Symphony Orchestra, followed a few weeks later by a grand Carnegie Hall recital. This resulted in a world-famous series of concerts in Europe and America, including a memorable occasion with the Berlin Philharmonic under Bruno Walter, playing concertos by Bach, Beethoven and Brahms. He made his London debut playing the Brahms Concerto with the London Symphony Orchestra, followed by an Albert Hall recital. Thus was launched the spectacular career of the infant prodigy of the violin. In 1934 came a world tour, including concerts in Australia and the Antipodes, but in 1936, Menuhin retired from all public performances for two years, which were spent with his family in California. At the age of 20 he returned to the world platforms in a further series of concert hall performances. In 1945 he came to England to record music for the Gaumont-Gainsborough film *The Magic Bow*, in which Stewart Granger takes the part of Paganini on the screen, with Yehudi Menuhin doubling for him on the sound track.

MEWTON-WOOD, NOEL. Composer and Concert Pianist. Famous concert hall pianist. He wrote the music for *Tawny Pipit* (Two Cities, 1944).

MEYER, H. ERNST. Composer and Special Sound Effects Expert. Born in Berlin, 1905. He went to classical school in Berlin and studied music, musicology, philosophy and acoustics in Berlin and Heidelberg. His teachers included Hanns Eisler, famous film music composer now living in America, and Paul Hindemith, film music expert, in whose film music class at the Microphone Experimental Department of the Berlin State Academy Meyer studied. He came to England in 1933, and began here as a musical journalist, composer, teacher and lecturer, giving various University music lecture courses and running classes for the W.E.A. In addition, he worked as a choral conductor, wrote a book on the history of instrumental music in England, and composed many songs (largely political and anti-Fascist) as well as a good deal of chamber music. He entered films in 1937 in association with Cavalcanti and the G.P.O. documentary film unit. Since then he has been closely associated with various documentary units, with the M.O.I. and the Admiralty during the war, and with Len Lye, the cartoonist, and Halas-Batchelor during the last two years. Meyer has done a great deal of unique work in the use of sound effects, including the study and practise of surrealism in sound, and the recording of " Orchestrated Sound " in such films as *A Few Ounces A Day* (Paul Rotha, 1941), and *When The Pie Was Opened* (Paul Rotha, 1941). He has carried out various dubbing jobs for Russian films as well as a great deal of musical scoring and editing. In addition to composing the music, conducting at the recording sessions, recording and operating special sound effects, and collaborating on the production of numerous cartoon films, he also does a good deal of his own film editing. He is a great believer in the value of film music as a means of bringing the musician into close contact with reality, as when he went to sea with the fishing fleets and lived in the homes of the fishing community before scoring for the film *North Sea* (G.P.O. Unit, 1938). His pictures are many and include : *Roadways* (Cavalcanti-G.P.O. Unit, 1937), *The Londoners* (Realist, 1938), *British Made* (G.P.O. Unit, 1939), *Oil From The Earth* (Shell Film Unit, 1939), *Musical Posters, Lambeth Walk* and *Colour Flight* in conjunction with Len Lye (for the British Council and Imperial Airways), *Point Of View*, series Nos. 1 and 2 (Spectator Films, 1939), *Collective Adventure* (Jewish Agency for Palestine, 1940), *Ship Control* (for the Admiralty), *When The Pie Was Opened* (Paul Rotha, 1941), *A Few Ounces A Day* (Paul Rotha, 1941) *Mobilise Your Scrap* (M.O.I., 1941), *Filling The Gap* (Realist, 1942), *Work Party* (Realist, 1942), *Newspaper Train* (Realist, 1942), *Subject For Discussion* (Ministry of Health, 1943), *Tanya* and *Volga-Volga* (Re-recording and dubbing of Soviet films, 1944), *Cameramen At War* (Realist, 1944) and *Lady Nicotine* (Grand National, 1945).

MILHAUD, DARIUS. Composer. Born in Aix-en-Provence, 1892. In 1910 he went to the Paris Conservatoire, where he studied under Gedalge, Widor and D'Indy. In 1919 he joined " Les Six," the group of French composers representing the modernist trends in music, influenced by the music of Erik Satie and by the aesthetics of Jean Cocteau. This group included two other film music composers, Auric and Honegger. In 1941, Milhaud went to America, being active in composition, conducting and presentation of his own music. He was associated with the cinema from 1924 onwards. His scores include *Actualites* (1928), *L'Inhumaine*, *Madame Bovary* (Jean Renoir, 1934), *L'Hippocampe* (" Sea Horses " by Painleve, an experimental film), *Tartarin De Tarascon*, *Voix D'Efants*, *Mollenard* (1938) and *Days Of Hope*. He also scored one G.P.O. Film Unit production—*The Islanders*.

MILNER, CECIL. Composer. He has provided orchestration for about 35 films; and composed music for about 20, usually in collaboration with other composers. Composition contributions include : *Bank Holiday*, *The Lady Vanishes*, *Hey, Hey, U.S.A.*, *The Citadel*, *They Drive By Night*, *Inspector Hornleigh*, *So This Is London*, *A Window In London*, *Good Old Days*, *Murder Will Out*, *Confidential Lady*, *Dressed To Kill*, *Hoots Mon*, *The Midas Touch*, *Two For Danger*, *George And Margaret*, *Busman's Honeymoon*, many of these being in collaboration with Bretton Byrd, who was responsible for the main score, but received additional items from Cecil Milner. Milner scored the two documentaries *Down At The Local* and *Some Like It Rough*, with Clive Richardson in 1944.

MOISEIWITSCH. Pianist. Famous concert hall pianist. He appeared with the London Philharmonic Orchestra in *Battle For Music* (Strand Films, 1944).

MUNRO, RONNIE. Composer. Well-known B.B.C. personality. *The Warning* (British National : A.R.P. Film, 1939), *Laugh It Off* (British National, 1939) and *Meet The Navy* are amongst the films on which he has worked.

NOBLE, PETER. Composer and Song Writer. *My Learned Friend* (song " You Do Things to Me." Ealing, 1941), and a musical film *Walking On Air* (Goodman Films, 1946). Peter Noble is the well-known writer and journalist who wrote " British Film Yearbook " and other volumes on the film, stage and music world which form companion volumes to this book.

O'DONNELL, R. P. Music Director. Wing-Commander R. P. O'Donnell is director of music to the Royal Air Force, and has been advisory music officer to the R.A.F. Film Unit at Pinewood, occasionally conducting at recording sessions. *Sportsmen All* series (John Betts Productions, 1937-38), *Spirit Of The Service* (R.A.F. Film Unit).

PAKEMAN, KENNETH. Composer. *Aircraft Carrier* (Paul Rotha, 1946), *Pacific Hitch-Hike* (Paul Rotha, 1946), *North-East Corner* (Greenpark, 1947), *October Man* (Two Cities, 1947).

PALMER, KING. Composer. *The Production Of High Quality Steel* (Verity, 1945).

PARKER, CLIFTON. Composer. Born in London, 1905. He has spent a life-time as an orchestral player, composing and orchestrating in every type of music. It was not until the outbreak of war, however, that he turned his attention to films, his first score being for the picture *It Started At Midnight*, originally titled *The Good Soldier Schweik* and based on the book of that name. There followed the Herbert Wilcox feature *The Yellow Canary* (R.K.O. Radio-British, 1943), then *Battle Is Our Business* (" Into Battle " series No. 3, Spectator Films, 1944), *Western Approaches* (Crown Film Unit, 1944), *Steam* (1945, documentary short film), *Acacia Avenue* (Sydney Box, 1945), *Johnny Frenchman* (Ealing, 1945),

Perfect Strangers (M.-G.-M. British, 1945), *Beyond The Pylons* (1945) and *Towards The Offensive, Mine Gapping, Conversation Piece, Jungle Patrol* (all made at Pinewood for the R.A.F. and Army Film Units), while his most recent films include the score for the Crown Film Unit production *Children On Trial* (1946), *The Man Within* (Sydney Box, 1947) and *The Silver Darlings* (Holyrood Productions, 1947).

PARR-DAVIES, HARRY. Composer. Famous song writer of many hit tunes. He has frequently written special numbers for British films, including *This Week Of Grace* (Twickenham Studios, 1931) and other Gracie Fields films, *It Happened One Sunday* (Welwyn Studios, 1944), *Sailors Three* (Ealing, 1942), *Lisbon Story* (British National, 1946).

POSFORD, GEORGE. Composer. *The Good Companions* (Gainsborough ; collaborated on the score), *Hi, Gang!* (song : " It's a Small World." Gainsborough, 1942), *Don Chicago* (British National, 1945), *Gaiety George* (Warner Bros., 1946).

RAWSTHORNE, ALAN. Composer. Born at Haslingden, Lancashire, 1905. He intended to become a dentist at first, but later went to the Royal Manchester College of Music, studying piano, 'cello and composition. Next, he went abroad for four years, continuing his training with Egon Petri. On his return he became a teacher at Dartington Hall and musician to the School of Dance-Mime there. In 1938, he had a work for two violins played in London at the Festival of the International Society of Contemporary Music, and has since composed a number of concert hall works. His film scoring dates from 1937 (when he did a short film for the Shell Unit), but it was during the war period that his music in films came to the fore. Pictures to note are *The City* (G.P.O. Film Unit, 1939), a set of films scored while he was in the army—*Tank Tactics, United States, Street Fighting* and the feature *Burma Victory*. After " demob," he did *The Captive Heart* (Ealing Studios, 1946) and *School For Secrets* (Two Cities, 1946).

RAYBOULD, CLARENCE. Composer. Professor of Music at the Guildhall School of Music in London, Clarence Raybould was one of the first composers to write original scores for British documentary films. In 1933 he scored the Paul Rotha production *Rising Tide* (Empire Marketing Board Film Unit, re-issued in 1935 as *Great Cargoes*) and *Contact*, also by Paul Rotha, made for Imperial Airways at about the same time. His other scores include *Flight To India* and *Where The Road Begins* (Steuart Films, 1933). Raybould has since left films to make a name for himself in other fields of music.

REYNDERS, JOHN. Composer and Music Director. John Reynders, usually with his own orchestra, has supplied music for a number of travel and interest films. These include : *Facts And Figures* (Central Film Productions), *High Hazard* (Stanley Watson) and *Father Thames* (Peter Collen) in 1935 ; in 1936 the following pictures : *The Dragon Of Wales* (W. B. Pollard Productions), *In Search Of Gold* (H. L. Sheridan Productions), *The Seventh Day* (A. P. Barralet), *Bassetsbury Manor* (Cyril Jenkins), *Elephant City* (A. P. Barralet), *Fire Fighters* (Peter Collen) and *Happy Hampstead* (Fairfax-Pearce Productions), and *Grey Seal* (Bury Productions, 1937). He conducted the British International Picture Orchestra for the recording of Hubert Bath's score to the first British all-talking film *Blackmail* (Alfred Hitchcock).

RHIND, AL. Music Recordist. *Steel Goes To Sea, Queen Cotton, Looking Through Glass, Teeth Of Steel, Switchover, National Health, Steel, Battle For Music.*

RICHARDSON, CLIVE. Composer. Famous as an arranger of music to such radio programmes as Tommy Handley's " Itma," he has contributed compositions, orchestrations and special arrangements to films : *Some Like It Rough* and *Down*

At The Local (with Cecil Milner), *It's That Man Again* (film version), *Woman In The Window, George And Margaret* (1938), *French Without Tears* (in collaboration with Nicholas Brodszky), *Miss London Limited* (Gainsborough, 1943), *Oh, Mr. Porter* (Gainsborough : Will Hay), *Convict 99* (Gainsborough : Will Hay), *Alf's Button Afloat* (The Crazy Gang ; Gainsborough), *Two For Danger, Strange Boarders, Sailing Along* (Jessie Matthews) and *Those Were The Days* (Max Miller).

ROFE, ESTHER. Music Director. *Duchy Of Cornwall* (Strand, 1938).

ROYLS, ERNEST. Music Recordist. Chief sound and electronics engineer to Warner Bros. First National Productions in England. He was for four-and-a-half years with the B.B.C. in the pioneer days of broadcasting, being on the engineering staff of the Liverpool and Manchester stations. In 1928 he left the B.B.C. to enter the field of sound pictures. For six-and-a-half years, he was with the Western Electric Company prior to joining Warner Bros. First National Productions, Ltd., in 1936. Since then he has been their sound supervisor, and has co-operated with a number of music directors in experimental work designed to improve the recording technique of British film music. It was Ernest Royls who recorded the music for *Flight From Folly* in a garage, following the destruction of Teddington Studios by a flying bomb. It was during the making of *Flight From Folly* that an unusual system of producing echo effects was worked out by Royls. A scene called for a deep, reverberating voice, but the normal methods of echo effect did not satisfy the sound chief. So powerful loudspeakers were directed down the shafts of the main drainage installation and microphones placed over manhole covers in other parts of the studio picked up the sound as it echoed through the myriad of tunnels and pipes below ground. The effect was perfect. However, an unexpected problem arose. Far away from these experiments, the sound recordists on Stage I were puzzled to find music rising up as if by magic from underground, making it impossible to shoot dialogue. Not until they heard about Royls' experiments did they realise the " music from nowhere " was actually coming from a grill in the studio which led to the main drainage system. Some of the best sound tracks of the buzz bomb were made by Ernest Royls. Two of them cut-off at a point which sounds directly overhead ; " I was inside the recording van, and could see nothing," says Royls. " I heard them cut-off in my headphones and just sat at the control panel, still recording, and waiting for the crash that might blow us all to blazes. It was very hectic, but we got our sound tracks, and they were later broadcast and sent over to the States." The buzz bomb sounds, along with some church bell recordings, were sent to the Warner Bros. studio in Hollywood with a message to Jack Warner from " Doc " Salomon, the studio manager at Teddington. He recorded his message in the afternoon with Ernest Royls, and stayed on to work late in his office. That evening a flying bomb scored a direct hit on the plant, and " Doc " Salomon was killed outright. Royls arrived two or three minutes afterwards to find the studio in flames ; he should have been there earlier, but his train was held up from London. He is now engaged in supervising the acoustical design of the new sound stages being built at Teddington, and also looking after the sound side of the alterations and repairs being carried out on studios at Elstree belonging to his company. For this, he has conducted a series of special tests on the sound-absorbent qualities of various materials, and has made an extensive study of the properties of rock wool, used for sound-proofing in most modern studios. His hobby is amateur radio transmission, and he operates his own telephony station G.3Q.R. He recorded the music for *The Briggs Family, That's The Ticket, George And Margaret, Two For Danger, Fingers, The Prime Minister, Atlantic Ferry, This Was Paris, Flying Fortress, The Peterville Diamond, The Night Invader, The Dark Tower, The £100 Window, They Met In The Dark, One Exciting Night, Mr. Emmanuel, Great Circle, Candlelight In Algeria, To-morrow We Live, Flight From Folly* and many others.

ROZSA, MIKLOS. Composer. Born in Budapest, Hungary, 1907. After receiving his early training in Budapest, he entered the Leipzig Conservatory at the age of 18, and soon had a number of his chamber music works published. In 1931, he came to Paris, where he stayed for four years, and in 1935, arrived in London for the production of his Hungarian Ballet. It was in 1936 that he scored his first film *Knight Without Armour* (London Films, 1936), and since then, he has remained closely associated with the cinema. His scores for Alexander Korda at Denham Studios include : *Thunder In The City* (1936), *The Squeaker* (1937), *Divorce Of Lady X* (1937), *Four Dark Hours* (1937), *The Four Feathers* (1938), *South Riding* (1938), most of which were made by London Films at Denham. In addition : *U-Boat* 29 (1939), *Ten Days In Paris* (Joseph Somlo, 1939) and *The Thief Of Baghdad* (London Films, 1940). Continuing his association with Alexander Korda, Rozsa went to the United States in 1941 to score *Lady Hamilton* and *Jungle Book*, both made by Alexander Korda in Hollywood. In 1943 he wrote the music for Zoltan Korda's picture *Sahara*, and since then has remained in Hollywood, scoring many American films : *Sundown* (Walter Wanger, 1942), *Lydia, So Proudly We Hail, To Be Or Not To Be, The Hour Before Dawn, Five Graves To Cairo, The Man In Half Moon Street, Woman Of The Town, Double Indemnity, Dark Waters, Blood On The Sun, The Lost Weekend, Lady On A Train, Spellbound* and the Chopin film *Song To Remember*, for which he wrote the incidental music. His music to the film *Jungle Book* was issued on gramophone records by the R.C.A.-Victor Company in America as an album set, and was the first American film music ever to receive such recognition. In 1938 he was awarded Hungary's highest musical honour, the " Francis Joseph Prize " for composition, and in 1943, he was awarded the citation of merit by the National Association for American Composers and Conductors for outstanding service to American music during the season 1942-43. The music to *Spellbound* has also been issued in the States on records, and has received a lot of radio performances both here and over there.

RUSSELL, KENNEDY. Composer and Music Director. *Laugh It Off, Dreaming, Heaven Is Round The Corner, Give Me The Stars, The Common Touch, Let The People Sing, Those Kids From Town, Theatre Royal, The Dummy Talks, Salute John Citizen, Asking For Trouble, Crooks Tour, The Shipbuilders* and *What Would You Do Chums* ? all made by British National Studios at Elstree.

RUSSELL, THOMAS. Orchestral Player. Well-known as a member-organiser of the London Philharmonic Orchestra, Russell appears in *Battle For Music* (Strand Films, 1944). He has written an account of the filming of the L.P.O. in his book " Philharmonic Decade."

SARGENT, MALCOLM. Conductor. World-famous conductor, born in 1895, and associated with almost every musical organisation in the country. He has had a number of connections with the film industry, notably for a picturisation based on the opera " Carmen," in the film story of the London Philharmonic Orchestra *Battle For Music*, and in the Crown Film Unit production of 1946 *Instruments of the Orchestra*, based on a composition by Benjamin Britten (from a theme by Purcell) and directed by Muir Mathieson.

SAUNDERS, MAX. Composer. Born in New Zealand, he came to England in 1932 and has since done a good deal of orchestration and arranging for film scores. His pictures include *Battle Of Britain* (M.O.I., 1944) in collaboration with Hubert Clifford.

SCHROEDER, KURT. Musical Director. Opera conductor from the Continent, Schroeder was associated with Alexander Korda at the beginning of London Film Productions. He scored *Stambul* on the Continent in 1932, and handled the music for the famous British success *The Private Life Of Henry VIII* (London Films, 1933).

SEIBER, MATYAS. Composer. Born at Budapest, Hungary, 1905. He studied at the Royal Academy of Music in Budapest, taking lessons in composition under Zoltan Kodaly. From 1928-33 he was professor at Hoch Conservatory in Frankfurt. In 1935 he came to live in England. He has made a special study of folk music, sixteenth century lute music and modern jazz. His composition includes orchestral, piano and chamber music. His first film score was written in 1938 for *Paper People Land*, made by Cyril Jenkins. Since then he has specialised in cartoon and short films, working as composer to the Halas-Batchelor British cartoon unit in Soho Square. His films include : in 1943, *Coupon Hearers*, *Abu Zeid And The Dungeon*, *Abu Zeid And The Poisoned Well* and *Abu Zeid's Harvest* ; in 1944, *Abu Zeid Builds A Dam*, *Good King Wenceslas*, *Six Little Jungle Boys* ; and in 1945, *The Big Top* and *Old Wives' Tales*. All these were for Halas-Batchelor Films. In 1945, he scored *Job For The Future* (Merlin Films) and in 1946 wrote the music for a Technicolor cartoon *The Magic Canvas* (Halas-Batchelor).

SELLICK, PHYLLIS. Pianist. Concert pianist. She recorded the piano part for the score of *49th Parallel*.

SEWELL, B. C. Music Recordist. Born in Lowestoft, 1910. He entered the film industry at the beginning of talkies, and was with British and Dominions Film Corporation from 1930-35. He then went to Pinewood Studios where he was engaged partly on re-recording, and partly on the investigation and control of the technique of sound film processing. After ten years' experience thus gained on the Western Electric Sound System, he joined the Gainsborough Studios at Shepherd's Bush in December, 1939, where he became sound supervisor to the British Acoustic Sound System which is used for all Gainsborough pictures. During this period, Sewell has been responsible for the recording of the music in the following films : *The Young Mr. Pitt* (1941), *Uncensored* (1942), *The Ghost Train* (1941), *Kipps* (1941), *Cottage To Let* (1941), *Back Room Boy*, *We Shall Rise Again*, *It's That Man Again* and *King Arthur Was A Gentleman* in 1942, *Miss London Limited*, *The Adventures Of Tartu*, *We Dive At Dawn*, *The Man In Grey*, *Millions Like Us*, *Dear Octopus* (all in 1943), *Bees In Paradise*, *Fanny By Gaslight*, *Time Flies*, *Give Us The Moon*, *2,000 Women*, *Love Story* and *Madonna Of The Seven Moons* in 1944, *Waterloo Road*, *A Place Of One's Own*, *They Were Sisters*, *I'll Be Your Sweetheart*, *The Rake's Progress* and *The Wicked Lady* in 1945, in 1946 *Remember The Unicorn*, *Caravan*, *The Magic Bow* and *Root Of All Evil*, and in 1947 *The Man Within* and *The Brothers*.

SHEPHERD, HORACE. Composer and Music Director. He has made musical arrangements for a large number of short films, mainly for Inspiration Pictures. He composed " Triumph of Empire " for the film *A Musical Masquerade*, in which Shepherd conducted the London Symphony Orchestra.

SHERWIN, MANNING. Composer and Song Writer. Born in Philadelphia, 1910. He composed music for a number of shows in New York, and later went to Hollywood under contract to Paramount, where he composed for the following films : *Stolen Holiday*, *Blossoms On Broadway* and *Swing, Teacher, Swing*. In 1938, he wrote songs for *Vogues Of 1938* (Wanger). He came to England in 1938 and since then has been extensively engaged on compositions for the British screen and stage. Among the films are : *A Girl Must Live* (Gainsborough), *He Found A Star* (Corfield), *Hi, Gang!*, *King Arthur Was A Gentleman*, *Miss London, Limited* and *Bees In Paradise*, all for Gainsborough. In 1945 he composed songs for *I'll Be Your Sweetheart* (Gainsborough).

SOWANDA, FELA. Composer and Music Director. Composer, music director, well-known organist and African music expert, Sowanda has contributed to a number of Colonial Office films, being responsible for the special African music tracks on such productions.

SPEAR, ERIC. Composer. A B.B.C. producer, Eric Spear has contributed music to a number of films, including the Warner Bros. British musical made at Teddington in 1944 *Flight From Folly*. He also scored the documentary *The Mosquito* (Merton Park Films for De Havilland Aircraft, 1945).

SPOLIANSKY, MISCHA. Composer. Born in Bialystok, Russia, in 1898. He received his first tuition in piano and composition at the age of 5. He grew up in a musical background, the youngest of three children, his brother, a 'cellist, his sister a pianist, and his father an opera singer. Later he came to Europe, where he continued his studies, meeting the celebrated theatrical producer Max Reinhardt, who commissioned Spoliansky to write music for one of his productions. This was the beginning of his career as a composer for the theatre and the films. He is famous for his Paul Robeson songs in *Sanders Of The River* (1935) and *King Solomon's Mines* (1936); in 1943 he gave a recital of his own film music in London. Other films include : *The Lucky Number* (1932), *Tell Me To-night* (Anatole Litvak, 1933), *My Song For You* (1934), *The Private Life Of Don Juan* (London Films, 1934), *The Ghost Goes West* (London Films, 1936), *Over The Moon* (London Films, 1938), *Jeannie* (Hellman, 1941), *Talk About Jacqueline* (M.-G.-M. British, 1942), *Secret Mission* (Harold French, 1943), *Mr. Emmanuel* (Two Cities, 1944), *Don't Take It To Heart* (Two Cities, 1944), *The Man From Morocco* (Associated British, 1945), *Song Of The People* (Horizon Films, 1945), *Fiddlers Three* (Ealing, 1944), *Wanted For Murder* (Excelsior, 1946), *Meet Me At Dawn* (Excelsior-Twentieth Century, 1947) and *Temptation Harbour* (Associated British Picture Corporation, 1947).

STEVENS, BERNARD. Composer. *The Upturned Glass* (Sydney Box, 1947).

STEVENS, C. C. Music Recordist. Born in Andover, 1907. Educated at Andover Grammar School, at Mill Hill School, and at the City and Guilds (Eng.) College. He worked for the International Telephone and Telegraph Laboratories in London and Paris, and in 1930, joined the staff of the Paramount Studios in Paris where he recorded his first film music. Since then he has been at the British and Dominion Studios and at Pinewood from 1932-37, and at Denham Studios from 1937 onwards, where he is now chief production mixer. He has been connected with two Academy nominations for sound recording; in 1939 for the sound recording of *Goodbye, Mr. Chips,* and in 1943 for the special sound effects for *One Of Our Aircraft Is Missing.* The films for which he has recorded the music (as distinct from the production and floor recording) are : *Bitter Sweet* (1934), *Dreaming Lips* (1936), *The Street Singer* (1937) and the recording of the Bach Toccata and Fugue in *A Canterbury Tale* (Archers, 1944). Academic qualifications : A.C.G.I., B.Sc., A.M.I.E.E.

STONE, LEW. Composer and Music Director. Lew Stone, well-known dance band leader, was composer and music director for the Jack Hulbert production *Under Your Hat,* filmed in 1939.

SULIKOKSKI, J. Musical Arranger. *Scottish Mazurka* (Seven League, 1943).

TAUSKY, VILEM. Composer. Polish composer. Scored the film *Seven Years* for Crown Unit.

TOCH, ERNEST. Composer. *Catherine The Great.*

TOYE, GEOFFREY. Composer and Music Director. Born in 1899, he studied at the Royal College of Music and made his debut as a musical director when he conducted "The Blue Bird" at the Haymarket Theatre. Later he conducted works at the Savoy Theatre and Queen's Hall. After war service, he entered Lloyd's and there revived the Lloyd's Operatic Society and founded the Lloyd's Choir. He became a director of the Royal Philharmonic Society, and in 1925, a Governor of the Old Vic and later of Sadler's Wells. Two of his ballets were performed there successfully—" Douanes " and " The Haunted Ballroom." In 1932 he was appointed managing director of Covent Garden and organised two seasons of opera in collaboration with Sir Thomas Beecham. He was responsible at that time for the modernisation of the Royal Opera House, and arranged the appearance of Grace Moore at Covent Garden in " La Boheme." For several seasons he was musical director and advisor to the D'Oyly Carte Opera Company and became the foremost authority in the country on the Gilbert and Sullivan operas. It was Toye who first secured the film rights of these operas, and he was responsible for the artistic preparation of the film scenario of *The Mikado*, the Technicolor film which he musically directed at Denham in 1939. His first film work was as composer and conductor of a special music score for British Movietone's " Coronation " film. Other film scores of his include the Charles Laughton film *Rembrandt* and *Men Are Not Gods*.

TRITTON, NORMAN. Composer. *Let's See* (Merton Park, 1945).

TRYTEL, W. L. Music Recordist. As head of a company specialising in the provision of " ready canned " music for short films, W. L. Trytel has recorded a considerable amount of picture music, and in many cases has fitted the tracks to the film as well. An example of his work is the film *Boys Of The Old Brigade* (Butchers, 1945).

TURNER, JAMES. Composer. *Candlelight In Algeria* (British Aviation Pictures, 1944).

VALE, WALTER. Composer. *For All Eternity* (Strand, 1935 : with Greville Cooke).

VINTER, GILBERT. Composer. *Story Of Omolo* (Crown Film Unit).

WALSWORTH, IVOR. Composer. Born in London, 1909. He studied at the Royal Academy of Music under film composer William Alwyn, and while at the Academy, some of his work was performed at the Promenade Concerts by Sir Henry Wood. During this time he won a Macfarren Scholarship, and later his Rhapsodic Dance for orchestra was taken to America by Eugene Goossens as an example of modern English music. He has only recently entered films with scores for a few documentary pictures which include *Papworth Village Settlement* (World Wide for the British Council, 1945), *American Hospitals, Unity Of Strength* and *Star And The Sand*.

WALTER, GEORGE. Composer and Music Director. See under Walter Goehr. The composer and conductor Walter Goehr also uses the name of George Walter. Films for which the music credits have been shown as " George Walter " include *Spellbound, For Freedom* and *The Ghost Train*. These will be found listed under " Walter Goehr " along with the films which appeared with credit titles indicating his real name.

WALTON, WILLIAM. Composer. Born in Oldham, Lancashire, 1902. At the age of 10 he entered Christchurch Cathedral Choir School, and at 15 he passed the first examination for the degree of Bachelor of Music. When 16, he became an undergraduate of Christ Church College, Oxford. To a large extent, Walton was self-taught, but among the musical people who came in contact with him in his early training were Sir Hugh Allen, Ansermet and Busoni. Before the age of 16 he had composed a large number of songs, motets and Magnificats, but it was in 1923 that he first came into prominence as a composer, when a string quartet of his was performed at the Annual Festival at Salzberg of the International Society for Contemporary Music. In the same year came the first public performance at the Aeolian Hall of the work " Facade," still one of Walton's most popular concert hall items. It was originally written as a musical accompaniment to a set of poems by Edith Sitwell; his connection with the Sitwell family has been of long standing, and the three movements of the Sinfonia Concertante, written in 1927 and revised in 1943, are dedicated respectively to Osbert, Edith, and Sacheverell Sitwell. This work is described by Ralph Hill, the well-known music critic, as one of the " most important works for piano and orchestra of our time." Other important music by Walton includes the overture " Portsmouth Point " (first performed at the Zurich Festival of the International Society for Contemporary Music in 1926), " Siesta " (performed at the Aeolian Hall first in 1926), a viola concerto in 1929, a symphony (first performed at the Queen's Hall with the B.B.C. Orchestra conducted by Sir Hamilton Harty in 1935), the Coronation March of 1937 " Crown Imperial," a violin concerto first presented in New York in 1939, and the famous work for orchestra, baritone solo and mixed chorus " Belshazzar's Feast," which dates from 1931. William Walton entered films in 1935 with a score which was written in a very short space of time for the Elizabeth Bergner picture *Escape Me Never*. This was followed a year later by a score to the Shakespearian production made by 20th Century-Fox British Films *As You Like It*. He then left films for the time being, returning again in 1939 for another Bergner picture *Stolen Life*. In 1941, Gabriel Pascal, famous director and producer of *Caesar And Cleopatra* fame, obtained the music for *Major Barbara* from Walton, following which he entered on a period of concentrated work for the films. Thus, in 1942, he scored *Next Of Kin*, *The Foreman Went To France* and *Went The Day Well?* all for Ealing Studios. In 1942 he wrote one of his finest scores; the music to the Leslie Howard picture *First Of The Few*, with its stirring Spitfire Prelude and Fugue. Finally, in 1944-45, he wrote the music for Laurence Olivier's production of Shakespeare's *Henry V*, and as with *First Of The Few*, the music has received concert hall performances. As one of the most promising and significant figures in modern British music, his contribution to films has been of the greatest importance in the development of film·music in this country.

WARRACK, GUY. Composer. Well-known B.B.C. personality, Guy Warrack has composed music for documentary films, including *The Last Shot* (Crown Unit), *A Defeated People* (Crown Unit), both in 1945, and *Theirs Is The Glory* (1946). In *Defeated People* he secured two musical effects that immediately put him in the front rank of documentary composers. To shots of the gutted steel shell of the Krupps Essen factory, the music gives great drama by musically reconstructing the air raid that originally destroyed the plant; one scene shows a conversation between an S.S. man on the run and a British interrogation officer done entirely by music with no actual speech whatsoever. Both items showed considerable imagination by the composer.

WATKINS, A. W. Music Recordist. Born in Kidderminster, 1897. After an extensive educational and technical grounding (Watkins is an A.M.I.E.E., F.R.P.S. and an F.R.S.A.), he entered the film industry in 1928 at the beginning of talkies with the Western Electric Company (as recording superintendent). Two years after he became recording director to the newly-formed London Film Company, and in 1935, he planned the acoustics of the great Denham studios, including the design of the recording stages for music purposes. After fifteen years, he left Denham and the old home of London Films to become recording director to M.-G.-M. British Film Productions, the company founded by the originator of London Films, Alexander Korda. Watkins has recorded the music for, literally, hundreds of films; among them are included: *The Little Damosel* (his first film music recording), *Pimpernel Smith*, *Meet The Tiger*, *Breach Of Promise*, *Unpublished Story*, *They Flew Alone*, *A Day Will Dawn*, *The Way To The Stars*, *The Life And Death Of Colonel Blimp*, *A Canterbury Tale*, *The Great Day*, *Secret Mission*, *Talk About Jacqueline*, *Brief Encounter*, *Beware Of Pity*, *49th Parallel*, *The Four Feathers*, *The Spy In Black*, *The Lion Has Wings*, *The Silent Battle*, *Over The*

Moon, Goodbye, Mr. Chips, A Window In London, Contraband, Wings Of The Morning, The Private Life Of Henry VIII, The Scarlet Pimpernel, The Thief Of Baghdad, Major Barbara, The Ghost Goes West, Conquest Of The Air, Hatter's Castle, Jeannie, Dangerous Moonlight, King Solomon's Mines, One Of Our Aircraft Is Missing, Old Bill And Son, The Arsenal Stadium Mystery, The Citadel, A Yank At Oxford, Catherine The Great, Sanders Of The River, Elephant Boy, In Which We Serve, Service For Ladies, Four Dark Hours, The First And The Last, The Challenge, The Drum, Dinner At The Ritz, He Was Her Man, The Rat, Q Planes, Sixty Glorious Years, Prison Without Bars, That Night In London, On The Night Of The Fire, This Man In Paris, Twenty-One Days, Busman's Honeymoon, Gaslight, The Saint's Vacation, Henry V, The Way Ahead, Perfect Strangers, Men Of To-morrow, Just My Luck, Strange Evidence, Cash, Counsel's Opinion, The Private Life Of Don Juan, Moscow Nights, Things To Come, The Man Who Could Work Miracles, Forget Me Not, Rembrandt, Men Are Not Gods, Love In Exile, Land Without Music, Dark Journey, Storm In A Teacup, Action For Slander, South Riding, Fire Over England, Farewell Again, Under The Red Robe, Victoria The Great, Divorce Of Lady X, Southern Roses, Honour Bright, Love From A Stranger, Dreaming Lips, Moonlight Sonata, Knight Without Armour, The Squeaker, Paradise For Two, The Return Of The Pimpernel, A Call To Arms, Miss Knowall.

WHYTE, IAN. Composer. Born in Dunfermline, 1903. He studied at the Royal College of Music and also on the Continent. He was the first director of music of the Scottish Regional station of the B.B.C., and is an expert on Scottish music of all types. He has remained closely associated with the B.B.C., regularly conducting the B.B.C. Scottish Orchestra. He has written music for documentary films, of which the most well-known are the two Paul Rotha productions *Power In The Highlands* and *Highland Doctor*, made in 1943, and distinguished by Ian Whyte's arrangements of old Scottish folk songs.

WILLIAMS, CEDRIC. Composer. Cedric Williams is a cameraman of documentary films, but he has written music for films, including *The Churchill Tank* (Army Kine Service, 1944).

WILLIAMS, CHARLES. Composer and Music Director. Born in London, 1893. He studied under K. H. Betjemann (of the Royal Academy of Music). Williams has had extensive experience in every type of theatre and picture music, and is well-known as the conductor of the Queen's Hall Light Orchestra. His conducting work for the B.B.C. is familiar, while he has been associated with films since the silent days. He has contributed, either as conductor or composer (or both) to : *Thursday's Child* (Associated British), *Warn That Man* (Associated British), *Medal For The General* (British National), *Kipps* (Gainsborough), *The Young Mr. Pitt* (Gainsborough), *My Wife's Family* (Associated British), *Women Aren't Angels* (Associated British), *Candles At Nine* (British National), *Twilight Hour* (British National), *It Happened One Sunday* (Associated British), *Tower Of Terror* (Associated British), *This Is Britain* (a series for the British Council, 1945). He conducted the music for *English Without Tears* (score by Nicholas Brodszky) ; *Colonel Blimp* and *The Silver Fleet* (scores by Allan Gray) ; *Carnival, Beware Of Pity* and *The Way To The Stars* (scores by Brodszky), in his capacity as music director to these productions. He composed and directed the music for *The Night Has Eyes* (the theme song of which became popular as a light music item) and *Quiet Weekend*.

WILLIAMS, ERIC. Music Recordist. Born in Sunningdale, 1906. He received his specialised training at the Polytechnic and other technical institutions. Next, he was engaged in various branches of the radio and electrical engineering industry, including a period with the B.B.C. and the film and research departments of H.M.V. There followed some years on equipment design for British International Pictures prior to his present appointment of chief engineer and technical supervisor to Ealing Studios, which he assumed in 1933. Eric Williams has been responsible for all recording at Ealing since then, including the recording of the music for all their pictures, a list of which would roughly coincide with the films quoted under the name of Ernest Irving in this index. Williams was awarded the M.B.E. in 1946.

WILLIAMS, RALPH VAUGHAN. Composer. Born at Down Ampney, Gloucestershire, 1872. He studied at the Royal College of Music and at Cambridge at the time when Tchaikowsky, Brahms and Verdi were still alive. His association with the Royal College has been life-long, and many of our younger composers have studied under his guidance. At the beginning of the present century, Vaughan Williams began his research into English folk music, a subject which later became a passion with him, and which colours a great deal of his composition. Much of his early life was spent travelling the countryside of East Anglia and Herefordshire, collecting and noting down the music of the farm labourers and the country folk. With the coming of World War I, he joined the Army at the outset and served in France and in the Balkans, returning afterwards to a life of composing and continued research into English music. During this period up to the coming of World War II, his range of works has been extremely varied, through the majestic " London " and " Sea Symphonies," the masque " Job," the delightful " Serenade to Music," a musical comedy " The Poisoned Kiss," the opera " Sir John in Love," to test pieces for brass band festivals, choral and orchestral works of many types, songs, church music, other operas, and the major task of editing the English Hymnal. The strong influence of his folk music studies is indicated in what is, perhaps, his best known piece—the setting of the beautiful Elizabethan melody " Greensleeves." To-day he lives quietly at his home in Dorking, Surrey, for Vaughan Williams has shunned publicity and public honours to a large extent, though he was awarded the Order of Merit in 1935. Over six feet, his tall, energetic, somewhat lumbering figure represents one of the most distinguished personalities in modern music. For despite his age (he is now 74 years old), he has remained amazingly active and up-to-date in his outlook, always maintaining that a composer must not work in an ivory tower, aloof from reality, but that he should never lose contact with the everyday life of the people around him. And so it was that at the beginning of the recent war, Vaughan Williams found himself wishing to take an active part in the battle for freedom, yet not knowing just how to go about it. In 1940, music director Muir Mathieson called at the house in Dorking and suggested that he should write music for Britain's latest documentary and feature films as a direct contribution to the new developments in the cinema world, now geared to wartime needs of entertainment and factual reporting of the battle fronts. Thus, a composer, who was once a contemporary of Tchaikowsky and Brahms, now in his seventies, was able, nevertheless, to turn his attention to an entirely new form of composition, and in 1941, the forerunner of the highly successful " fictional-documentary " school of British cinema *49th Parallel* carried a music score written by Ralph Vaughan Williams. The music was an immediate success, and in 1946, the composer turned it into a full orchestral suite and an established concert hall work. This was followed in 1942 by music to the Crown Film Unit production *Coastal Command*, which the B.B.C. later recorded and broadcast as a suite, dedicated now to the R.A.F. Then in 1943, Vaughan Williams scored *The People's Land*, a documentary made by Strand Films, dealing with the work of the National Trust. In the same year came *Flemish Farm* (Two Cities), performed as an orchestral item at the 1945 Promenade Concerts. Finally, in 1945, we had the score to *Stricken Peninsula*, a film made by the Army Unit. Vaughan Williams has, during the last five years, shown considerable enthusiasm for this new medium of composition, having written articles on the subject in the R.C.M. Magazine and in other journals, besides devoting so much time to the actual composition and subsequent orchestral arrangement of some of the finest music ever written for films in any part of the world. In 1947 he scored *The Loves of Joanna Godden* (Ealing Studios, 1947).

WILLIAMSON, W. L. Conductor. *A Matter Of Life And Death* (Archers, 1946). Orchestrated and planned music for *Edge Of The World* (Michael Powell, 1937).

WOOLDRIDGE, JOHN. Composer. Born in Barnstaple, Devon, 1911. An unusual combination of music composer and R.A.F. hero, Wooldridge was educated at London's famous St. Paul's School. His first job was secretary to a boys' preparatory school in Norfolk. All his spare time was spent in flying for the R.A.F. Volunteer Reserve and studying music under Lukno, a Swedish-Finn and disciple of Sibelius, now residing in England. Six months before the war, Wooldridge transferred to the regular Air Force as a Sergeant Pilot. In this capacity, he took part in the first air raid of the war—the one on Kiel on 4th September, 1939. He brought his damaged aircraft home safely and was awarded the D.F.M. Commissioned in August, 1940, he quickly rose to be a Flight-Commander and in that capacity, flying Lancasters, with the rank of Flight-Lieutenant, he was awarded the D.F.C. in the middle of 1942. This was for a 1,000 bomber raid on Cologne. When, in early 1943, he completed the 80th of his ultimate total of 87 successful missions he received the Bar to his D.F.C. By this time he was a Wing Commander and O.C. of a low level Mosquito Bomber squadron. During the first three years of the war, and in between flying, he wrote his first musical work—a symphonic poem entitled " The Constellations," working alternately on borrowed pianos and the local padre's organ. In 1944, Wooldridge went to America to acquaint the U.S. Service Chiefs of British plans for " Pluto " and " Fido " in so far as they affected the Air Forces. He took with him the score of " The Constellations " which was performed by the New York Philharmonic under Arthur Rodzinski. In November, 1944, he returned by invitation and with the special permission from the R.A.F. to attend the British concerts. A further composition called " A Solemn Prelude " was performed four times. Other works on the same programme were : Walton's " Belshazzar's Feast " and Vaughan Williams' " Fifth Symphony." Homeward bound from his first visit, and flying a Mosquito, he broke the Atlantic record. Bombing landing barges at Calais for three nights successively early in 1940, he was wounded when an A.A. shell burst in the cockpit and the injury eventually caused him to be invalided out of the R.A.F. in October, 1945, when he held the post of Chief Flying Instructor. Since being " demobbed " he has completed scores of " The Saga Of The Ships," for narrator and orchestra and " A Prelude For A Great Occasion " for orchestra and organ. His latest is an English Rhapsody entitled " Song Of The Summer Hills," dedicated to the Boyd Neel String Orchestra, and a " Largo." This most remarkable of composers is 6 foot tall, weighs 150 pounds, with brown hair and blue eyes, and describes himself as " an ordinary chap." He is inclined to be irritated with people who expect composers to be eccentric or queer. He is mild in manner and his typical " Bomber Command " moustache is the only clue to his Air Force exploits. He entered films in 1946 with the Boulting Brothers, scoring *Fame Is The Spur* (1947), and has a contract at present for two more films.

WOOD, HENRY J. World-famous Conductor, father of the Promenade Concerts and an outstanding figure in British contemporary music for sixty years up to the time of his death in the later years of the war ; Sir Henry J. Wood was associated with the films in *Calling The Tune* (Phœnix Films, 1936), a story set against the background of a gramophone factory, and also as musical advisor to a set of four films produced by the " News of the World " in aid of the King George V Playing Field Fund. These were entitled *Heritage Of The Air*, *Heritage Of Defence*, *Heritage Of The Sea* and *Heritage Of The Soil*. They were directed by Widgey Newman and issued in 1937.

WRIGHT, GEOFFREY. Composer and Song Writer. Geoffrey Wright has written a very large number of songs for numerous stage revues and musical shows ; he has also contributed items to a number of films, including *Ships With Wings* (Ealing) and *Fiddlers Three* (Ealing). During the war he served with the Royal Navy as a signaller.

WYCK, ARNOLD VAN. Composer. *The Eighth Plague* (Crown Film Unit).

ZWAR, CHARLES. Australian Composer. He has written music for two films : *Hello Fame* (Andrew Buchanan, 1938) and *Australian Army At War* (Army Kine Service, 1944).

FILM MUSIC ORCHESTRAS

There are virtually no permanent film music orchestras in this country. The requirements of music in pictures are so varied that each music session needs individual consideration as to the number of players necessary and the type of instrumentalists best suited to the sort of music that is going to be used with the film in question. Composers vary greatly in their methods of scoring for the film music microphone ; some prefer to work with small groups of 20 or 30 players, while others write for orchestras of 60 or 70. In some cases, cost may have to be considered ; one film may be allowed a full symphony orchestra, while another may be requested to curtail music costs to an orchestra of the light music type.

However, our leading musical directors have in many cases established a central pool of musicians as it were from which they form their regular recording group, while others have their own concert hall orchestras and use them for all their film work. Where established concert orchestras are used in films, they are usually given a credit title at the beginning of the film, for example, the music for *Caesar And Cleopatra* was recorded by the National Symphony Orchestra. Here then is a list of some orchestral groups and organisations that have contributed to the recording of music in British films.

1. THE LONDON SYMPHONY ORCHESTRA

The London Symphony Orchestra was formed in 1904 by a group of players from the Queen's Hall Orchestra, principally due to what they called the " vexed question as to the right deputies." It began its operations with a series of concerts under the leadership of the famous Hans Richter. Since then, along with distinguished soloists, it has engaged for itself other outstanding conductors such as Nikisch, Arbos, Koussevitzky, Mendelberg, Elgar, Beecham, Damrosch, Coates, Sokoloff and Goossens. The London Symphony Orchestra has, perhaps, done more film work than any other, mainly under the leadership of Muir Mathieson, who has described it as " the perfect film orchestra." These musicians recorded the music for all the London films made at Denham by Alexander Korda, and were known as the London Film Symphony Orchestra, under which title they broadcast a series of six film music concerts with Muir Mathieson in 1938. It was about this time that the film reviewer of the " New York Herald Tribune " wrote " Despite the fact that American screen music has been improving at a rapid pace, no permanent symphonic ensemble in the United States, ranking with the London orchestra, has yet the record in the screen world that the English group has."

Since then, the London Symphony Orchestra has a fine and continuous record of film work for a very extensive collection of documentaries, numerous feature films made at Denham during the war and after, Crown Unit and Service Film Unit productions, and indeed, has made contributions to every possible aspect of film music, including many concert hall and broadcast performances of film music works. In recent years, it has appeared on the screen in such pictures as *The Seventh Veil, Girl In A Million, I'll Turn To You* and the Crown Film Unit picture on the instruments of the orchestra, so that we have come to know such familiar concert hall figures as George Stratton and Gordon Walker on the screen as well as we know them at the Albert Hall.

Among the films for which it has recorded are included such titles as *49th Parallel, Things To Come, Dangerous Moonlight, Escape To Danger, The Flemish Farm, Victoria The Great, Elephant Boy, Burma Victory, Sanders Of The River, Blithe Spirit* and *The Four Feathers.*

2. THE LONDON PHILHARMONIC ORCHESTRA

Founded in 1932 by Sir Thomas Beecham, the London Philharmonic Orchestra is mainly known in the film world for its work with Ernest Irving at Ealing Studios. For many years it handled the major music scores at this plant and its films include: *They Came To A City, Painted Boats, Pink String And Sealing Wax, Dead Of Night, Johnny Frenchman, Next Of Kin, San Demetrio* and two films dealing with the lives of composers—*Whom The Gods Love* (Mozart) and *The Great Mr. Handel*, both musically directed by Ernest Irving. Perhaps there is one film with which the London Philharmonic Orchestra will always be especially associated—*Battle For Music*, the film story of the orchestra itself (which is reviewed elsewhere in this book).

3. THE NATIONAL SYMPHONY ORCHESTRA

The National Symphony Orchestra is a comparative newcomer to the film studio, but it has already recorded some important scores, including the music for *The Rake's Progress, Brief Encounter, Love Story* and *Caesar And Cleopatra.*

4. THE PHILHARMONIA ORCHESTRA

Like the N.S.O., this is a recently formed group for film recording purposes. It has come to the studios at Ealing so far with Ernest Irving to play the music for *The Captive Heart* and *The Overlanders.*

5. THE R.A.F. ORCHESTRA

During the war years various R.A.F. recording groups were assembled to provide music for service film productions under the control of Wing-Commander R. P. O'Donnell of the R.A.F. Central Band. Pictures made by the R.A.F. Orchestra include: *Target For To-night, The Big Pack, Coastal Command, Sons Of The Air, Operational Height* and *Journey Together.*

6. THE GAUMONT-BRITISH SYMPHONY ORCHESTRA

This is about the nearest approach to a permanent film music orchestra in this country, but again it varies in its composition depending on the type of picture being made. With its famous conductor Louis Levy, the Gaumont-British Symphony, with the strains of the well-known march "Music from the Movies," are well-loved by radio listeners in its broadcasts of the lighter type of film music. Recently, it gave a very successful Albert Hall concert of film music. However, although a group of regular players for broadcasting and concert purposes, when the Gaumont company go to the H.M.V. Studios at St. John's Wood for film background work, the unit is often considerably changed ; Louis Levy himself never conducts at a recording session. However, it does nevertheless record a good deal of Gainsborough Picture music, and particularly did it do great work for many early Shepherd's Bush successes like the Jessie Matthews and Jack Hulbert series, the Will Hay pictures and a number of Gainsborough's more recent hits as *I'll Be Your Sweetheart.* The Gaumont-British Symphony has built up a reputation of having only the best players of the lighter and dance music type in its ranks, building up a tradition of symphonic playing from this basis as distinct from the usual procedure in British pictures of employing full-scale, existing symphony orchestras.

7. OTHER ORCHESTRAS

Finally, we come to the various orchestras who have only made occasional visits to the studio recording theatre for specific film jobs. A few examples will help to illustrate the type used for these sessions :—

THE QUEEN'S HALL LIGHT ORCHESTRA. Conducted by Charles Williams.
Night Train To Dublin, It Happened One Sunday.

SADLER'S WELLS ORCHESTRA. Conducted by Constant Lambert.
Merchant Seamen.

ALBERT SANDLER AND HIS PALM COURT ORCHESTRA
I'll Turn To You, For You Alone.

ORCHESTRA OF THE ROYAL MARINES, CHATHAM DIVISION
Close Quarters

THE BOYD NEEL ORCHESTRA
Dreaming Lips.

THE BLECH STRING QUARTET
The Magic Canvas.

EXAMPLES OF SERIOUS MUSIC FEATURED IN BRITISH FILMS

WHOM THE GODS LOVE (Ealing Studios, 1936)
The music of Mozart, including extracts from " The Marriage of Figaro " and " The Magic Flute."
The London Philharmonic Orchestra conducted by Sir Thomas Beecham. Musical direction by Ernest Irving.

MOONLIGHT SONATA (Pall Mall Productions, 1937)
Beethoven Moonlight Sonata, Minuet by Paderewski, and music by Brahms. Ignace Jan Paderewski.

THE COMMON TOUCH (British National, 1940)
Tchaikowsky Piano Concerto No. 1 in B Flat Minor.
Mark Hambourg with the London Symphony Orchestra. Musical direction by Kennedy Russell.

THE GREAT MR. HANDEL (G.H.W. Productions, 1943)
The music of Handel, including extracts from " Messiah," " Largo," etc.
The London Philharmonic Orchestra conducted by Ernest Irving.

LISTEN TO BRITAIN (Crown Film Unit, 1942)
Mozart Concerto K.453 in G Major.
Dame Myra Hess with a section of the R.A.F. Orchestra.

THE PROUD VALLEY (Ealing Studios, 1939)
Mendelssohn's " Elijah " (extracts).
Paul Robeson. Musical direction by Ernest Irving.

C.E.M.A. (Strand Films, 1943)
Tchaikowsky Piano Concerto No. 1 in B Flat Minor. " Greensleeves " (R. Vaughan Williams).
The Jacques Symphony Orchestra.

BATTLE FOR MUSIC (Strand Films, 1944)
Extracts from "Tristan and Isolde" (Wagner).
Symphony No. 2 (Sibelius).
" La Calinda " (Delius).
Fifth Symphony (Beethoven).
Symphony No. 40 (Mozart).
Piano Concerto No. 2 (Rachmaninoff).
Piano Concerto in A Minor (Grieg).
Cockaigne Overture (Elgar).
Romeo and Juliet Overture (Tchaikowsky).
Eileen Joyce, Moisewitsch, Sir Adrian Boult, Constant Lambert, Warwick Braithwaite, Dr. Malcolm Sargent.
The London Philharmonic Orchestra.

THEY CAME TO A CITY (Ealing Studios, 1944)
" The Divine Poem " (Scriabin).
The London Philharmonic Orchestra conducted by Ernest Irving.

A CANTERBURY TALE (Archers Films, 1944)
Toccata and Fugue in D Minor (Bach).
Musical direction by Allan Gray.

PINK STRING AND SEALING WAX (Ealing Studios, 1945)
Songs by Handel, John Gay, James Cook and Sir Henry Bishop.
Musical direction by Ernest Irving.

BRIEF ENCOUNTER (Noel Coward Productions, 1945)
Piano Concerto No. 2 in C Minor (Rachmaninoff).
Eileen Joyce with the National Symphony Orchestra conducted by Muir Mathieson.

THE SEVENTH VEIL (Sydney Box Productions, 1945)
Prelude No. 7 (Chopin).
Pathetique Sonata (Beethoven).
Piano Concerto in A Minor (Greig).
Sonata in C Major (Mozart).
Overture " Merry Wives of Windsor " (Nicolai).
Piano Concerto No. 2 in C Minor (Rachmaninoff).
Eileen Joyce with the London Symphony Orchestra conducted by Muir Mathieson.

A GIRL IN A MILLION (Sydney Box Productions, 1946)
Symphonic Variations (César Franck).
Eileen Joyce with the National Symphony Orchestra conducted by Muir Mathieson.

DANCE BANDS FEATURED IN BRITISH FILMS

A typical selection taken at random from the many British films that have featured our leading dance orchestras.

AMBROSE AND HIS ORCHESTRA
Soft Lights And Sweet Music (1937).

IVY BENSON AND HER BAND
The Dummy Talks (1943).

PHIL CARDEW AND HIS BAND
Song Of The People (1945).

JOHNNY CLAES AND HIS BAND
George In Civvy Street (1946).

BILLY COTTON AND HIS BAND
Music Hall Parade (1939).

DON MARINO BARRETTO AND HIS BAND
Flight From Folly (1945).

ROY FOX AND HIS BAND
On The Air (1937).

GERALDO AND HIS ORCHESTRA
Laugh It Off (1939).
Limelight (1937).

CARROLL GIBBONS AND HIS ORCHESTRA
The Common Touch (1941).
I Live In Grosvenor Square (1945).

NAT GONELLA AND HIS BAND
Sing As You Swing (1937).

PHIL GREEN'S ORCHESTRA
It Happened One Sunday (1944).

HENRY HALL AND HIS ORCHESTRA
Music Hath Charms (1936).

JACK HYLTON AND HIS BAND
She Shall Have Music (1935).
Band Wagon (1940).

JACK JACKSON AND HIS BAND
Let's Make A Night Of It (1937).

FRANK KING AND HIS ORCHESTRA
Sweethearts Forever (1945).

MANTOVANI AND HIS ORCHESTRA
Sing As You Swing (1937).

JACK PAYNE AND HIS BAND
Sunshine Ahead (1937).

HARRY PARRY AND HIS SEXTET
Short film : *Harry Parry And His Sextet* (1943).
What Do We Do Now? (1946).
Short film : *Swingonometry* (1943).

LOU PRAEGER AND HIS BAND
Musical Masquerade (1946).

R.A.F. DANCE ORCHESTRA
One Exciting Night (1944).

233

R.A.F. DANCE BAND (CANADIAN SECTION)
I Live In Grosvenor Square (1945).

EDMUNDO ROS AND HIS BAND
Flight From Folly (1945).
What Do We Do Now ? (1946).

JACK SIMPSON AND HIS SEXTET
Strawberry Roan (1944).

DEBROY SOMERS AND HIS BAND
Stars On Parade (1937).
Shooting Stars (1937).

LEW STONE AND HIS BAND
Under Your Hat (1940).

FRANK WEIR AND HIS SEXTET
Dead Of Night (1945).
Happy Family (1946).

MAURICE WINNICK AND HIS BAND
Thunder In The City (1936).
Men Are Not Gods (1936).

ERIC WINSTONE AND HIS ORCHESTRA
Don Chicago (1945).

SERGEANT VICCART AND HIS G.I. BAND
I Live In Grosvenor Square (1945).

GEORGE MELACHRINO AND HIS ORCHESTRA
Appointment With Crime (1946).

LEW STONE AND HIS ORCHESTRA
Appointment With Crime (1946).

BUDDY FEATHERSTONEHAUGH AND HIS SEXTETTE
Appointment With Crime (1946).

LOU PREAGER AND HIS ORCHESTRA
Dancing Thru (1946).

B.B.C. FILM MUSIC BROADCASTS

The incidental music composed for radio features and plays has a good deal in common with film music, and it is, therefore, not surprising to find many film composers engaged on B.B.C. work. Men like Roy Douglas, Lennox Berkeley, Gordon Jacob and Jack Beaver write regularly for the radio, while Muir Mathieson has conducted and organised many incidental music scores in addition to conducting various sections of the B.B.C. Orchestras. The general policy is to use gramophone records as incidental music to radio plays and features. This method is simple, cheap and satisfactory in many cases, but, to a lesser extent, the principle that the association of ideas connected with known music can destroy the continuity of idea in a film is applicable to the radio feature. However, the expense of commissioning specially composed music for radio is only justified in the case of very special jobs. With the film, vast sums of money are available for production purposes, but with radio, the budget is not so liberal. The B.B.C. have proved to be progressive in their use of incidental music, and have established expert music departments to supply the script writers with original scores of considerable musical value, carefully integrated into the feature or play to produce a unity unobtainable with records. But that is a story in itself, as yet an untold story.

The B.B.C. have always encouraged contemporary music and from our point of view, they have been on the whole enthusiastic. Apart from the inclusion of much film music in such programmes as " Music From the Movies " (Louis Levy) and " March of the Movies " (Leslie Mitchell, Harry Alan Towers), there have been a number of programmes dealing exclusively with background film music, for which we have had to tune to the overseas wavelengths in most cases up to now.

1. In April, 1943, a half-hour programme was given on THE MUSIC TO THE FILM *MALTA G.C.* BY SIR ARNOLD BAX with the B.B.C. Symphony Orchestra conducted by Muir Mathieson. This went out on the African Service, Pacific Service, Eastern Service and the North American Service.

2. In July, 1943, a thirty-minute programme on MUSIC FROM BRITISH DOCUMENTARY FILMS, played by the London Symphony Orchestra conducted by Muir Mathieson, went out on the Pacific Service, the African Service, Overseas, North American (Red) and North American (Purple).

3. In October, 1943, a half-hour talk on BRITISH FILM COMPOSERS OF TO-DAY was illustrated by the B.B.C. Orchestra and went out on the African Service, the North America Service and the North American Service (Purple).

4. In the third quarter of 1944, MUSIC IN THE MAKING, five half-hour programmes were broadcast in the Eastern Service on Film Music. These were illustrated by B.B.C. discs and commercial records, and were presented by Muir Mathieson.

In the second quarter of 1945, thirteen programmes on CONTEMPORARY BRITISH FILM MUSIC were broadcast on Mondays from 3.35 p.m. to 4 p.m. in the Eastern Service. The programmes were entitled :—

1. Preliminary ·Discussion.
2. General Survey.
3. Dramatic use of Music.
4. The Music of Vaughan Williams.
5. Films about the War.
6. Music for Comedy in Films.
7. The Music of Arnold Bax—*Malta G.C.*
8. *The Gen*—R.A.F. Newsreel.
9. The Industrial Documentary.
10. The Music of William Walton.
11. War Films.
12. Films about the Sea.
13. The Social Documentary.

5. In December, 1945, in the MUSIC IN THE MAKING series, a half-hour programme on Music for the Films was given in the Eastern Service, with a script written and presented by Dr. Hubert Clifford and illustrated by B.B.C. discs.

6. Programmes of film music prior to 1939 included the following items, all conducted by Muir Mathieson and presented on the National Programme :—
Two Dances : *The Scarlet Pimpernel* (Arthur Benjamin).
Prelude : *The Ghost Goes West* (Mischa Spoliansky).

Things To Come (Arthur Bliss).
1. March.
2. Attack.
3. Ballet for Children.
4. World in Ruins.
5. Pestilence.
6. Epilogue.

Elephant Boy (John Greenwood).
    1. Overture.
    2. Indian Scenes.
    3. In the Temple.
    4. The Elephant Caravan.
    5. In the Jungle.
    6. The Elephant Dance.

Dances at a Montmartre Café : *The Rat* (Anthony Collins).

Carnival and Funeral : *The Private Life Of Don Juan* (Mischa Spoliansky).

Music to a Spy Melodrama : *Dark Journey* (Richard Addinsell).

Two Burlesques : *The Man Who Could Work Miracles* (Mischa Spoliansky).

Rembrandt (Geoffrey Toye).
    1. Rembrandt and Saskia.
    2. Return to the Mill.
    3. Hendrikje's Death.

Ballet : *Escape Me Never* (William Walton).

Wings Of The Morning (Arthur Bliss)..
    1. Overture.
    2. Riding Sketches.
    3. Prelude to Daybreak.
    4. Gypsy Scenes.
    5. At the Wishing Well.
    6. Derby Day March.

Music for an English Landscape : *South Riding* (Richard Addinsell).

Music to Thrillers : *The Squeaker* and *Four Dark Hours* (Miklos Rozsa).

March : *The Man Who Could Work Miracles* (Mischa Spoliansky).

March : *The Drum* (John Greenwood).

Scherzo : *Paradise For Two* (Mischa Spoliansky).

Music : *Knight Without Armour* (Miklos Rozsa).

Telegrams : *Sixpenny Telegram* (Benjamin Britten).

Music to a Cartoon : *The Fox Hunt* (Mischa Spoliansky).

Victoria The Great (Anthony Collins).
    1. The Ride to Kensington.
    2. The Wedding Breakfast.
    3. The Queen's Caprice.
    4. Portrait of Lord Melbourne on a Horse.
    5. Victoria Regina.

Music : *The Divorce Of Lady X* (Miklos Rozsa).

Conquest Of The Air (Arthur Bliss).
    1. The Wind.
    2. The Vision of Leonardo da Vinci.
    3. Stunting.
    4. Gliding.
    5. Over the Arctic.
    6. March : Conquest of the Air.

7. Two recent B.B.C programme series have given many special presentations of film music items. They are March of the Movies (produced by Pat Osborne and written by Harry Alan Towers) and Picture Parade (produced by Peter Eton).

B.B.C. FILM MUSIC ITEMS

The B.B.C. have given many performances to individual film music works; in addition, they have made numerous special records of film scores, using their own orchestras for the recording. Here is a selection of these works, giving details of the conductor, orchestra and year of recording in a number of cases :—

March : *The Lion Has Wings* (Richard Addinsell).
    Recorded by the B.B.C. Northern Orchestra, conducted by Muir Mathieson, 1943.

Suite : *Desert Victory* (William Alwyn).
    1. Prelude : El Alamein : Holding the Line.
    2. The Eighth Army in Training.
    3. Preparing for Battle.
    4. The Calm before the Storm.
    5. The Advance Begins.
    6. Rommel in Full Retreat : the Attack from the Air.
    B.B.C. Northern Orchestra. Muir Mathieson, 1943.

March : *Tunisian Victory* (William Alwyn).
    B.B.C. Northern Orchestra. Muir Mathieson, 1943.

March : *They Flew Alone* (William Alwyn).
    B.B.C. Northern Orchestra. Muir Mathieson, 1943.

N.F.S. March : *Fires Were Started* (William Alwyn).
    B.B.C. Northern Orchestra. Muir Mathieson, 1943.

March : *The Way Ahead* (William Alwyn).

"Java" and "On the Beach" : *Hotel Reserve* (Lennox Berkeley).
    B.B.C. Northern Orchestra. Muir Mathieson, 1944.

Music to the film : *Malta G.C.* (Arnold Bax).
    1. Opening Fanfare.
    2. Prelude and Convoy.
    3. Old Valetta.
    4. Air Raid.
    5. Ruins.
    6. Gay March.
    7. Intermezzo.
    8. Work and Play.
    9. March.
    B.B.C. Symphony Orchestra. Muir Mathieson, 1943.

Theme of Reconstruction : *Things To Come* (Arthur Bliss).
    B.B.C. Military Band. 1942.

Film Music : *Conquest Of The Air* (Arthur Bliss).

March : *Things To Come* (Arthur Bliss).

March : *The Gen*—R.A.F. Newsreel (Hubert Clifford).

Suite : *Victoria The Great* (Anthony Collins).

Prelude : *In Which We Serve* (Noel Coward).
    B.B.C. Northern Orchestra. Muir Mathieson, 1943.

"On the Seashore" : *Man Of Aran* (John Greenwood).
    B.B.C. Theatre Orchestra. Stanford Robinson, 1943.

Waltz : *Pimpernel Smith* (John Greenwood).

Battle Sketch "Landing Party" : *The Gen*—R.A.F. Newsreel (Norman Delmar).
    B.B.C. Northern Orchestra. Muir Mathieson, 1944.

"Ferry Flight" : *Maintenance Command* (Gordon Jacob).
    B.B.C. Northern Orchestra. Muir Mathieson, 1944.

Suite : *Merchant Seamen* (Constant Lambert).
  1. Fanfare and Convoy in Fog.
  2. The Attack.
  3. Safe Convoy.
  4. Finale. March : " Merchant Seamen."
  B.B.C. Symphony Orchestra. Constant Lambert, 1943.
March : *Target For To-night* (Leighton Lucas).
  B.B.C. Northern Orchestra. Muir Mathieson, 1943.
Prelude to *Western Approaches* (Clifton Parker).
Prelude to *49th Parallel* (Vaughan Williams).
  B.B.C. Northern Orchestra. Muir Mathieson, 1943.
Suite : *Coastal Command* (Vaughan Williams).
  1. Prelude.
  2. The Island Station.
  3. Hudsons take off from Iceland.
  4. The Sunderland goes in close.
  5. Beaufighters.
  6. We search and strike.
  B.B.C. Northern Orchestra. Muir Mathieson, 1943.
Dawn scene : *Flemish Farm* (Vaughan Williams).
  B.B.C. Northern Orchestra. Muir Mathieson, 1944.
Spitfire Prelude and Fugue : *First Of The Few* (William Walton).
Suite : *Henry V* (William Walton).
  1. Overture : " The Globe Playhouse 1600."
  2. Passacaglia : " The Death of Falstaff."
  3. The Agincourt Song.
  B.B.C. Northern Orchestra. Muir Mathieson, 1944.
Variations and Fugue on a theme by Purcell (Benjamin Britten). (From the film *Instruments Of The Orchestra*).
  B.B.C. Symphony Orchestra. Conductor : Malcolm Sargent.

BRITISH FILM FESTIVAL CONCERT IN PRAGUE, OCTOBER, 1946
Programme

1. Spitfire : Prelude and Fugue *First Of The Few* (William Walton).
2. Suite from the film *49th Parallel* (Ralph Vaughan Williams).
3. Calypso Music : *The Rake's Progress* (William Alwyn).
4. Suite from the film *Henry V* (William Walton).
5. Variations and Fugue on a theme by Purcell *Instruments Of The Orchestra* (Benjamin Britten).
6. Seascape : *Western Approaches* (Clifton Parker).
7. Suite from the film *Things To Come* (Arthur Bliss).
8. Waltz into Jig : *Hungry Hill* (John Greenwood).
9. Suite from the film *Malta G.C.* (Arnold Bax).
  Presented by the Filmovy Symfonicky Orchestra. Conducted by Muir Mathieson.

ITEMS FROM LOUIS LEVY FILM MUSIC CONCERTS

1. March : *Things To Come* (Arthur Bliss).
2. " A Voice In The Night " (from *Wanted For Murder*) (Mischa Spoliansky).
3. Music from *Piccadilly Incident* (Vivian Ellis and Anthony Collins).
4. March : " Heroique " (*Theirs Is The Glory*) (Guy Warrack).
  Presented by Louis Levy and his " Music From The Movies " at the Royal Albert Hall, London.

GRAMOPHONE RECORDS QF BRITISH FILM MUSIC

(Years shown in parentheses indicate year of completion of each film)

1. **THINGS TO COME.** (Director : William Cameron Menzies).
   Music by Arthur Bliss.
   1. March.   2. Attack : Melodrama.
   3. Ballet for Children.   4. The World in Ruins.
   5. Pestilence.   6. Epilogue.
   Recorded by the London Symphony Orchestra, conducted by the composer.
   (1935). Decca 810, 811, 817.

2. **DANGEROUS MOONLIGHT.** (Director : Brian Desmond Hurst).
   (American title : *Suicide Squadron*).
   Music by Richard Addinsell.
   The Warsaw Concerto.
   Recorded by the London Symphony Orchestra, conducted by Muir Mathieson.
   Pianoforte : Louis Kentner.
   (1941). Columbia DX.1062.

3. **THE FIRST OF THE FEW.** (Director : Leslie Howard).
   (American title : *Spitfire*).
   Music by William Walton.
   Spitfire Prelude and Fugue.
   Recorded by the Hallé Orchestra, conducted by the composer.
   (1942). H.M.V. C.3359.

4. **LOVE STORY.** (Director : Leslie Arliss).
   Music by Hubert Bath.
   The Cornish Rhapsody.
   Recorded by the London Symphony Orchestra, conducted by the composer.
   (1944). Columbia DX.1171.

5. **BLITHE SPIRIT.** (Director : David Lean).
   Music by Richard Addinsell.
   Prelude and Waltz.
   Recorded by the London Symphony Orchestra, conducted by Muir Mathieson.
   (1945). Columbia DX.1186.

6. **THE WAY TO THE STARS.** (Director : Anthony Asquith).
   Music by Nicholas Brodszky.
   Recorded by the Two Cities Symphony Orchestra, conducted by Charles Williams.
   (1945). Columbia DB.2180.

7. **HENRY V.** (Director : Laurence Olivier).
   Music by William Walton.
   1. Death of Falstaff.   2. Touch Her Soft Lips and Part.
   Recorded by the Philharmonia String Orchestra, conducted by the composer.
   (1945). H.M.V. C.3480.

8. **COLONEL BLIMP.** (Director : Michael Powell).
   Music by Allan Gray.
   Commando Patrol.
   Recorded by the R.A.F. Dance Orchestra.
   (1943). Decca F.8364.

9. **RHODES OF AFRICA.** (Director : Berthold Viertel).
   Music by Hubert Bath.
   March : " Empire Builders."
   Recorded by Louis Levy and his Gaumont-British Symphony.
   (1936). Columbia FB.2380.

10. **TARGET FOR TO-NIGHT.** (Director : Harry Watt).
Music by Leighton Lucas.
March : " Freihausen, Here we come."
Recorded by the Central Band of the Royal Air Force.
(1941). H.M.V. R.A.F.11.

11. **DESERT VICTORY.** (Army and R.A.F. Film Units).
Music by William Alwyn.
March : " Desert Victory."
Recorded by H.M. Grenadier Guards Band, conducted by Lieut. F. Harris,
A.R.A.M.
(1943). Columbia DB.2140.

12. **NINE MEN.** (Director : Harry Watt).
Music by Eric Coates and John Greenwood.
March : " The Eighth Army."
Recorded by H.M. Grenadier Guards Band, conducted by Lieut. F. Harris,
A.R.A.M.
(1943). Columbia DB.2140.

13. **GAUMONT-BRITISH NEWS.**
Music by Louis Levy.
March : " Music from the Movies."
Recorded by Louis Levy and his Gaumont-British Symphony.
Columbia FB.2380.

14. **THE PRIVATE LIFE OF DON JUAN.** (Director : Alexander Korda).
Music by Mischa Spoliansky.
Song : " Senorita." (Arthur Wimperis and Mischa Spoliansky).
Recorded by John Brownlee, Baritone.
(1934). H.M.V. B.8218.

15. **SANDERS OF THE RIVER.** (Director : Zoltan Korda).
Music by Mischa Spoliansky.
1. Canoe Song.   2. Love Song.
3. Killing Song.   4. Congo Lullaby.
Recorded by Paul Robeson, with orchestra conducted by Muir Mathieson.
(1935). H.M.V. B.8315 and 8316.

16. **THE PROUD VALLEY.** (Director : Pen Tennyson).
Musical direction by Ernest Irving.
1. Land of My Fathers.   2. Ebenezer.
3. All Through the Night.
Recorded by Paul Robeson.
(1939). H.M.V. B.9020 and 9021.
4. Deep River (arr. Ernest Irving) and Rehearsal Scene (including Baal
Chorus and Lord God of Abraham from " Elijah.") Sound track
recording.
Recorded by Paul Robeson, with orchestra conducted by Ernest Irving.
(1939). H.M.V. B.9024.

17. **SONG OF FREEDOM.** (Director : J. Elder Wills).
1. Sleepy River.   2. Song of Freedom.
3. Lonely Road.   4. The Black Emperor.
Recorded by Paul Robeson.
(1936). H.M.V. B.8482 and 8483.

18. **KING SOLOMON'S MINES.** (Director : Robert Stevenson).
Music by Mischa Spoliansky.
1. Ho ! Ho ! (Wagon Song).   2. Climbing Up (Mountain Song).
Recorded by Paul Robeson.
(1936). H.M.V. B.8586.

19. **JERICHO.** (Director : Thornton Freeland).
    1. Deep Desert.   2. My Way.
        Recorded by Paul Robeson.
                    (1937). H.M.V. B.8621.

20. **LORNA DOONE.** (Director : Basil Dean).
          Musical direction by Ernest Irving.
    1. Love's Wisdom. (Mordaunt Currie and Armstrong Gibbs).
    2. Lorna's Song. (R. D. Blackmore and Rutland Boughton).
Recorded by Victoria Hopper, accompanied by the Associated Talking Pictures Studio Orchestra, conducted by Ernest Irving.
                    (1934). H.M.V. B.8249.

21. **CHAMPAGNE CHARLIE.** (Director : A. Cavalcanti).
          Musical direction by Ernest Irving.
    1. Everything will be lovely.   2. The Man on the Flying Trapeze.
    3. 'Arf of 'Arf and 'Arf.   4. Come On, Algernon.
Sound track recordings.
            (1944). Columbia FB.3050 and 3051.

22. **WANTED FOR MURDER.** (Director : Lawrence Huntingdon).
          Music by Mischa Spoliansky.
          A Voice in the Night.
Recorded by the Queen's Hall Light Orchestra, conducted by Charles Williams. Piano solo : Eric Harrison.
                  (1946). Columbia DX.1264.

23. **SPELLBOUND.** (Director : Alfred Hitchcock).
Music by Miklos Rozsa. (British film composer up to 1940 ; Hungarian by birth ; now in Hollywood).
          Spellbound Concerto.
Recorded by the Queen's Hall Light Orchestra, conducted by Charles Williams.
        (1946, American). Columbia DX.1264.

24. **THE RAKE'S PROGRESS.** (Director : Sidney Gilliat).
          Music by William Alwyn.
          Calypso
Recorded by the London Symphony Orchestra, conducted by Muir Mathieson.   (1946). Decca K.1544.

25. **WESTERN APPROACHES.** (Director : Pat Jackson).
          Music by Clifton Parker.
          Seascape.
Recorded by the London Symphony Orchestra, conducted by Muir Mathieson.   (1944). Decca K.1544.

26. **MEN OF TWO WORLDS.** (Director : Thorold Dickinson).
          Music by Arthur Bliss.
          " Baraza."
Recorded by Eileen Joyce with the National Symphony Orchestra and Male Chorus, conducted by Muir Mathieson. Recorded at the Kingsway Hall, London.
                  (1946). Decca K.1174.

27. **VILLAGE HARVEST.**
          Music by Benjamin Britten.
          " Irish Reel."
Recorded by the Charles Brill Orchestra.
                       Decca K.874.

28. **THE NIGHT HAS EYES.** (Director : Leslie Arliss).
          Music by Charles Williams.
Recorded by Charles Williams and the Queen's Hall Light Orchestra.
                  (1942). Columbia DB.2272.

29. **CARNIVAL.** (Director : Stanley Haynes).
Music by Nicholas Brodszky.
Intermezzo.
Recorded by the Two Cities Symphony Orchestra, conducted by Charles Williams.
(1946). Columbia DB.2225.

30. **PICCADILLY INCIDENT.** (Director : Herbert Wilcox).
Music by Anthony Collins and Vivian Ellis.
Piccadilly, 1944, composed by Vivian Ellis.
Boogie Woogie Moonshine (includes " You Are My Sunshine " and Beethoven's Moonlight Sonata).
Recorded by Louis Levy and his " Music From The Movies."
(1946). Decca K.1559.

31. **INSTRUMENTS OF THE ORCHESTRA.** (Director : Muir Mathieson).
Music by Benjamin Britten.
A Young People's Guide to the Orchestra : Variations and Fugue on a Theme by Purcell.
    1. Themes—Full Orchestra : Woodwind, Brass, Strings, Percussion.
    2. Variations : Clarinets, Bassoons, Violins (First and Second), Violas.
    3. Variations : Cellos, Double Basses, Harp.
    4. Variations : Horns, Trumpets, Trombones and Bass Tuba, Percussion.
    5. Fugue.
Recorded by the Liverpool Philharmonic Orchestra, conducted by Dr. Malcolm Sargent.
(1946). H.M.V. DX.1307, 1308 and DXS.1309.

32. **49TH PARALLEL.** (Director : Michael Powell).
Music by Ralph Vaughan Williams.
Epilogue. (1941).

33. **THEIRS IS THE GLORY.**
Music by Guy Warrack.
March : Men of Arnhem. (1946). Decca K.1571.

34. **MALTA G.C.** (Army, R.A.F. and Crown Units).
Music by Arnold Bax.
Quiet Interlude.
Gay March. (1943).

35. **HUNGRY HILL.** (Director : Brian Desmond Hurst).
Music by John Greenwood
Waltz into Jig. (1947).

36. **MAINTENANCE COMMAND.** (R.A.F. Film Unit).
Music by Gordon Jacob.
Ferry Flight. (1944).

37. **THE CAPTIVE HEART.** (Director : Basil Dearden).
Music by Alan Rawsthorne.
Prisoners' March. (1946).

38. **EDGE OF THE WORLD.** (Director : Michael Powell).
Music by W. L. Williamson.
Last Walk. (1937).

39. **CONQUEST OF THE AIR.** Director : Alexander Korda-Charles Frend).
Music by Arthur Bliss.
Visions of Leonardo da Vinci Gliding. (1940).

40. **THE OVERLANDERS.** (Director : Harry Watt).
Music by John Ireland (1946).

242

41. **WRENS.** (Ministry of Information).
Music by Richard Addinsell.
March. (1941).
(Records 32-41 form part of the Decca " Incidental Music from British Films "
series, and are all recorded by the London Symphony Orchestra, conducted
by Muir Mathieson).

42. **A MATTER OF LIFE AND DEATH.** (Director : Michael Powell).
Music by Allan Gray.
Prelude.
Recorded by the Queen's Hall Light Orchestra, conducted by Charles Williams.
(1946). Columbia DX.1320.

43. **THIS MAN IS MINE.** (Director : Marcel Varnel).
Music by Allan Gray.
Theme.
Recorded by the Queen's Hall Light Orchestra, conducted by Charles Williams.
(1946). Columbia DX.1320.

44. **THE SOUND TRACK**
The following records provide an opportunity to study the composition of
the sound track containing dialogue, natural sound and music.

1. CONVICT 99
Sound track excerpt from the film.
Will Hay, Moore Marriott and Graham Moffatt.
(1938). Columbia FB.2040.

2. THE VOICE OF THE STARS SERIES
Among a large collection of short extracts from the sound track of many
American and British films, the following are of special interest despite
the fact that the individual excerpts are very brief :—

Cavalcade (Diana Wynyard).

The Private Life Of Henry VIII (Charles Laughton).

Knight Without Armour (Robert Donat).

The Ghost Goes West (Robert Donat).

Vessel Of Wrath (Charles Laughton).

Divorce Of Lady X (Merle Oberon).

I, Claudius (Charles Laughton ; an extract from a film that was never
completed).

A Yank At Oxford (Robert Taylor).

Victoria, The Great (Anna Neagle).

Wings Of The Morning (John McCormack) and the voices of Jack
Hulbert, Gracie Fields, Jessie Matthews, Richard Tauber, Victoria
Hopper, Jack Buchanan, Elsie Randolph, Will Hay, Max Miller,
Paul Robeson, George Formby, Evelyn Laye, Leslie Henson, Gordon
Harker, George Arliss, Bobby Howes and Cicely Courtneidge in
brief glimpses from numerous British films.

Regal Zonophone VS.1, VS.2, VS.3, VS.4, VS.5, MR.1234 and MR.2722.

3. The British Film Festival of 1946, organised by the " Daily Mail," and
held at the Leicester Square Theatre.

These records contain a series of reconstructed scenes from British films
made between 1939 and 1945.

(a) March from the film *Desert Victory* (William Alwyn).

243

(*b*) Scene from *The Way Ahead* with Raymond Huntley, Stanley Holloway and Hugh Burden.

(*c*) Scenes from *The Way To The Stars* with Michael Redgrave, Rosamund John and John Mills.

(*d*) George Formby sings " Get Cracking."

(*e*) Scene from *The Man In Grey* with Margaret Lockwood and Phyllis Calvert.

(*f*). Scenes from *49th Parallel* with Eric Portman and Anton Walbrook.

(*g*) Scene from *The Young Mr. Pitt* with Robert Donat.

Music from the films played by a symphony orchestra directed by Sidney Torch. Script and production by Harry Alan Towers.

Columbia DX.1241 and 1242.

BIBLIOGRAPHY

I. ARTICLES ON FILM MUSIC

1933

Music and the Film. Sight and Sound. Autumn.

Music in Films (Alfred Hitchcock). Cinema Quarterly. Vol. 2, No. 2.

1934

The Musician and the Film (Walter Leigh). Cinema Quarterly. Vol. 3, No. 2.

1935

Music and the Film. Sight and Sound. Summer.

Music and the Movies. Harpers Magazine. July.

Background Music is a Help (Louis Levy). Flickers. 1935.

1936

Film Music (Muir Mathieson). Royal College of Music Magazine. Vol. XXXII. No: 3.

Film Music (Darius Milhaud). World Film Newa. April.

Music and Film (Hans Eisler). World Film News. May.

Music and Film (Maurice Jaubert). World Film News. July.

1937

Music in Films (Leslie Perkoff). World Film News. April.

Music in Films (Cavalcanti). World Film News. July.

Film Music (Arthur Benjamin). Musical Times. July.

The Story of British Film Music (Ralph Hill). Radio Times. 31.12.37.

Music and the ' Cellulose Nit-Wit' (Alan Frank). The Listener. 29.12.37.

1938

Music from the Movies Radio Programme (Louis Levy). Radio Pictorial. 21.1.38.

1940

Music and the Film. New Statesman. 13.4.40.

Film Music (Muir Mathieson). Documentary News Letter. September.

1941

The Functions of Music in Sound Films. Musical Quarterly (N.Y.). April.

Film Music Notes of America commenced publication in 1941. (Nine issues annually).

1943

Recent Film Music (John W. Klein). Musical Opinion. June.

Music in Films (Ernest Irving). Music and Letters. Vol. XXIV. No. 4.

1944

Film Music (John Huntley). Sight and Sound. January.

Film Music (Darrel Catling). Sight and Sound. April.

British Film Music (Hubert Clifford). Tempo. September.

Film Music (R. Vaughan Williams). Royal College of Music Magazine. Vol. XL. No. 1.

Background Music to the Fore (Sam Heppner). Sound Illustrated. December.

Walton's Henry V Music (Hubert Clifford). Tempo. December.

Aspects of Film Music (Muir Mathieson). Tempo. December.

Music and World News (John Huntley). Sound Illustrated. December.

Music and the Cinema (Alexander Brent Smith). Piping Times. Vol. IV. No. 3.

Film Music (R. Vaughan Williams). Piping Times. Vol. IV. No. 1.

Film Music (Ken Cameron and Muir Mathieson). Piping Times. Vol. IV. No. 2.

British Film Music (John Huntley). Film Music Notes. April.

Film Music in England (John Huntley). Film Music Notes. December.

1945

Film Scores (Arthur Kleiner). Sight and Sound. January.

Tchaikowsky, Walton, Addinsell (John Huntley). Sound Illustrated. May.

Music and the Film (Harold Rawlinson). British Journal of Photography. 16.3.45.

Criticism from London (John Huntley). Film Music Notes. September.

Music from the Films (Hubert Clifford). Tempo. March, June and December issues.

Classical Music in Films. Picture Show.

Music for All (John Huntley). Film Music Notes. September.

Music of the Cinema (Arthur Unwin). Music Parade.

Getting the Gen : A Course in Film Music (John Huntley). Film Music Notes. October.

Dramatists in Music (Muir Mathieson). Talkabout.

Film Music News from England (John Huntley). Film Music Notes. November.

1946

Newsreel Music (John Huntley). Film Music Notes. April.

Film Music (John Huntley). Penguin Film Review.

Music from the Films (Ernest Irving). Tempo. June, September.

Film Music : A Teacher's Aspect (Music Master). Music in Education. July, 1946.

Putting in the Sound Track (Edward Silverman). Our Time. October.

Fitting the Music to the Picture (Walter Goehr). Sound Illustrated. October.

How a Music Recording Theatre Was Made From a Sound Stage (Cyril Crowhurst). Kinematograph Weekly. 26th September.

1947

Notes on Film Music (John Huntley). Penguin Film Review.

Scoring for Films (Muir Mathieson). Penguin Film Review.

Film Music Reviews (Ernest Irving). Tempo.

Background For British Pictures (Muir Mathieson). Musical Express. 3.1.47.

The British Musical Film (Muir Mathieson). Melody Maker. January.

This Concerto Business (George Maffery). Keynote.

Film Music (John Huntley). Film Music Notes. March, 1947.

British Film Music and World Markets (John Huntley). Sight and Sound. First Issue, 1947.

2. BOOKS CONTAINING FILM MUSIC REFERENCES

Film and Theatre (Nicoll). Harrup, 1939.

Our New Music (Aaron Copland). U.S.A., 1940.

Film (Roger Manvell). Pelican, 1944.

Things to Come (Film script by H. G. Wells). Cresset Press, 1936.

Henry V (C. Clayton Hutton). London, 1945.

Music in the Modern World (Rollo H. Myers). Edward Arnold, 1937.

Meeting at the Sphinx (Marjorie Deans). Macdonald, 1946.

Footnotes to the Film (Davy). Includes article on " Music on the Screen " by Maurice Jaubert. Lovat Dickson, 1937.

Behind the Screen. Includes article by Herbert Stothart on film music at M.-G.-M. Studios. U.S.A., 1939.

Talking Pictures (Kiesling). U.S.A., 1939.

British Film Yearbook (Peter Noble). British Yearbooks, 1946.

Transatlantic Jazz (Peter Noble). British Yearbooks, 1946.

Documentary Film (Paul Rotha). Faber and Faber, 1936 and 1939.

Music for the Films (Sabaneev). Pitman, 1935.

Film Music (Kurt London). Faber and Faber, 1936.

Sound and the Documentary Film (Ken Cameron). Pitman, 1947.

ADDENDUM

CAMERON, KEN. Music Recordist. Born in Wendover, Bucks, in 1915. He was educated at Glasgow Academy and Glasgow University, where he took his B.Sc. (Electrical Engineering) in 1938. After a period of apprenticeship in the G.P.O. Film Unit while still at the University, Cameron joined them again after graduation, and in September, 1938, he was given charge of the G.P.O. Film Unit Sound Department. During the course of his acoustical researches, he found that King George V Hall attached to the Central Telegraph Office in London was excellent for music recording (and incidentally cost the G.P.O. Unit nothing !). As a result it was used a great deal until it was finally burnt down during the London Blitz. Since then, Cameron has been responsible for the " discovery " of a number of Town Halls near London which are suitable for the type of film music recording he has developed, for he is the foremost advocate of using an unorthodox amount of reverberation in music recording. He was the first recordist to use Watford Town Hall, now a great favourite amongst studio sound men. Cameron remained with the G.P.O. Unit when they became known as the Crown Film Unit, and in 1944 he went to Hollywood to study recording technique, bringing back with him the American method of " multi-microphone " recording which is now used by most studios in this country. Cameron is today one of the foremost music recording experts in the country and he personally supervises and handles all the music recording done by Crown. His films include : *Men In Danger, Forty Million People, The Islanders, The City, Squadron 992, Men Of The Lightship, Merchant Seamen, Christmas Under Fire, The Heart Of Britain, Target For Tonight, Ferry Pilot, Wavell's 30,000, Listen To Britain, Coastal Command, We Sail At Midnight, Malta G.C., Fires Were Started, Lili Marlene, Western Approaches, A Diary For Timothy, Instruments Of The Orchestra* and *Myra Hess.*

The Arno Press Cinema Program

THE LITERATURE OF CINEMA

Series I & II

American Academy of Political and Social Science. **The Motion Picture in Its Economic and Social Aspects,** edited by Clyde L. King. **The Motion Picture Industry,** edited by Gordon S. Watkins. *The Annals,* November, 1926/1927.

Agate, James. **Around Cinemas.** 1946.

Agate, James. **Around Cinemas.** (Second Series). 1948.

Balcon, Michael, Ernest Lindgren, Forsyth Hardy and Roger Manvell. **Twenty Years of British Film, 1925-1945.** 1947.

Bardèche, Maurice and Robert Brasillach. **The History of Motion Pictures,** edited by Iris Barry. 1938.

Benoit-Levy, Jean. **The Art of the Motion Picture.** 1946.

Blumer, Herbert. **Movies and Conduct.** 1933.

Blumer, Herbert and Philip M. Hauser. **Movies, Delinquency, and Crime.** 1933.

Buckle, Gerard Fort. **The Mind and the Film.** 1926.

Carter, Huntly. **The New Spirit in the Cinema.** 1930.

Carter, Huntly. **The New Spirit in the Russian Theatre, 1917-1928.** 1929.

Carter, Huntly. **The New Theatre and Cinema of Soviet Russia.** 1924.

Charters, W. W. **Motion Pictures and Youth.** 1933.

Cinema Commission of Inquiry. **The Cinema: Its Present Position and Future Possibilities.** 1917.

Dale, Edgar. **The Content of Motion Pictures.** 1935.

Dale, Edgar. **How to Appreciate Motion Pictures.** 1937.

Dale, Edgar. **Children's Attendance at Motion Pictures.** Dysinger, Wendell S. and Christian A. Ruckmick. **The Emotional Responses of Children to the Motion Picture Situation.** 1935.

Dale, Edgar, Fannie W. Dunn, Charles F. Hoban, Jr., and Etta Schneider. **Motion Pictures in Education: A Summary of the Literature.** 1938.

Davy, Charles. **Footnotes to the Film.** 1938.

Dickinson, Thorold and Catherine De la Roche. **Soviet Cinema. 1948.**

Dickson, W. K. L., and Antonia Dickson. **History of the Kinetograph, Kinetoscope and Kinetophonograph. 1895.**

Forman, Henry James. **Our Movie Made Children. 1935.**

Freeburg, Victor Oscar. **The Art of Photoplay Making. 1918.**

Freeburg, Victor Oscar. **Pictorial Beauty on the Screen. 1923.**

Hall, Hal, editor. **Cinematographic Annual, 2 vols. 1930/1931.**

Hampton, Benjamin B. **A History of the Movies. 1931.**

Hardy, Forsyth. **Scandinavian Film. 1952.**

Hepworth, Cecil M. **Animated Photography: The A B C of the Cinematograph. 1900.**

Hoban, Charles F., Jr., and Edward B. Van Ormer. **Instructional Film Research 1918-1950. 1950.**

Holaday, Perry W. and George D. Stoddard. **Getting Ideas from the Movies. 1933.**

Hopwood, Henry V. **Living Pictures. 1899.**

Hulfish, David S. **Motion-Picture Work. 1915.**

Hunter, William. **Scrutiny of Cinema. 1932.**

Huntley, John. **British Film Music. 1948.**

Irwin, Will. **The House That Shadows Built. 1928.**

Jarratt, Vernon. **The Italian Cinema. 1951.**

Jenkins, C. Francis. **Animated Pictures. 1898.**

Lang, Edith and George West. **Musical Accompaniment of Moving Pictures. 1920.**

L'Art Cinematographique, Nos. 1-8. 1926-1931.

London, Kurt. **Film Music. 1936.**

Lutz, E [dwin] G [eorge]. **The Motion-Picture Cameraman. 1927.**

Manvell, Roger. **Experiment in the Film. 1949.**

Marey, Etienne Jules. **Movement. 1895.**

Martin, Olga J. **Hollywood's Movie Commandments. 1937.**

Mayer, J. P. **Sociology of Film: Studies and Documents. 1946.** New Introduction by J. P. Mayer.

Münsterberg, Hugo. **The Photoplay: A Psychological Study. 1916.**

Nicoll, Allardyce. **Film and Theatre.** 1936.

Noble, Peter. **The Negro in Films.** 1949.

Peters, Charles C. **Motion Pictures and Standards of Morality.** 1933.

Peterson, Ruth C. and L. L. Thurstone. **Motion Pictures and the Social Attitudes of Children.** Shuttleworth, Frank K. and Mark A. May. **The Social Conduct and Attitudes of Movie Fans.** 1933.

Phillips, Henry Albert. **The Photodrama.** 1914.

Photoplay Research Society. **Opportunities in the Motion Picture Industry.** 1922.

Rapée, Erno. **Encyclopaedia of Music for Pictures.** 1925.

Rapée, Erno. **Motion Picture Moods for Pianists and Organists.** 1924.

Renshaw, Samuel, Vernon L. Miller and Dorothy P. Marquis. **Children's Sleep.** 1933.

Rosten, Leo C. **Hollywood: The Movie Colony, The Movie Makers.** 1941.

Sadoul, Georges. **French Film.** 1953.

Screen Monographs I, 1923-1937. 1970.

Screen Monographs II, 1915-1930. 1970.

Sinclair, Upton. **Upton Sinclair Presents William Fox.** 1933.

Talbot, Frederick A. **Moving Pictures.** 1912.

Thorp, Margaret Farrand. **America at the Movies.** 1939.

Wollenberg, H. H. **Fifty Years of German Film.** 1948.

RELATED BOOKS AND PERIODICALS

Allister, Ray. **Friese-Greene: Close-Up of an Inventor.** 1948.

Art in Cinema: A Symposium of the Avant-Garde Film, edited by Frank Stauffacher. 1947.

The Art of Cinema: Selected Essays. New Foreword by George Amberg. 1971.

Balázs, Béla. **Theory of the Film.** 1952.

Barry, Iris. **Let's Go to the Movies.** 1926.

de Beauvoir, Simone. **Brigitte Bardot and the Lolita Syndrome.** 1960.

Carrick, Edward. **Art and Design in the British Film.** 1948.

Close Up. Vols. 1-10, 1927-1933 (all published).

Cogley, John. **Report on Blacklisting. Part I: The Movies.** 1956.

Eisenstein, S. M. **Que Viva Mexico!** 1951.

Experimental Cinema. 1930-1934 (all published).

Feldman, Joseph and Harry. **Dynamics of the Film.** 1952.

Film Daily Yearbook of Motion Pictures. Microfilm, 18 reels,
   35 mm. 1918-1969.

Film Daily Yearbook of Motion Pictures. 1970.

Film Daily Yearbook of Motion Pictures. (Wid's Year Book).
   3 vols., 1918-1922.

The Film Index: A Bibliography. Vol. I: The Film as Art. 1941.

Film Society Programmes. 1925-1939 (all published).

Films: A Quarterly of Discussion and Analysis. Nos. 1-4, 1939-1940
   (all published).

Flaherty, Frances Hubbard. **The Odyssey of a Film-Maker:
   Robert Flaherty's Story.** 1960.

General Bibliography of Motion Pictures, edited by Carl Vincent,
   Riccardo Redi, and Franco Venturini. 1953.

Hendricks, Gordon. **Origins of the American Film.** 1961-1966. New
   Introduction by Gordon Hendricks.

Hound and Horn: Essays on Cinema, 1928-1934. 1971.

Huff, Theodore. **Charlie Chaplin.** 1951.

Kahn, Gordon. **Hollywood on Trial.** 1948.

New York Times Film Reviews, 1913-1968. 1970.

Noble, Peter. **Hollywood Scapegoat: The Biography of Erich
   von Stroheim.** 1950.

Robson, E. W. and M. M. **The Film Answers Back.** 1939.

Weinberg, Herman G., editor. **Greed.** 1971.

Wollenberg, H. H. **Anatomy of the Film.** 1947.

Wright, Basil. **The Use of the Film.** 1948.